# THE MAN FROM NAZARETH

*Other Books*
*by*
Harry Emerson Fosdick

★

# THE MAN FROM NAZARETH

As His Contemporaries Saw Him

*By*

HARRY EMERSON FOSDICK

HARPER & BROTHERS · NEW YORK

To

My Grandchildren

PATRICIA DOWNS

STEPHEN FOSDICK DOWNS

# CONTENTS

[ 7 ]

# Prologue

WHEN one has been fascinated by the personality of Jesus, the desire to see him as one would have seen him had one been his contemporary is inevitable. Even in the earliest records of the New Testament we have an interpreted Jesus, already thought of in current theological and messianic terms. How to pierce behind those interpretations and to recover the Man of Nazareth as he would appear could we moderns directly see him, has been the object of endless research, especially during the last century.

The results of this endeavor have been far from satisfactory. The attempt, as it were, to leap into the self-consciousness of Jesus, to by-pass the Gospel's thoughts about him and to recover the uninterpreted personality, as he was before being set in inherited patterns of theology, is an all but impossible task. Even if Jesus were only a genius, it requires a genius to get inside the mind of a genius. How, then, can we project ourselves into the inner life of the Master, and be sure that we are truly recovering the historic personality and understanding him? The Gospel records themselves are an inadequate basis for such an endeavor, leaving open to endless debate many central questions, such as whether he regarded himself as, in any traditional sense, the Messiah and, if so, what he meant by his messiahship.

[ 9 ]

The frustration which one experiences when one tries thus to detour around the first interpretations of the Master and to come immediately into the presence of the "historic Jesus" is made evident in the many diverse ideas of him which have resulted. The difference between the picture of Jesus given us, with only slight variations, in Matthew, Mark and Luke, and the picture presented in the Fourth Gospel is familiar. That, however, is nothing as compared with the difference between Ernest Renan's sentimentalist, Bouck White's social revolutionist, Bruce Barton's expert in salesmanship, Schweitzer's apocalypticist, Thomas N. Carver's economist, Binet-Sanglé's paranoiac, and Middleton Murry's man of genius. That invaluable contributions have been made to our knowledge and appreciation of the Master by attempts to get directly at him, and that such attempts will and should go on, is to be taken for granted. Nevertheless, what each man sees, when he tries this method of direct attack, is what he brings eyes to see, and the portrait he paints is commonly so highly colored by subjective factors that it is more a revelation of himself than of Jesus.

This book is an endeavor to try an indirect method of approach. To project ourselves into the self-consciousness of history's supreme personality may be beyond our power, but to see from the inside the way Pharisees and Sadducees felt and thought, to put ourselves into the places of first-century outcasts and sinners, women and children, patriotic nationalists, believers in God's world-wide kingdom, and even the first disciples, is far more within our range. Moreover, there is a vast amount of specific information, both in the New Testament and outside it, concerning such groups, their convictions and prejudices, their customary ways of thinking, and their personal and social needs. What if we should start with them,

[ 10 ]

identify ourselves with their attitudes, and look at Jesus through their eyes? We might at least see Jesus as they saw him and, in the end, achieve a composite portrait of him as these varied folk, friendly and hostile, looked at him.

Such is the endeavor which this book undertakes. To be sure, I have tried not to let this method enslave and shackle me. The aim is still to see what manner of man the historic Jesus was, what he thought and taught and did, and how he felt. Wherever the insight of his contemporaries makes clear the kind of person they were looking at, I have tried to bring that out; and often, in attempting to portray the way he appeared to them, I have used whatever evidence I could find to show what it was in him that made such appearance possible. Nevertheless, my major approach to the Master has been indirect, by way of the responses to him of the men and women who saw and heard him.

The last half century of research has brought to light revealing information about the life and times of Jesus. For the most part this is known to scholars only, hidden in learned volumes which only specialists are likely to read. Today, however, the desire to know all that we can know about the Man of Nazareth is widespread, and not intellectual curiosity alone but profounder motives of personal and public need awaken hunger for all available information about Jesus. I have hoped, therefore, that a modest volume, such as this, written not by a technical New Testament scholar, might be of use in presenting to the ordinary reader some of the results of recent study.

I am under no illusion that I have avoided the subjective element, which colors all portraits of the Master. Inevitably one's own predilections and biases get in the way of one's endeavor to draw a true picture of him. But I have done my best and, to that end, have tried to make clear by apposite quotations and by specific references the objective evidence on which the opinions of this book are based.

As for my indebtedness, that is far too extensive to be covered by any printed acknowledgment. The list of selected books in the appendix will indicate a portion of it. This list, however, has been compiled mainly with the non-technical reader in mind, and it comprises only books which are available in English. To Dr. John Knox, Professor of Sacred Literature in the Union Theological Seminary, New York City, I owe a special debt. He read the manuscript of this book with painstaking care and, while he must not be accused of holding all the opinions which the book expresses, his critical judgment has made it a much better piece of work than it would otherwise have been.

The material in four of the chapters was used as the basis of the Shaffer Lectures at the Yale Divinity School in 1948; and a few paragraphs in Chapter IV are repeated substantially from an article of mine which appeared in *Life* magazine, entitled, "The Personality That Christmas Celebrates." To Mrs. Dorothy Noyes I am grateful for the tireless care she has expended on the preparation of the manuscript for the publisher. As for the rest, I must trust the imagination of the reader and the evidence of the footnotes to indicate my many and varied obligations.

Quotations from the Old Testament are ordinarily from the Standard Edition of the American Revised Version, issued in 1901. In quoting the New Testament I have regularly used the Revised Standard Version, issued in 1946. Both are published by Thomas Nelson and Sons, New York. Occasionally

Dr. James Moffatt's rendering, published by Harper & Brothers, has been used, and this has been indicated by an "M" after the footnote.

HARRY EMERSON FOSDICK

*Boothbay Harbor, Maine*
*July 1, 1949*

# THE MAN FROM NAZARETH

## CHAPTER I

# A Real Man, Not a Myth

THE personality of Jesus, as portrayed in the Gospels, is
so vivid, his individual characteristics are so lively and
unmistakable, he stands out so distinctively himself and not
anyone else, that the story leaves the intense impression of a
real man, dealing with real people, in an actual historic situation.

Nevertheless, some have thought that Jesus of Nazareth
never lived—that he was only a myth.

Some religions have been built around mythological figures,
while others have had historic founders. No reputable scholar
now doubts that Gautama founded Buddhism, Zoroaster
Zoroastrianism, Mohammed Islam, and that at the source of
Judaism stands Moses. Jupiter, Juno, Venus and Mars, however, never lived as real persons; Isis and Osiris, Adonis, Attis
and Dionysus were mythological; Mithra was a mythical
figure, around whose legends and rituals a religion developed
so powerful that, for a time, in the third century, it threatened
to outdo Christianity.

To which category, then, does the Christian religion belong?
Was Jesus a real historic personality or a myth?

As the record in the Gospels stands—granting the legendary
accretions there—the mythical interpretation of Jesus seems

at first grotesque. Here are people, whose attitudes and prejudices we know from extra-Biblical sources—Pharisees, Sadducees, Romans like Pilate, taxgatherers like Zacchaeus and all the rest—dealing with Jesus in ways so apt to the historic situation, so native to the land and time, so appropriate to their own predilections, that common sense protests that this is not the way a myth is made. Does mythology construct a god by picturing a man like this—a carpenter by trade, loving flowers and children, talking about garments that need patching and about poor folk buying two sparrows for a penny; telling stories in a style so characteristically his own that they cannot be reduplicated; being weary and hungry and angry and out of heart; called "beside himself" by his family, a heretic by his church, a traitor by his government? This is not the way mythical gods are made. Nor can the intense historic realism of the response Jesus called out from the legalism of the Pharisees, from the collaborationist alliance of the Sadducees with Rome, from the spiritual hunger of the outcasts, from the fiery hopes of those who looked for a Messiah, be reasonably fitted in to a process of myth-making with no vivid, vital, powerful personality at the center of it.

Nevertheless, the idea that Jesus never actually lived has been seriously argued, and if we are to see him through the eyes of his contemporaries, we must start with the proposition that they saw him as a real man and not a myth.

At the very end of the eighteenth century a few French writers classed Christianity among the mythical religions, but the first person of acknowledged modern scholarship to deny that Jesus actually lived was Bruno Bauer, who died in 1882. That is a long time to wait for doubt to arise about the existence of a transcendently important historic personality.

Christianity from the beginning had bitter enemies, shrewd and powerful, who sought every available weapon of attack. Had there been factual basis for the supposition that this Christ the Christians worshiped was an invented fable, would they not have used it? Yet, so far as is known, no one thought of such a possibility until close to the beginning of the nineteenth century.

The cogency of this fact is especially evident when one considers Jewish testimony to the reality of the historic Jesus. From the beginning of the Christian church the Jews were hostile to it for reasons whose force any loyal Jew would have felt. To be sure, the powerful Rabban Gamaliel, when the nascent Christian church was less than a decade old and the disciples were still faithful observers of the law, defended the apostles from punishment as heretics. He doubtless saw little peril to Judaism in this futile sect of unimportant folk who called the crucified Jesus the Messiah.[1] Such liberal tolerance, however, soon faded out, and hostility between church and synagogue became bitter. Jesus was a heretic, the Jews thought; claiming messiahship, he had misled the people; and now, the Christian movement, spreading across the Roman Empire, was splitting synagogues asunder, making converts to a false Messiah, inviting persecution from the Romans who might confuse Christians with Jews, and in every way hurting and troubling Israel. In the early documents of the New Testament, such as the letters of Paul, the conflict arising between Jews and Christians is evident.

Had Jesus not really lived, none would have known it better than the Jews and, had it been possible, they surely would have raised that issue. Upon the contrary, all Jewish attacks on Jesus take for granted his life and death in Palestine. Says the Talmud: "On the eve of the Passover Jesus of Nazareth was hung. During forty days a herald went before him crying aloud: 'He ought to be stoned because he has practiced magic, has led Israel astray and caused them to rise in rebellion. Let him who has something to say in his defense come forward and declare it.' But no one came forward, and he was hung on the eve of the Passover."[2]

In Jewish writings—none contemporary with Jesus, some centuries later—we are told these things about Jesus: he was the illegitimate son of a Roman soldier;[3] his mother's name was Mary, and she was a dresser of women's hair; he was a "revolutionary" and he "scoffed at the words of the wise"; he worked miracles by means of magic brought out of Egypt; he had devoted personal disciples, who healed diseases in his name; he was a heretic who sinned and caused the multitude to sin, and he "led astray and deceived Israel"; he was about thirty-three years old when he was put to death; and he was executed on the eve of the Passover. One thing, however, which the Jewish enemies of Jesus never thought of saying was that he had not existed.[4]

Josephus, the Jewish historian, was born in Jerusalem in the year A.D. 37 or 38, and thus narrowly missed being Jesus' contemporary. In two passages in his *Antiquities*, he mentions Jesus. The first (18,3,3) has so evidently been expanded by later hands that, while it probably started with a bona fide core,[5] its use may be questioned. If an authentic core be granted, as it is by many scholars both Jewish and Christian, then Josephus tells us that Jesus came into prominence about the time a popular uprising opposed Pilate's attempt to use temple revenues to improve Jerusalem's water supply; that Jesus was "a wise man," "a doer of wonderful works"; that "when Pilate, at the suggestion of the principal men among us had condemned him to the cross, those who loved him at the first ceased not to love him"; and that "the race of Christians, so named from him, are not extinct even now." Whatever may be one's judgment concerning this first passage, the second passage (20,9,1) appears so casually and naturally in Josephus' narrative that there is no valid reason to suspect its authenticity: "Ananias called a Sanhedrin together, brought before it James, the brother of Jesus who was called the Christ, and certain others . . . and he caused them to be stoned."

One naturally wishes there were more references to Jesus in early Jewish writings, but the far more important fact is that in whatever references we do have, even when most evidently motived by hostility, Jesus' life, ministry and death in Palestine are assumed as matters of unquestioned fact.

The same is true concerning the evidence from Roman writings. Scanty as that witness is, it might easily have been scantier. The Roman world was filled with religions, big and little, commonly despised by serious minds; and why this Messiah-cult from Palestine, scorned by the Jews themselves, concerned with a crucified felon, and attracting, insofar as it attracted at all, those whom the historians would regard as insignificant people, should claim attention from Roman writers is not evident. Inevitably early references to Jesus are few. Yet Tacitus, writing about A.D. 115, describes Nero's ruse when in A.D. 64 he blamed the burning of Rome on the Christians, and Tacitus adds: "This name comes to them from Christ, whom the Procurator Pontius Pilate, under the rule of Tiberius, had handed over to torture."[6] So few are the references to Jesus in Roman writings—Pliny's letter to Trajan, about A.D. 112, reporting meetings in Bithynia-Pontus where a hymn is sung "to one Christus as a god," and Suetonius' possible reference to Jesus when he reports that the Emperor Claudius, probably about A.D. 50, "banished from

Rome the Jews who made a great tumult because of Chrestus"[7] —that some say Jesus never lived. The more important fact, however, is that Jewish and Roman references to him when they do occur, take for granted his historic existence, confirm, as Tacitus does, some detail of his life, ministry or death, and breathe no faintest rumor that he was a myth.

Doubt concerning the historicity of Jesus was a passing vogue of the nineteenth century; no serious scholarship now upholds it. After centuries of credulity concerning the infallibility of the Bible, the new historical criticism, glorying in its scepticism, destroyed one supposed certainty after another, until even the existence of personalities like Moses and Jesus was denied, and, as Professor McCown says, "It seemed that every scholar in Germany who was even remotely connected with theology had to write a brochure with the title, 'Did Jesus Ever Live?' "[8]

At the height of this vogue in 1854, Professor Wilson, of Oxford University, read a paper before the Royal Asiatic Society of London, maintaining that the supposed life of Buddha was a myth and "Buddha himself merely an imaginary being." Dr. T. W. Rhys Davids' comment would be generally agreed with: "No one would now support this view."[9] A similar reversal has taken place with regard to the historicity of Jesus. The day of Arthur Drews in Germany, John M. Robertson in England and W. B. Smith in the United States, with their mythological theory of Christ, has gone, and they have left no disciples of any importance in the field of scholarship.

The nearest approach, in present-day New Testament study, to the mythological school of thought is to be found among certain exponents of "Form Criticism." Scholars of this school have made notable contributions to the understanding of the Gospels. They have analyzed the patterns in which the earliest oral traditions about Jesus were probably transmitted; have subjected these component units to searching examination; have emphasized the way the needs and convictions of the Christian communities, at the time our Gospels were written, must have affected the selection, formulation and transmission of this inherited material; and, in many cases, have thus cast doubt upon the historical reliability of the Biblical record. This approach to the Gospel narratives must now be taken seriously into account in all studies of the historic Jesus, but even the most extreme exponents of "Form Criticism," like Rudolf Bultmann, do not for a moment question that Jesus of Nazareth was a real person, who lived and taught in Palestine, and died on Calvary.

Moreover, the idea toward which the more extreme Form-critics tend, that the later Christian community *created* the major features of Jesus' life and teaching as portrayed in the Gospels, meets increasing incredulity. Communities, as such, are not thus creative—not in music, art, philosophy, science, morals or religion. Communities can furnish favorable conditions for creativity, can help at the start and radically modify and amplify the result afterwards, but it takes creative personalities to account, in all such realms, for the unique, original discoveries. Johann Sebastian Bach's music was largely lost sight of for a century, and then gathered around it an enthusiastic following of those who hailed Bach as the prince of all musicians. To suppose, however, that this fellowship of followers produced the music, and that Bach was a more or less imaginary mouthpiece through which the community spoke, would be preposterous. Nothing like the originality of Bach's music or Jesus' unique contribution to ethical and religious life and thought is ever explicable without creative personality. On that matter New Testament scholarship is increasingly agreed.

The idea that Jesus never lived involves the assumption that the New Testament's witness is untrustworthy, and that his existence must be proved, if proved at all, by extra-Scriptural evidence. The fallacy of this assumption becomes clear when one thinks not first of the Gospels but of Paul. No serious scholar now doubts that he really lived, and at least eight letters attributed to him are today taken for granted as authentic. If ever a distinctive personality was revealed in valid, firsthand documents, Paul is so revealed in these vivid letters —with his convictions, traditions, handicaps and repentances, his enthusiasm and downheartedness, his troubles with himself and his tussles with opponents. Moreover, if one still insists on further evidence, we have a long letter written to the Corinthians by Clement of Rome in A.D. 95, reminding them that, only a scant forty years before, Paul had founded their church, and exhorting them to read and reread "the epistle of the blessed Paul," written to them "in the beginning of the Gospel," in which he warned them against divisive party spirit.[10]

Paul was a contemporary of Jesus. He studied under Gamaliel in Jerusalem while Jesus was alive. He was converted probably within three years after the crucifixion. Perhaps he even saw Jesus, although his clause, "Even though we have known Christ after the flesh,"[11] probably has another meaning. Certainly he knew the Christian movement from its very start. Among its first persecutors, he was informed and concerned about it, and bitter with hostility against it. After his conversion and before his Christian ministry began, as his letter to the Galatians, probably written about A.D. 50, tells us, he "went up to Jerusalem to visit Cephas [Peter], and remained with him fifteen days," seeing, at the same time, he adds, "James the Lord's brother."[12] In his missionary activity he was allied with Barnabas, an associate of the first disciples, with Silas, another member of that earliest Christian community, with John Mark, whose mother's home in Jerusalem was headquarters for the first disciples, where John Mark himself lived[13] and to which Peter is said to have repaired when he escaped from prison.[14] Probably throughout his ministry, and certainly during the first fourteen years of his ministry, Paul was in communication with men who had known Jesus.

In the extravagant days of mythological interpretation, this Pauline witness was so obviously dangerous to the idea that Jesus was a myth that Paul also had to be liquidated. He too became only a ventriloquist's lay figure, and the real voice was supposed to be some unknown, pseudonymous writer who, long years afterwards, made up these letters to support the myth that had created "Christ." All this, however, has proved too preposterous to last. These letters are too vividly real, too authentically autobiographical, too intensely sincere for any such interpretation. Here a distinctive personality speaks, not out of some late generation but from the middle years of the first century, when eschatological hopes of Christ's immediate return, for example, were still fresh and strong— not yet translated from outward physical into inward spiritual terms as they were later in the Fourth Gospel. At every point the characteristic qualities and ideas of the letters reveal an author who was what Paul was said to be—a Pharisee, born in Hellenic Tarsus, educated in Jerusalem, and converted to a convinced faith that the Messiah at last had come.

That this historic Paul bears witness to an historic Jesus seems clear. Much has been made by the mythologists of the fact that few details of Jesus' life are mentioned in Paul's letters. Reading them, the charge runs, one would learn only that he was born a Jew, "under the law,"[15] that he ate a last supper with his disciples,[16] that he was crucified and rose from the dead. Paul's Christ, they say, is no such human personality as the Gospels present, but a supernatural deity, awaiting in heaven his second coming and meanwhile mystically dwelling in the hearts of believers.

Paul unquestionably did speak most frequently, not of the Jesus of history but of the coming Messiah, and of the Christ of experience, of whom he could say, "It is no longer I who live, but Christ who lives in me."[17] The real question, however, still remains: Was Paul's idea of this Christ, to whom the future belonged and whose indwelling spirit could take possession of men's lives, dominated by the historic Man of Nazareth?

To argue that the historic Jesus was unreal to Paul because so few details of his life are mentioned in the letters is, like many another argument from silence, dubious business. The life and teaching of Jesus were the common property of the Christian communities. Evangelism started with that. How else could it start, except with the story of Jesus? An indwelling Christ could have had no conceivable meaning unless the career and character, the nature and quality of him who was the Christ, had been made plain. The real explanation of Paul's silence about the details of Jesus' earthly life is not that he was unaware of it or unconcerned with it, but that, writing to Christian churches where it was the basis of all instruction, he took it for granted. The material that later went into the Gospels was already formulated in oral tradition, some of it already written down, all of it cherished, and transmitted to every new convert. Paul's letters were not intended to take the place of that; they started from that and assumed it.

The evidence for this seems convincing. One of Paul's most constant and loyal traveling companions was Luke.[18] Once Paul calls him his "fellow-worker";[19] again he alludes to him as "the beloved physician";[20] once again—if Second Timothy, as seems probable, contains a bona fide passage from Paul— he says, "Luke alone is with me."[21] But Luke wrote the third Gospel. Is it possible to imagine Paul and Luke as fast friends and fellow apostles, and to suppose Paul ignorant of Jesus' earthly ministry and unconcerned about it?

The fact is that Paul's letters are saturated with the ideas of Jesus, and his whole conception of Christ is dominated by the character and teaching of the Man of Nazareth. At this point, the argument from silence breaks down completely. There is no silence about what Jesus was and taught: "I, Paul, myself entreat you, by the meekness and gentleness of Christ";[22] "We who are strong ought to bear with the failings of the weak, and not to please ourselves. . . . For Christ did not please himself";[23] "We all with unveiled face, beholding as in a mirror the character of the Lord, are changed into the same image from character to character."[24] Jesus said, "Every one who exalts himself will be humbled, and he who humbles himself will be exalted."[25] Paul said, "Do not be haughty, but associate with the lowly; never be conceited."[26] Jesus said, "As you did it to one of the least of these my brethren, you did it to me."[27] Paul said, "Who is weak, and I am not weak? Who is made to fall, and I am not indignant?"[28] Jesus said, "Blessed are those who are persecuted for righteousness' sake."[29] Paul said, "For the sake of Christ, then, I am content with weaknesses, insults, hardships, persecutions, and calamities."[30] Jesus said, "Do not be anxious."[31] Paul said, "Have no anxiety about anything."[32] Jesus said concerning the laws of Kosher food, "There is nothing outside a man which by going into

[ 27 ]

him can defile him."[33] Paul said on the same subject, "I know and am persuaded in the Lord Jesus that nothing is unclean in itself."[34] Jesus said, "Judge not, that you be not judged."[35] Paul said, "Let us no more pass judgment on one another."[36] Jesus said, "Whoever says to this mountain, Be taken up and cast into the sea, and does not doubt in his heart . . . it will be done for him."[37] Paul said, "If I have all faith, so as to remove mountains."[38] Jesus said, "Love your enemies and pray for those who persecute you."[39] Paul said, "Bless those who persecute you; bless and do not curse them. . . . Repay no one evil for evil."[40] Jesus said that love of God and one's neighbor is the first of all the commandments.[41] Paul said, "Love is the fulfilling of the law."[42]

These are but samples of the constant reflections of Jesus' ways of thought and life in Paul. When he said, "Be imitators of me, as I am of Christ,"[43] what could he have meant, had he not been thinking of the character whom he and Luke together preached? As he put it in his Ephesian letter: "It is Christ whom you have been taught, it is in Christ that you have been instructed—the real Christ who is in Jesus."?[44]

Paul did emphasize the Christ of experience, but not by eliminating the Jesus of history. He rather distilled the essential quality and meaning of Jesus, and proclaimed the gospel that this same spirit could possess men's souls. What else could he have meant when he wrote: "My little children, with whom I am again in travail until Christ be formed in you"?[45]

Paul did stress the supernatural Messiah who would soon come upon the clouds of heaven, but in all the Jewish portraits of the Messiah there is nothing remotely like the quality which Paul ascribes to Christ. Paul's Messiah is utterly unique and his uniqueness is inexplicable save as we see its cause in the character of the historic Jesus. "Do nothing from selfishness or conceit, but in humility count others better than yourselves. Let each of you look not only to his own interests, but also to the interests of others. Have this mind among yourselves, which you have in Christ Jesus"[46]—for *that* kind of Messiah one looks in vain except among those like Paul, whose Christ was Jesus glorified.

There seems no escaping the conclusion that the historic Paul bears witness to the historic Jesus.

The attack of the mythologists on the factual reality of Jesus was, of course, centered on the Gospels. Presenting in vivid detail, as they seem to do, the characteristic qualities, activities and ideas of a genuine historic person, they had to be brushed aside as untrustworthy if Jesus was to be regarded as a myth. The Gospels were not the honest record of a life humanly lived in Palestine; they were the late, legendary endeavor to build a camouflaged foundation under the symbolic figure of a dying and a rising god—such was the necessary assumption of the mythologists.

Modern scholarship dealing with the Gospels, however, has rendered this position untenable. It nowhere fits the facts.

The very contrasts and contradictions within the Gospels, which at first were used to discredit their reliability now turn out to be a boomerang for the mythologists. To be sure, the Gospels disagree on many points in Jesus' life and teaching, from small matters, like the wording of the placard on the cross—"This is Jesus the King of the Jews," says Matthew; "The King of the Jews," says Mark; "This is the King of the Jews," says Luke; "Jesus of Nazareth, the King of the Jews," says John—to matters of graver import. Matthew's Beatitudes are spiritual—"Blessed are the poor in spirit, for theirs is the kingdom of heaven"[47]—while Luke's are stated in terms of

economic classes: "Blessed are you poor, for yours is the kingdom of God. . . . But woe to you that are rich!"[48] Matthew
says: "Blessed are those who hunger and thirst for righteousness," but Luke thinks the beatitude refers to literal penury:
"Blessed are you that hunger now, for you shall be satisfied."

Such distinctive slants and biases on the part of the writers
do sometimes turn Jesus' reputed sayings to varied meanings;
and, as for his life, so uncertain is the order of events, and so
irreconcilable are some of the narratives, that no biography
of him can be written with confidence about the sequence of
many incidents. Papias, an early Christian writer in the first
half of the second century noted this, and said: "Mark, having
become the interpreter of Peter, wrote down accurately whatsoever he remembered. It was not, however, in exact order
that he related the sayings or deeds of Christ. For he neither
heard the Lord nor accompanied him."[49]

Modern criticism, uncovering these discrepancies in the
Gospels, at first seemed to confirm the impression of their
unreliability, and to make it possible plausibly to say that,
even if there were a person named Jesus, we know little or
nothing trustworthy about him and what we have is only the
myth that grew up around him.

Now, however, the very inconsistencies in the Gospels, puzzling though they often are, turn out to be one reason why the
myth-theory has broken down. No mythological Christ, deliberately created by an adoring group, would ever have been
presented in documents like the Gospels. Their historic realism
is evident in these very differences that distinguish their narratives. This is no concocted myth, but the honest endeavor
to record an actual story, with all the effects of oral transmission involving diverse renderings, and with the writer's dis-
similar backgrounds and temperaments resulting in divergent

interpretations. The total impression now made upon New Testament scholars by these records, with their natural, casual, often explainable contrasts, is one of bona fide authenticity.

These Gospels are genuine historical documents, subject to gaps in information, failures of memory, and individual coloring, with no artificial inspiration saving them from dissimilarities that inevitably sprang from varied authorship, legendary accretions, the vagaries of verbal transmission, and the effect of special needs and interests in the different Christian communities for which they were written. Not the less, but the more because of their inconsistencies, they now appear as valid portrayals of a real personality of whom they are honestly trying to present a true picture.

This becomes the more clear when one turns to details. If Christianity began not with a living person but with a myth created around an allegorical figure, and if the human elements in the tradition were made up later to give it richer content, then one consequence must have followed: the earliest records would have presented a completely deified Christ, and the later records would have introduced for the first time his human qualities.

The precise opposite is true; the earliest Gospel record presents Jesus in the most human terms. Mark, the first of the Gospels, has no story of a virgin birth. Mark even represents Jesus as saying, "Why do you call me good? No one is good but God alone,"[50] which Matthew later tones down: "Why do you ask me about what is good?"[51] In one instance after another, comparing Mark with Matthew and Luke, one finds the miraculous powers of Jesus heightened in the later narratives. In Mark a fig tree denounced in the evening was wilted the next morning, while in Matthew the tree, cursed in the morning, "withered at once."[52] While in Mark one demoniac was healed at Gadara, in Matthew two were healed;[53] and two blind men, according to Matthew, were given sight at Jericho, whereas in Mark there was only one.[54] In Mark "one of those who stood by drew his sword, and struck the slave of the high priest and cut off his ear," but only later in Luke do we hear that Christ performed a miracle and restored the dissevered member.[55]

That the early tradition concerning Jesus moved not from a mythological figure toward an historic person but from an historic person into heightened theological interpretations of him becomes unmistakable when one contrasts the Jesus of the first three Gospels with the Jesus of the Fourth Gospel. There not only are hitherto unheard of exhibitions of miraculous power narrated—turning water into wine, curing a man born blind, raising Lazarus from the dead after he had been four days entombed[56]—but the whole concept of Christ is set in terms of pre-existent deity, and the theological interpretation of him dominates the narrative.

At first such facts as these deeply disturbed the faith of Christians, but now they have turned out to be not so much a problem to believers in an historic Jesus, the interpretation of whom deepened with the years, as an insurmountable obstacle to the mythologists. The earliest records start not with a myth but with an authentic person who said things—for example, that the end of the world would come before some of those who heard him speak had died[57]—which no one would have made up two generations later when the situation had turned out otherwise; and who did things, such as submitting to John's baptism, which very much perplexed the next generation of Christians. Facing a bitter conflict with John the Baptist's continuing movement, Christians of the second century would never have concocted the story of the baptism, which could so easily be used, as it was used, to give John priority.

In short, the earliest Christian tradition plainly started with the human personality of Jesus and the position of the mythologists is no longer supported by serious scholarship.

This becomes even more clear when we reconstruct, in the light of such information as we possess, the way our four Gospels came to be written.

At the beginning the Christian community relied on oral transmission of stories about Jesus' life and teaching. Papias, writing in Phrygia, in Asia Minor, sometime before A.D. 135, said: "I shall not be unwilling to put down, along with my interpretations, whatsoever instructions I received with care at any time from the elders, and stored up with care in my memory, assuring you at the same time of their truth. . . . If, then, any one who had attended on the elders came, I asked minutely after their sayings—what Andrew or Peter said, or what was said by Philip, or by Thomas, or by James, or by John, or by Matthew, or by any other of the Lord's disciples: which things Aristion and the presbyter John, the disciples of the Lord, say. For I imagined that what was to be got from books was not so profitable to me as what came from the living and abiding voice."[58]

This oral transmission which Papias so valued was clearly not haphazard and formless. In our written Gospels scholars now perceive the shapes and patterns it took on in a generation accustomed not so much to writing and reading as to listening and remembering. The narrative of Jesus' trial and death was evidently told and retold in ordered form. Illustrative anecdotes with an appended pronouncement by Jesus represent one of the most familiar patterns of recollection in the Gospels. "The sabbath was made for man, not man for the sabbath"[59] is appended to a story about the disciples plucking ears of corn on the sabbath day; "Let the children come to me, and do not hinder them; for to such belongs the kingdom of heaven"[60] is appended to a story about the disciples rebuking parents who brought children to the Master for his blessing; "Those who are well have no need of a physician, but those who are sick; I came not to call the righteous, but sinners"[61] climaxes an anecdote about Jesus eating with publicans and sinners.

The oral transmission of the early disciples' recollections about Jesus thus broke up the narrative into rememberable units, and the result is still manifest in the lack of continuity the reader often feels in our Gospels—for example, in detached narratives introduced by phrases such as, "On another day," "And it came to pass," "He arose from thence." Any thoughtful reader must be aware of these cells of which the body of the record is composed—parables, miracle stories, disconnected anecdotes, sayings of Jesus set in familiar Hebrew poetic forms, such as

> If ye love them that love you,
>     What thank have ye?
> For even sinners love those that love them.

> If ye do good to them that do good to you,
>     What thank have ye?
> For even sinners do the same.

> If ye lend to them of whom ye hope to receive,
>     What thank have ye?
> Even sinners lend to sinners to receive
>     again as much.

But love your enemies, and do good, and lend,
   Never despairing!
   And your reward shall be great,
   And ye shall be sons of the Most High.[62]

Far from invalidating the record, therefore, this period of oral transmission made the record an affair of the whole Christian community. These units of recollection were no matter of individual remembrance only but were used by the church in the winning and instruction of converts, the confuting of opponents, and probably in public worship to keep fresh the Lord's memory.

Nevertheless, while even Papias, with written Gospels in his hands, might prefer personal testimony by word of mouth, written records became inevitable, and their beginning scholars now push back to a date far earlier than used to be supposed. In any case, the period of sole reliance on oral transmission was brief. Within thirty to forty years after Jesus' death Mark's Gospel—the earliest we now possess—was written, and before that the evidence indicates that written records were familiar. Certain sections in Mark are in themselves such distinct, self-consistent units, that they suggest previous narratives, taken over and incorporated in the Gospel. Certainly Luke was acquainted with numerous written accounts of Jesus: "Many have undertaken to compile a narrative of the things which have been accomplished among us."[63]

One such document was almost certainly a record of Jesus' sayings used, along with Mark's Gospel, by both Matthew and Luke. That these two writers had in their hands either an identical or a very similar document, mainly made up of the

[ 35 ]

words of Jesus, is so convincingly indicated that few now question it. Papias says that Matthew, the disciple, "put together the oracles of the Lord in the Hebrew language, and each one interpreted them as best he could."[64] This certainly was not our present Gospel of Matthew, which was written in Greek, but it may well have been an early record of Jesus' teaching by one of the first disciples, which in its original form we no longer possess, but which the writers of our first and third Gospels knew and used. At any rate, the evidence is so convincing that written records lay behind our present Gospels and that the authors of the first and third Gospels had in their hands not only Mark and an early collection of Jesus' sayings but other material as well, that the historical reality of Jesus becomes increasingly difficult to question.

That these earlier writings passed out of existence when our four Gospels were at the disposal of the churches was natural. They probably were partial, incomplete, covering distinct areas of Jesus' life and ministry—his Passion, his sayings, stories of his birth, and so on—and the need became urgent for inclusive narratives that would tell the whole story.

Why this need was not felt in the church's earliest years is easy to guess. The immediate return of Christ was ardently expected. Since he so soon would be back again in glory, the need of gathering the detailed memories of his earthly ministry, setting them down in order, and preserving them for future generations was not evident. When, however, Christ did not return, when attention was increasingly centered not so much on the expected end of the world as on the expanding church in the world, that necessity became urgent. The church was making converts whose indoctrination in the truth about the Savior's life, death and resurrection was imperative. The

church was facing enemies whose slanders had to be refuted
by authentic records of the Founder's life and teaching. The
church confronted early Gnosticism, making Christianity an
abstract theosophy, and the need of presenting the gospel's
factual, historic, personal origin became acute. The church
was inwardly perplexed by controversies in dealing with which
knowledge of any relevant and applicable words of Jesus was
anxiously desired. Our Gospels were not written for the purpose of satisfying historic curiosity; they are in no sense the fruit
of academic biographical research; they were called into being
by the pressing needs of the churches. Luke undertook the
writing of his Gospel with intellectual conscientiousness—"It
seemed good to me also, having followed all things closely for
some time past, to write an orderly account for you, most
excellent Theophilus"—but the motive that drove him to it
was one of those practical necessities that confronted the expanding church, the instruction of converts, or perhaps the
enlightenment of an influential official: "that you may know
the truth concerning the things of which you have been informed."[65]

Thus our four Gospels were written between A.D. 65 and
100. Their authors did the best they could, but despite the
rememberable units of oral transmission and many written
records, they faced grave difficulties, whose nature reveals an
authentic historic situation.

Incidents in Jesus' life had been forgotten. Only one is recorded from the years before his public ministry began, although his brother, James, could have told, and doubtless did
tell, how many! The order of events in Jesus' ministry had
grown obscure, so that, for example, Luke dates the time when
he preached in Nazareth at his ministry's beginning while
Mark puts it later;[66] and as between the first three Gospels and

the fourth, the cleansing of the temple is put by Matthew, Mark, and Luke at the close of his ministry, and by John at the beginning.[67] The setting of Jesus' sayings had in some cases grown uncertain, so that Matthew puts the Lord's Prayer in his first recorded sermon, while according to Luke it was taught to the disciples after the final journey to Jerusalem had begun.[68] The words of Jesus had been variously remembered, as in the case of the Beatitudes; and even the versions of the Lord's Prayer and of the golden rule in Matthew and Luke are not the same.[69] Moreover, legendary elements had been added to the tradition, so that while in Mark we have only the symbolic rending of the temple veil at Jesus' death, in Matthew "the earth shook, and the rocks were split; the tombs also were opened; and many bodies of the saints who had fallen asleep were raised; and coming out of the tombs after his resurrection they went into the holy city and appeared to many."[70]

This realistic situation confronting Jesus' biographers cannot be successfully fitted into the supposition that they were constructing a myth around an allegorical figure. Our Gospels spring from a bona fide historical background, not to be mythologically interpreted.

Mark's Gospel was most probably written in Rome, where all early tradition associates John Mark with the ministry of Peter. So, at least, Clement of Alexandria, in the middle of the second century, understood the facts: "The Gospel according to Mark had this occasion. As Peter preached the word publicly at Rome . . . many who were present requested that Mark, who had followed him for a long time and remembered his sayings, should write them out. And having composed the Gospel he gave it to those who had requested it."[71] Certainly Mark wrote for some Gentile community. He translates every

Aramaic phrase he uses;[72] he explains the Palestinian coinage
—the widow's two copper coins equal a penny;[73] he explains
the season when ripe figs are to be expected in Palestine;[74] he
explains Jewish ceremonial customs which his readers might
not understand;[75] and whereas under Jewish law no woman
could divorce her husband, while under Roman law she could,
Mark citing Jesus' condemnation of divorce, includes the
guilty woman as well as the guilty man.[76]

Matthew's Gospel was almost certainly written in some city
where the constituency of the Christian community was
largely Jewish—perhaps Antioch in Syria, where the disciples
of Jesus were first called Christians. Old Testament prophecies, brought to fulfillment in Jesus, are a major concern in
this Gospel, and interest in Jesus' attitude toward the Jewish
law bulks large. Who the author was we do not know—the
writing is anonymous, the present title a late addition—and
no early tradition, as in the case of Mark, throws light on the
problem. That the author, however, was a Jewish Christian,
writing for a church where the relationship between Judaism
and the Christian gospel was of front rank concern seems
certain.

Luke's Gospel suggests a Gentile author, writing, as a not
improbable early tradition says, in some Gentile community
in Greece.[77] That "Luke, the beloved physician," Paul's
traveling companion, wrote it is far and away the most likely
hypothesis. This certainly was the early church's tradition,
and this also is the natural inference from the opening words
of the Book of Acts: "In the first book, O Theophilus, I have
dealt with all that Jesus began to do and teach, until the day
when he was taken up." Moreover, according to those passages in the Book of Acts where "we" is used, apparently including the author, Luke had ample opportunity to get at firsthand

testimony concerning Jesus' life and ministry. Early in Paul's mission he worked for a time in company with Silas, a member of the early Jerusalem church.[78] Later he spent several years in Palestine, mainly in Jerusalem and Caesarea, where he had ample opportunity to meet those who had known Jesus.[79] He was present with Paul at interviews with James, the Lord's brother, and with leaders of the church.[80] At Caesarea he lodged, along with Paul, at the house of Philip the evangelist.[81] Still later at Rome he was the companion of John Mark.[82]

John's Gospel, latest of all, was probably written in Ephesus, not by John, the immediate disciple of Jesus, but by John the Elder, a leader of the Ephesian church. One of the earliest traditions we have about the matter comes from Clement of Alexandria: "Last of all, John, perceiving that the external facts had been made plain in the gospel, being urged on by his friends, and inspired by the Spirit, composed a spiritual gospel."[83]

Our four Gospels, therefore, were written not only by different persons, but in different communities, such as Rome, Antioch in Syria, some city in Greece, and Ephesus in Asia Minor. They were composed to meet the needs of widely separated churches and the marvel is not their differences but their agreement. Seen against the background of the historic situation out of which they came they are authentic endeavors to deal with bona fide recollections of a real personality.

All such evidence as we have canvassed for the historic reality of Jesus comes to its fulfillment when we take into account the impressive mass of information uncovered during the last half century about Palestine in Jesus' day. Whether one thinks of its now familiar geography, of the revelations of archaeology, of the then current estate of Judaism and its various problems and parties, of the meaning of Roman rule, of the prevalent ideas and hopes of the people, or of the social and economic conditions in Galilee and Judea, one faces a situation into which the Gospel record fits with such entire congruity that a mythological interpretation of Jesus is ruled out.

This Palestine, which the visitor sees even yet, is the veritable land where he lived and taught. The incidents narrated in the Gospels, the pictures drawn in the parables, the Master's casual metaphors and similes, the background assumed by the story's outline and filled in by its details, fit the scene like a hand in a glove. Nazareth, the Sea of Galilee, the coasts of Tyre and Sidon, Mount Hermon and the Jordan, Esdraelon and Samaria, Jericho and the Judean wilderness, Bethlehem and Jerusalem—it is all too consistent with the Gospels to leave any doubt about the factual basis of the record.

Here in the Gospels are vineyards, surrounded by hedges and guarded by towers; fields, sometimes beautiful with flowers, sometimes overgrown with thorns. Here are fig trees, needing cultivation, herbs such as mint and rue, and, as well, tares and dry grass for fuel in primitive home ovens. Here are pits into which an animal might fall, and houses, made of clay bricks, in danger from downpouring rain. Along the Jordan are reeds shaken by the wind and on the uplands mustard trees in which birds make their nests. Here are all the typical animals of Palestine—foxes, wolves, dogs, calves, asses, oxen, goats, kids, sheep and lambs. Here vultures gather about their prey, sparrows fall, and ravens, doves, hens and chickens are familiar. Here the farmer, the husbandman, the shepherd go about their daily tasks, businessmen make their investments and artisans ply their trades. Within poor homes are problems of patched garments and cheap food, and by the roadside blindness is a commonplace and beggars flourish. This is Palestine as all the evidence we have, past and present, shows it to have been, and to suppose that such verisimilitude was concocted is incredible.

Moreover, when one turns from the outward scene to the inner thinking of that first band of disciples, one finds in the Gospels ideas which the church two generations afterward would never have invented. Illustrations of this fact we shall repeatedly face in this book. When the Gospels were written, for example, the Gentile mission had long been taken for granted, and the universality of the gospel, including Jew and Greek, Scythian, barbarian, bond and free, was accepted doctrine. Support for that was found in Jesus' teaching, but other sayings of the Master are recorded that never would have been made up, if they had not been set down in the original recollections of the first disciples. Would the later church, predominantly Gentile, have invented a Jesus who said, "I was sent only to the lost sheep of the house of Israel"?[84] That goes veritably back to Palestine, where Jesus, however universal his outlook, faced the practical necessity of concentrating his attention on the immediate task of reaching his own people. So, in one realm after another, one finds in the Gospels ideas and emphases that never could have been invented two generations after Jesus, and, as well, one finds two generations after Jesus prevalent customs and doctrines, from speaking with tongues to the allegorizing of Jewish eschatology, that in the first three Gospels are not found at all.[85]

Here, then, we may confidently start: whatever else his contemporaries saw in Jesus, they saw *him;* he was a real man and not a myth.

[ 42 ]

## CHAPTER II

# As the Crowds Saw Him

T HE unpopularity of Jesus among his own people in Palestine had become, by the time the Fourth Gospel was written, a major factor in the portrayal of his life. John retains echoes of the earlier tradition that "a multitude followed him,"[1] and even adds an incident, not elsewhere recorded, that the crowd once sought to "take him by force to make him king."[2] John's main emphasis, however, is on the fact that "he came to his own home, and his own people received him not,"[3] and, attacking the Jews as a whole, John's indictment is sweeping: "The Jews sought to kill him."[4] That the Jewish populace was thus massed in opposition to Jesus is an idea naturally reflecting the harsh hostility between Jews and Christians at the close of the first century, but it does not accord with the earlier records.

According to them, Jesus' popularity was one of his most dangerous problems. When Jesus began his ministry, says Mark, he caused a great stir, and "his fame spread everywhere throughout all the surrounding region of Galilee."[5] When he entered Capernaum, "many were gathered together, so that there was no longer room for them, not even about the door."[6] Once, at the lakeside, he spoke from a boat, "because of the crowd, lest they should crush him";[7] once, when his family came to seek him, "a crowd was sitting about him,"[8] so that they could not reach him; once the crowd so pressed upon the disciples that "they could not even eat";[9] and once, "the whole city was gathered together about the door."[10] When Jesus noted a woman's beseeching touch on his garment and asked who it was, the disciples exclaimed: "You see the crowd pressing around you, and yet, you say, 'Who touched me?' "[11] Indeed, Mark says that "a great multitude from Galilee followed; also from Judea and Jerusalem and Idumea and from beyond the Jordan and from about Tyre and Sidon a great multitude, hearing all that he did, came to him."[12]

These descriptions of throngs crowding about Jesus may involve enthusiastic exaggeration, as, for example, in such phrases as "the whole city," but Galilee in Jesus' day was a populous land. Josephus says that it contained "two hundred and forty cities and villages," the least of which numbered fifteen thousand souls,[13] and while such statistics are questionable, the picture Josephus draws of a rich and fruitful country, thickly settled and busy with varied trades is doubtless true. As late as A.D. 600 Antoninus, the Martyr, visiting Galilee, reported: "The province is like paradise, rivalling Egypt in its grain and cereals, and, while small indeed, it surpasses Egypt in wine and oil and fruit."[14] Gennesaret—the plain, some four miles wide along the lake's western shore—was especially the "garden" of Galilee, and Josephus called it "the ambition of nature." Not only in fishing and agriculture were the lakeside and uplands rich in possibilities, but merchant routes led travelers by way of the lake to varied destinations. Galilee's population, therefore, was not purely Jewish; Judeans commonly condescended to its people as a motley racial mixture. Not only were Roman officers and soldiers there, but Greek colonists, settlers from Phoenicia, emigrants and travelers from

Syria, Arabia and the East.[15] It was in this teeming, busy region that Jesus began his public ministry, and was met by so popular a response that it might easily have cost his life. Far from facing neglect and rejection, he was greeted with a mounting outburst of public favor.

The consequence of this popularity enables us, with some confidence, to reconstruct the order of events in Jesus' early ministry. Impossible as it is, in our modern sense, to write his biography, certain outlines in his career seem evident. He came from Nazareth. At first associated with the movement launched by John the Baptist, he later parted company with it, and began an independent ministry in Galilee. The popular interest which he called out, with crowds attending him, was brought to the attention of Herod Antipas, Tetrarch of Galilee, whose superstitious fears were aroused that John the Baptist, though beheaded, had come back again.[16] Certainly Herod could not allow the public agitation caused by Jesus to continue. A dilemma thus confronted the Master—either to leave Galilee or to be executed. This choice, Luke reports, was plainly presented to him by "certain Pharisees," who said to him, "Get away from here, for Herod wants to kill you."[17] Were those Pharisees really friendly, desiring to protect Jesus? Or did they see a chance to frighten him away and so rid the country of his disturbing presence? Or were they emissaries sent by Herod himself, who hoped to solve his own problem by scaring Jesus into exile? Jesus' reply to the Pharisees suggests that the last was his interpretation. He bade them return to Herod: "Go and tell that fox, 'Behold, I cast out demons and perform cures today and tomorrow, and the third day I finish my course.' "[18]

The dilemma which Jesus faced was a real one. Then was

not the time for him to die, nor was Galilee the place; "It cannot be" he told the Pharisees, "that a prophet should perish away from Jerusalem."[19] Leaving Galilee, therefore, he retired to the Mediterranean coasts at Tyre and Sidon, until the commotion should die down, and even there "he entered a house, and would not have any one know it; yet he could not be hid."[20]

The picture of Jesus, therefore, as a rejected man, with the massed hostility of his people arrayed against him, must be given up. He was, instead, a popularly arresting figure in Palestine. He caught the public imagination. He alienated those who feared him as a heretic and hated him as a disturber of the peace, but large numbers of common people were drawn to him. Even after religious leaders had organized their opposition and political leaders were deciding to get rid of him, he entered Jerusalem in triumph, while "the crowds that went before him and that followed him shouted, 'Hosanna to the Son of David! Blessed be he who comes in the name of the Lord! Hosanna in the highest.' "[21] The Fourth Gospel's representation of the way the Pharisees felt at this evidence of Jesus' acceptance by the masses is not improbable: they "said to one another, 'You see that you can do nothing; look, the world has gone after him.' "[22] As though to leave no doubt of Jesus' popular following that last week in Jerusalem Mark tells us that "the mass of the people listened with delight to him."[23]

A familiar interpretation of this popularity has stressed its fickle nature, and the crowd that cried "Crucify him" at the Passion Week's end has been commonly supposed to be the same crowd that cried "Hosanna" at the week's beginning. There is no evidence for this, and such data as we have casts doubt upon it. The claque that cried "Crucify him" in Pilate's court were most probably the organized hirelings of the high

[ 46 ]

priests, the hangers-on of Judea's collaborationist government. Still the "multitude" stood by Jesus. When his foes plotted to seize him, "they feared the people."[24] When they arrested him they bribed Judas, and through his information chose night-time in Gethsemane, when the people could not intervene. Even when he went to the cross, "there followed him a great multitude of the people, and of women who bewailed and lamented him,"[25] and after the dreadful deed was done on Calvary, "all the multitudes who assembled to see the sight, when they saw what had taken place, returned home beating their breasts."[26]

Who made up this "multitude"? The Jews of Palestine in Jesus' day are now commonly thought of as divided into parties—Pharisees, Sadducees, Essenes, Zealots—but parties never adequately describe a population. Parties have their inner core of eager, even fanatical, adherents and their larger circle of more or less loyal followers, but always, there are the vague, uncertain hangers-on, and beyond all parties the general mass of human beings to whom party lines are of small or no concern.

"It is the task of Gospel Criticism," says a modern scholar, "to make ourselves the contemporaries of Jesus."[27] One who tries to do this faces at the very start these crowds made up of plain folk rather than partisans, who saw in Jesus a challenging personage. As with all crowds, what they saw did not reach the spiritual depths, but it is nonetheless important to the understanding of Jesus. Can we make ourselves one of them, and through their eyes catch at least a glimpse of him?

That they saw him as one of themselves, a Jew of the common people, is clear. He spoke their familiar dialect, drew his similes and parables from their familiar experiences, shared

[ 47 ]

with them the current mental categories of his generation, and in his teaching they heard the affirmations of their traditional faith. He dressed as they did, with tassels on the corners of his garment to show he was a Jew—so distinctive a uniform that no Jew was permitted to sell a garment to a Gentile until the tassels were removed.[28] At the height of Jesus' popularity in Galilee we read that "they would lay their invalids in the marketplace, begging him to let them touch even the tassel of his robe."[29]

They saw him as a faithful exemplar of Jewish piety, observing their festivals, going on pilgrimage to the temple in Jerusalem, regularly worshipping in their synagogues.[30] Indeed despite his attacks on Phariseeism, they must have seen that he himself was closer to that most numerous and devout party in Israel than to any other. He certainly was not a Sadducee; he had no kinship with the high priestly group that ruled in Jerusalem, collaborated with Rome to make their tenure secure, and said that "there is no resurrection, nor angel, nor spirit."[31] He was not a Zealot; he stood completely apart from militant hopes of a violent insurrection against Rome. He was not an Essene; they were ascetics—according to early tradition numbering only some four thousand souls—living in communistic communities separate from the general life of Israel, and practicing severe austerities, whereas Jesus was accused by his foes of being "a glutton and a drunkard."[32]

Despite their faults, the Pharisees were the hope of Israel, the Puritans of Palestine, with the deplorable legalism of Puritanism which Jesus condemned, but with its sturdy virtues too, its convinced faith, stubborn conscientiousness, devout loyalty. Of all the parties in Israel Jesus was closest to them. If he visited special censure on them it was because in them he saw the best hope of his people and to their reform dedi·

cated his attention. What he said in rebuke of the Pharisees, orthodox Jewish literature also said. Among the evils that "destroy the world," the Mishna lists "the plagues of the Pharisees."[33] A very ancient *Baraita* describes seven kinds of Pharisees, of which only one clearly and one other doubtfully are to be admired.[34] Nevertheless, the great heritage of Jewish religion in Jesus' day was in the keeping not of the Sadducees, Zealots, or Essenes but of the Pharisees; to them in criticism and appeal his attention was given; and to them, as the crowds must have sensed, he was closer than to any other group in Israel.

The fascination with which Jesus drew crowds around him, however, is not explicable simply by the qualities and attitudes that made him seem one of themselves. No such phenomena as greeted his appearance beside the Sea of Galilee can be accounted for without presupposing a distinctive personality, vigorous, aggressive, outstanding, challenging. To be sure, the manner of his teaching in parables was familiar. The Jewish rabbis also spoke in parables. Did Jesus tell of a father's mercy toward a prodigal? "A king's son fell into evil courses," runs an ancient rabbinic parable. "The king sent his tutor to him with the message, Repent, my son. But the son sent to his father to say, How can I return? I am ashamed before thee. Then the father sent to him to say, Can a son be ashamed to return to his father? If you return, do you not return to your father?"[35] Such teaching in stories was not strange to the crowds that surrounded Jesus, but never such parables as he told had they heard before. Considered only from the literary point of view, one feels about them still, as about some passages in Shakespeare—not an unfamiliar word in them, yet breathtaking in effect.

[ 49 ]

One hesitates to use the word "artist" about Jesus, because he was so much more, but one does not understand him and his impact on his contemporaries, if one fails to see him as that too. In his thinking about God, the soul and the profound concerns of religion with which he dealt, he was never a speculative theologian, working out a formal religious philosophy, but an artist, seeing truth with visual vividness and embodying it in similes, metaphors, parables, which mankind has never been able to forget. If the common folk who heard him were to understand serious teaching at all, they would best understand *that*.

This does not imply that the crowds easily grasped the meaning of his parables; we are explicitly told that they did not.[36] Indeed, to many of the multitude he and his teaching mattered not at all. They stood in the presence of one, concerning whom nearly two millenniums later a man like H. G. Wells could say that he is "easily the dominant figure in history," and they saw and heard nothing worth attending to. Like the guests in his parable, invited to a royal banquet, they were busy with their farms, their oxen, and their families, and making their excuses, passed him by.

This, however, is not the whole story. On many of the common folk those parables struck home. Not only what he said but the way he said it—with the impact of a personality whose mysterious, powerful *plus*, though indescribable, they felt— fascinated and challenged them. During the early days of his ministry, so Mark reports, the crowds, watching his deeds and hearing his words, "were all so amazed that they discussed it together, saying, 'Whatever is this?' 'It is new teaching with authority behind it!' "[37]

It is a commonplace in history that while empires fall and all the ostentatious bigness on which contemporary interest is centered proves ephemeral, those things at long last are most treasured and preserved which are beautifully done. Great literature and music far outlast the external settings of the centuries that produced them, and even remnants of creative beauty, such as the Parthenon, and fragile embodiments of supreme artistry, such as great paintings, are preserved when all else perishes. We should not have the parables of Jesus now, had they not been so consummately well told. Even the common people, dull of understanding though they were, felt a uniqueness they could not explain.

To many of the crowd, however, something besides this in Jesus' teaching must have been arresting. The crowd always loves a fight and Jesus provided one. He attacked with unsparing vigor evils that the "multitude" may well have been pleased to hear attacked. The pride of the scribes and Pharisees was not popular, and the outlawing of the *amme ha-arez,* "the people of the land," from the community of faithful Israel, because they did not and often could not keep the minutiae of scribal legalism, was resented. Josephus said of the Pharisees that "they valued themselves highly upon the exact skill they had in the law of their fathers, and made men believe they were highly favored by God."[38] When, therefore, Jesus criticized pharisaical pomp and circumstance, when he hit with hard epithets those who tithed mint, anise, and cummin and neglected the weightier matters of the law, when he called well-known types of religionists whitewashed tombs and blind leaders of the blind, the crowd, with no conscious disloyalty to the nobler sort of Pharisee, was probably with him. He was saying what they commonly felt but did not dare to say.

There is no understanding the impact of Jesus on the

[ 51 ]

crowds without stressing this hard-hitting vigor of his speech. The "Gentle Jesus, meek and mild," who satisfies the imagination of many moderns, cannot explain what happened in Galilee. In painting and poetry we have sentimentalized him, made him what Thomas Dekker, the English dramatist at the beginning of the seventeenth century, described as,

> A soft, meek, patient, humble, tranquil spirit,
> The first true gentleman that ever breathed.

That some of the qualities Dekker names were his is true, but the total picture is fallacious. No man of merely soft, patient, tranquil spirit did the crowds in Galilee come out to hear. He was exciting, uncompromising, stormy, formidable.

A man's style of speech reveals him. Dekker's lines tell us more about Dekker than about Jesus. Jesus' speech was packed with energy—vehement, vigorous, exuberant, often extravagant. One listening to him saw men straining out gnats and swallowing camels;[39] men with logs in their own eyes trying to take specks from others' eyes;[40] herdsmen offering pearls to swine;[41] men plucking out their eyes and cutting off their hands in order to escape hell;[42] offenders with great millstones about their necks thrown into the ocean.[43] Hyperbole was his native language—a man forgiven a debt of twelve million dollars denies forgiveness to a man who owes him seventeen dollars;[44] a mountain, because a man prayed that it be done, is "taken up and cast into the sea";[45] a sycamine tree, commanded by a man of faith to be rooted up and "planted" in the ocean, obeys the order;[46] the disciples are to be at one and the same time like serpents and like doves;[47] a camel goes through a needle's eye;[48] dead men bury dead men.[49] There is no mistaking the kind of person who speaks like that. Young, dynamic, tremendously in earnest, such a person the crowds heard, and were convinced that something unique in their experience was happening.

To be sure, homelier qualities in Jesus doubtless drew the common people to him, especially his extraordinary gift of being at ease with all sorts of persons. His was a time when caste lines were sharply drawn, but with unembarrassed ease he ate alike with Simon, the Pharisee, and with tax collectors and sinners. It was a time when stiff conventionalities limited social intercourse between the sexes, but alike in public and in private he associated with men and women on equal terms. He was at home with little children in their innocence and strangely enough at home too with conscience-stricken grafters like Zacchaeus. Respectable home-keeping women, such as Mary and Martha, could talk with him with natural frankness, but courtesans also sought him out as though assured that he would understand and befriend them. He lost from his discipleship the "rich young ruler" but Mark says he "loved him"[50] and, as for the poor, his heart was always theirs. He was a loyal Jew, yet in a good Samaritan he portrayed incarnate unselfishness, and in a Roman centurion he found more faith than he had found in Israel.[51]

This inclusiveness of Jesus, his strange unawareness of boundaries that hemmed ordinary people in, is one of his most characteristic qualities. Even in the Fourth Gospel, where his deity rather than his humanity is stressed, the recollection of this human quality is still fresh and strong; he was equally at ease with a learned rabbi, Nicodemus, and with a questionable woman of Samaria. He was, as Dekker said, a "gentleman." The common people would be quick to feel such openheartedness to all sorts and conditions of men and women. Jesus hated pose. Long prayers made for show and ostentatious

[ 53 ]

almsgiving "to be seen of men" aroused his indignation. He despised the façades that men built to shut themselves in and others out and, by-passing social, economic and pietistic distinctions, he went straight for people as human beings, and touched a responsive chord in common folk.

Nevertheless, it was not such ingratiating qualities alone that drew the fascinated crowds. There was power in Jesus, force and drive of personality, daring ideas, strong language. He never minced matters. He felt so intensely that he stretched his words into superlatives before he trusted them to carry what he wished to say. Getting good conduct from bad character was like picking figs from thistles;[52] God, in his care for men, counted every hair on their heads;[53] children were imagined asking for bread or fish and receiving from their fathers stones or snakes.[54] As for denunciation, when Jesus faced selfish greed or cruelty or sham his indignation was explosive. To point out that overstatement is characteristically oriental and that some of Jesus' extreme expressions were doubtless current idiom does not change the picture. In the Babylonian Talmud, written in the Euphrates valley where elephants were known, not a camel but an elephant is imagined trying to pass through a needle's eye.[55] That Jesus seized upon such similes and, along with those of his own invention, used such hyperbole to express his thought, reveals the man. He was not restrained, tame, moderate. He intended his words to be taken seriously—but not literally. Like Beethoven, composing music for whose expression no existent instruments were adequate, the drive of Jesus' thought stretched to the limit his available vocabulary and wanted more.

All this, of course, the crowds did not fully comprehend, but the general effect they must have felt. Jesus was not like anyone they had ever heard before. The content of his teaching they might not understand, but the unique power of both teaching and teacher aroused their wonderment: "The crowds were astonished at his teaching, for he taught them as one who had authority, and not as their scribes."[56]

Naturally, however, not so much Jesus' teaching as his miracles first brought the crowds thronging around him. At that point for moderns to become his contemporaries requires a change of mental outlook so radical as to be almost beyond our power. We start with the idea of nature as an ordered system, in which by law-abiding processes everything moves from cause to consequence. Not in all the Bible, however, is there any such concept as natural law. The Old Testament contains no word that can be translated "nature," and in the New Testament the word so rendered refers not to cosmic order but to the specific constitution of some particular thing, such as an olive tree, wild by nature.[57] Whatever happened in the world of Jesus' day was conceived as happening by personal volition; God, Satan, angels, demons, and men did things, sometimes in usual and to-be-expected ways, sometimes in ways extraordinary and marvelous. No organized knowledge of natural laws limited credulity; miracles, challenging attention and awakening wonder, were expected and counted on; the doors were wide open for any unusual event to be taken as a miracle and for its marvelousness to grow with the retelling.

Indeed, our word "miracle," carrying the implication of broken law, completely misrepresents the thinking of Jesus' day. There is no one word in the New Testament for miracles. Extraordinary events are called mighty works, powers, wonders, signs.[58] Such surprising expressions of power, even when mercifully exhibited in healing the sick, might not be divine

[ 55 ]

at all. Jesus' foes said of him, "He casts out demons by Beelze-bub, the prince of demons,"[59] and Jesus himself is reported as saying: "False Christs and false prophets will arise and show signs and wonders, to lead astray, if possible, the elect."[60] Nor were such wonderworks so uncommon as to constitute unique authentication; "If I cast out demons by Beelzebub," said Jesus, "by whom do your sons cast them out?"[61] This clear indication in the Gospels of the familiarity of miracles—divine, satanic, angelic, demonic, human—corresponds with what we know of the whole world in Jesus' day. In Greece the god Asclepius was credited with endless feats of healing, and the inscriptions discovered in the ruins of the Asclepieion at Athens or of the temple of Epidaurus in Argolis give long lists of marvelous cures. The wonder-works attributed to Apol-lonius of Tyana (born about 4 B.C.) by Philostratus, his biog-rapher, are so strikingly like those attributed to Jesus, that the similarity was once widely ascribed to conscious intent, but now is understood to be the reflection of an all but universal way of thinking. As for Palestine, both the Talmud and Mid-rash describe typical miracles performed by Rabbi Johanan ben Zakkai and his disciple, Rabbi Eliezer ben Hyrcanus, contemporaries of Jesus.[62] Moreover, magicians like Elymas whom Paul defied,[63] and books of sorcery whose spells could even raise the dead, were familiar.

Into such a world came Jesus and, healing the sick as he undoubtedly did, faced in the multitudes who sought his help one of the most embarrassing problems of his ministry.

A contrast seems evident between Jesus' attitude toward "mighty works" and that of his contemporaries. The crowds gathered to see his miracles, partly from curiosity and love of the marvelous, but mostly from desperate need. Beneath Galilee's prosperity were grim factors of poverty and disease.

[ 56 ]

The oppression of Herod and the Romans was cruel to the bodies and maddening to the minds of the Jews. Resentment seethed; unemployment and mendicancy existed alongside the wealth of a few; and behind bodily ills which no known medicine could cure, mental ills flourished alike on the outward wrongs that seemed to have no end and on inward bitterness that could see no hope. As a result—so Dr. Klausner describes it—"Palestine, and especially Galilee, was filled with the sick and suffering and with those pathological types which we now label neurosthenics and psychosthenics . . . and especially hysterical women and all manner of 'nerve cases'—dumb, epileptics, and the semi-insane—were numerous."[64]

When Jesus, therefore, "healed many," all Galilee soon heard of him and throngs gathered. At the center of his ministry, as they saw it, not his teaching but his "mighty works" were paramount. To them he was first and foremost a miracle man, and this disturbed him. Repeatedly, as Mark records it, he admonished those whom he had healed and those standing by to tell no one.[65] Only in recent years have students of the Gospels begun to take the full measure of that fact. Jesus felt himself in danger, and in danger he surely was. He came with a prophetic message; his was a spiritual mission to redeem Israel and to proclaim a gospel of salvation; and instead of being so understood he was being followed by curious, clamoring crowds as a wonder-worker.

To be sure, Jesus valued his power to heal the sick. "If it is by the Spirit of God that I cast out demons," Matthew quotes him as saying, "then the kingdom of God has come upon you";[66] and to imprisoned John the Baptist, so both Matthew and Luke report, he sent word of his healing ministry.[67] Jesus could not have been himself without rejoicing in his power to help afflicted minds and bodies. One fact of

[ 57 ]

crucial importance to him, however, made the multitudes who followed him solely because of his miracles an unwelcome sight: their amazement at the curing of a sick man was no guarantee that either the healed man or those who saw the healing would be spiritually won to Jesus' message and morally transformed. The crowds might exclaim, "We have seen strange things today,"[68] or "We never saw anything like this!"[69] but with that gaping wonder the whole effect might end, and that was not Jesus' goal. After a certain healing, though "all men marveled," the district's inhabitants thought only of getting rid of this wonder-worker, and "began to beg Jesus to depart from their neighborhood."[70] After another healing, his critics, far from being won to him, "were filled with fury and discussed with one another what they might do to Jesus."[71] Let him do his merciful best in healing the sick, his foes could still ascribe his power to the prince of demons,[72] and despite his miracles, that, as he said, might well have converted Tyre and Sidon, the cities where they were wrought, Chorazin, Bethsaida and Capernaum did not repent.[73]

Jesus saw that wonderworks were not convincing; they proved nothing and did not necessarily lead to any good consequence. They were displays of power that men could marvel at while brushing off the major message of the one who worked them. So from his ministry's beginning he tried to keep them in the background. "He strictly charged them that no man should know this,"[74] was his characteristic word after a miracle of healing.

This attitude of Jesus came plainly out on an occasion, when "the crowds were thronging him,"[75] hoping to see some "mighty work." "This generation is an evil generation," said Jesus. "It seeks a sign [that is, a miracle] but no sign shall be given to it except . . ."[76] Then he pictured Jonah's ministry

[ 58 ]

in Nineveh, preaching the grace of God and the call to penitence, until Nineveh repented, although Jonah wrought no
miracle there; and, as well, Solomon, attracting the Queen
of the South from the ends of the earth to listen to his wisdom,
although no miracle is recorded as wrought by him. Jonah
and Solomon in what they were and taught were themselves
the "sign," said Jesus—"Jonah became a sign to the men of
Nineveh." They and their message *were* God's wonderwork,
and no outward marvels were needed to persuade the Queen
of Sheba to listen or Nineveh to repent. So, said Jesus, the
Queen of the South and the men of Nineveh will rise at the
judgment to condemn this "evil generation," clamoring for
marvels while impenitently deaf to the message and blind to
the person of a "greater than Jonah." Indeed, the earliest
Gospel pictures Jesus as profoundly depressed by the crowds'
obsession with miracles. When, apparently dissatisfied with
Jesus' acts of healing, they pestered him for some more preten-
tious wonderwork, "he sighed deeply in his spirit, and said,
'Why does this generation seek for a sign? Truly, I say to you,
no sign shall be given to this generation.' And he left them."[77]

The contrast between Jesus' attitude toward "mighty
works," and that of his contemporaries, therefore, seems clear,
and it extended beyond the crowds to his disciples and to the
recorders of his life. They, too, were of their own time, fascinated by the miraculous. They played up Jesus' marvelous
deeds, and with successive retelling his miracles grew in wonder. In Mark's Gospel there is no record that Jesus revived the
dead, for in the healing of Jairus' daughter, the father appealed
to him saying, "My little daughter is at the point of death,"
and while a messenger came later announcing her decease,
Jesus himself when he saw her said, "The child is not dead."[78]
By the time the Fourth Gospel was written, however, not only

was Lazarus, entombed four days, revived by a word from Jesus, but the miracles in general had moved into the center of the church's picture of him, and were used as proof of his divinity. Even in recording Jesus' attack on his generation for demanding a sign, Matthew interpolates a saying, unknown to Mark and Luke, comparing Jonah's deliverance from the sea-monster with Christ's resurrection from the dead—a comparison alien to the argument and almost certainly not a saying of Jesus himself,[79] but a reflection of the post-resurrection church.

The contrast between Jesus' reluctance to be known as a miracle worker and the ancient world's attitude comes out startlingly in the apocryphal lives of Christ, written in the second and third centuries. They undoubtedly intended to exalt and glorify Jesus, but how did they do it? When the Holy Family flees to Egypt dragons assail them, but when Jesus descends from his mother's bosom and stands before them they adore him. Lions and panthers reverently show Mary and Joseph the way, and palm trees bend their branches to furnish fruit. Jesus himself in early boyhood becomes a magician. He makes a dried fish live. He molds sparrows from clay, claps his hands, and they fly away. He slays with a word a boy who accidentally bumps into him, and, when the boy's parents complain, he strikes them blind. When one of Jesus' playmates falls from a roof and is killed, the dead boy's parents accuse Jesus of throwing him down, and Jesus brings the boy to life again just long enough to report that it was an accident. Repeatedly he revivifies the dead. When six years old he breaks his water pitcher at the well, but carries the water home nonetheless in the folds of his cloak. He makes clay animals walk, colors cloths all the hues the dyer wishes by dipping them in one tub of indigo, changes boys to kids and then back to boys

[ 60 ]

again, lengthens and shortens timbers by touching them to make Joseph's work easier, makes a serpent suck back the poison from a boy whom it has bitten so that the boy lives and the serpent dies, and even divides the river Jordan so that he can walk across it.[80]

Some of the miracles in our canonical Gospels tax modern credence but, in comparison with the wild extravagance of these later apocryphal Gospels, their sobriety stands out. To be sure, obsession with thaumaturgy in forms utterly incongruous with Jesus' character, does begin to appear in the later strata of our Gospels, as in Matthew's account of the hungry Jesus cursing a fruitless fig tree, which "withered at once,"[81] or in the late addition to Mark's Gospel where "they will pick up serpents, and if they drink any deadly thing, it will not hurt them"[82] is a sign of the true believer. Against the miracle-madness of his age the dread of Jesus that he might be taken for a wonder-worker and a magician does seem, as one scholar calls it "extremely modern."[83]

Here is one area where, in Matthew Arnold's phrase, we must see Jesus over the heads of his reporters. The passage about the evil generation that demands a sign could never have been made up later. It runs counter to the whole drift of current thought in Jesus' day. It is alien to the development of the early church's thought as evidenced even in the Fourth Gospel. It must be genuinely his. He did not think that a spiritual message could be authenticated by a wonderwork or that men and women, unconvinced by truth's appeal, could be savingly persuaded by a miracle. He said this explicitly and unmistakably: "If they do not hear Moses and the prophets, neither will they be convinced if some one should rise from the dead."[84]

With the coming of modern psychosomatic medicine Jesus'

healings have become increasingly understandable. He did do "mighty works," rejoicing in the succor brought to the afflicted, but he was apprehensive about their effect upon his ministry. His disciples, returning from a mission in Galilee, were jubilant about one thing most of all: "Even the demons are subject to us." Sharing their joy, Jesus confronted them with a warning: "Nevertheless do not rejoice in this, that the spirits are subject to you; but rejoice that your names are written in heaven."[85] Obsession with wonderworks, he saw, could crowd out that deeper matter in his disciples—their inner quality, their transforming spiritual message, their gospel of God's grace and man's salvation.

As for himself, he feared being misunderstood as a magician. Long afterward the Jewish Talmud called him a sorcerer. He dreaded that reputation among the crowds that sought him for his marvels. He was a teacher, a prophet, a savior—not a magician. He wanted his spiritual mission to be indubitably paramount, and even with the common people, despite their clamor for a sign, he did not altogether fail. At Caesarea Philippi he asked his disciples, " 'Who do men say that I am?' And they told him, 'John the Baptist'; and others, 'Elijah'; and others, 'One of the prophets.' "[86]

When the early church had separated from the synagogue, and Christianity had become a heresy dangerously disrupting Judaism, so that there were even "some believers who belonged to the party of the Pharisees,"[87] the division between Jews and Christians became ever more embittered. In Antioch in Syria, where both Judaism and Christianity were strong, Ignatius, bishop of the city near the end of the first century and the beginning of the second, saw no compromise between the two. "It is monstrous to talk of Jesus Christ," he wrote, "and to practise Judaism."[88] As for the Jews, the earliest mention of Christians in their first century literature is the curse contained in their daily prayer, the "Schemonè Esrè," at the century's close: "May the Nazarenes and the Minim perish."[89] In that generation the Jewish multitude was certainly against Jesus, as the Christian multitude was against the Jews. In our present Gospels, therefore, written as that bitter hostility developed, some of the harshest things said against Jews in general, and Pharisees in particular, may well be not historically authentic but reflections from the then raging controversy between church and synagogue. Obviously this is true in the Fourth Gospel;[90] quite probably it may be true of some passages in the first three. The whole trend and temper of the times when the Gospels were written would lead to emphasis on the hostility of the Jews to Jesus, and of Jesus to the Jews.

All the more impressive, therefore, is the witness of the Gospels, reflecting the original tradition, that the common people heard him gladly, and that to the end multitudes attended him. According to their varied interests and their capacities to comprehend they saw in him a wonder-worker, a teacher, a prophet, an understanding friend, a personality of challenging power, until to meet their anxious hopes of national release from humiliation and slavery the rumor spread that he might be the Messiah. At least the High Priest had heard that rumor concerning the popular response to him, and at the last asked him, "Are you the Christ, the Son of the Blessed?"[91]

It was not the Jewish common people by whom Jesus was despised and rejected. In their response, from the start to the end of his ministry, lay his best chance of winning Judaism to his leadership. The evidence seems convincing that at the beginning of his ministry he had hoped for this. When he laments those Galilean towns which would not repent,[92] or exclaims, "O Jerusalem, Jerusalem, killing the prophets and stoning those who are sent to you! How often would I have gathered your children together as a hen gathers her brood under her wings, and you would not!"[93] do we not hear the cry of a disappointed spirit that had hoped for a consummation of his mission now denied him?[94]

## CHAPTER III

# As the Scribes and Pharisees Saw Him

CONTRARY to common supposition among modern Christians, the Pharisees were Israel's progressive party. The Sadducees were the reactionaries, standing rigidly for the written Scripture as the sole authority for their faith and including in their Scripture only the five Books of Moses. Later innovations in Judaism, such as belief in the resurrection of the dead, they denied, along with the existence of angels and spirits. Precisionists in the interpretation of the law, they were harsh in its enforcement, requiring, for example, that in cases of personal injury the rule, "Eye for an eye," be literally enforced, whereas the Pharisees allowed compensation by a fine. This comparatively small group representing wealth and political power in Jerusalem were orthodox believers of the old school, of whom Josephus said: "Their doctrine reaches only a few men, but those who hold the highest offices."[1]

The Pharisees, however, based their faith and practice not only on the written Scriptures—Torah, Prophets and Sacred Writings—but on oral tradition as well, which they regarded as the true interpretation of the Scriptures. Devoutly faithful to the law, they nevertheless developed its applications, tried to make it relevant to their people's changing life, and wel-

[ 65 ]

comed new ideas which had emerged in the generations immediately preceding Jesus: the angelic and demonic world, the resurrection of the dead, the future life, and the hope of a coming Messiah who would redeem Israel.

Judaism in Jesus' day, therefore, was not at peace within itself but was riven by controversy and, as between Pharisees and Sadducees, the former, often alleviating the too strict enforcement of old laws on which the latter insisted, were the more popular. So Josephus says of the two parties that "great disputes and differences have arisen among them," and that "while the Sadducees are able to persuade none but the rich, and have not the populace obsequious to them, the Pharisees have the multitude on their side."[2]

The differences between Jesus and the Pharisees have been stressed in Christian thinking, as they are stressed in the Gospels, but his disagreements with the Sadducees were much more radical. Even when he criticized the Pharisees for displacing the written law by later oral tradition—"You leave the commandment of God, and hold fast the tradition of men"[3]—he did it for reasons quite unlike the Sadducees' reactionary attitude toward the Books of Moses. Jesus shared with the Pharisees doctrines which the Torah does not teach— belief in the resurrection, for example, which to the Sadducees seemed ridiculous. If a man has had seven wives, they asked, which wife would be his in the resurrection?[4] As for the coming Messiah, that expectation had no such place in Sadducean thinking as in the faith of the Pharisees. The Sadducees stressed man's power of choice and saw the nation's future depending on the uncertainties of that, rather than on the predestinating providence of God. The messianic hope, as the Pharisees held it, they could not find in the Torah and, being rich, powerful, on co-operative terms with Rome, they felt no flaming desire for a change in the *status quo* such as was setting the Jewish people, as a whole, afire. That the Sadducean priests at last conspired with Pilate to crucify Jesus was due not so much to theoretical differences with him as to fear of the public unrest he was causing, and to wrath at his cleansing of the temple, with its threat to their prestige and revenues. As between the Sadducees and the Pharisees, Jesus was mainly on the Pharisees' side.

Nevertheless, it was with the "scribes and Pharisees" that his trouble began. The scribes were the official teachers, who specialized in the interpretation of the law. Most of them were Pharisees, although the Gospels link them also with the Sadducean high priestly party;[5] and especially after the cleansing of the temple, "The chief priests and the scribes . . . sought a way to destroy him."[6] The Pharisees, however, were far more numerous than the Sadducees, and "the scribes of the Pharisees," as Mark calls them,[7] belonged to the party and with their revered authority guided the thought and swayed the judgment of this most popularly powerful and progressive religious group in Palestine.

What Jesus thought of the scribes and Pharisees the Gospels enlarge upon. While scholars feel confident that some of his most scathing epithets—"You brood of vipers,"[8] for example, in Matthew only—are not authentically his, but represent the later fierce hostility between Christians and Jews in the early church, yet Jesus' stern dislike of certain aspects of Phariseeism is unmistakable. Not, however, what Jesus thought of the Pharisees, but what they thought of him is at present our concern.

That some of them were attracted to him is evident. The earliest church in Jerusalem contained "some believers who

[ 67 ]

belonged to the party of the Pharisees,"[9] and Jews like Paul—
"I am a Pharisee, a son of Pharisees"[10]—were among the first
converts. In view of all the enmity between church and synagogue, grown virulent by the time our Gospels were written,
it is natural that in the record hostility between Jesus and the
Pharisaic rabbis should be stressed. All the more authentic,
therefore, must be every indication that some of the scribes
and Pharisees were drawn to him.

One scribe, Mark tells us, so heartily agreed with Jesus
about "which commandment is the first of all," that he exclaimed, "You are right, Teacher," and Jesus answered, "You
are not far from the kingdom of God."[11] In our latest Gospel,
"a man of the Pharisees, named Nicodemus," came to Jesus,
secretly by night, saying, "Rabbi, we know that you are a
teacher come from God."[12] Behind such recollections of Jesus'
appeal to scribes and Pharisees, so alien to the trend of the
times when the Gospels were written, one suspects forgotten
incidents, which, could we recover them, would put into truer
perspective Jesus' relationship with the religious leaders of his
people.

His own brother, James, according to all available data was
an ardent Pharisee, and he became head of the first church in
Jerusalem. Paul's account of him, makes clear his loyalty to
the Pharisaic laws,[13] and the Book of Acts confirms the picture.[14] So loyal a Jew was James, so assiduous in his attendance
at the temple and his practice of the law, that when Annas,
the High Priest, condemned him to death, Josephus says, the
Pharisees themselves protested this perversion of justice and
sent messengers to Agrippa II to complain of it.[15]

Not all scribes did Jesus find alien and hostile. "Every scribe
who has been trained for the kingdom of heaven," he said, "is
like a householder, who brings out of his treasure what is new

and what is old."[16] And, once, we read, "A scribe came up and said to him, 'Master, I will follow you wherever you go.' "[17]

Our accustomed emphasis upon the enmity between Jesus and Israel's religious leaders has obscured the fact that with many things which Jesus said the Pharisees heartily agreed, and that many things they said represented what Jesus thought. "Think not that I have come to abolish the law and the prophets; I have come not to abolish them but to fulfill them. For truly I say to you, till heaven and earth pass away, not an iota, not a dot, will pass from the law, until all is accomplished"[18]—was not that good Phariseeism? "The scribes and the Pharisees sit on Moses' seat; so practice and observe whatever they tell you"[19]—could religious leaders ask for more than that, even though scathing criticism of their deeds did follow?

As for the rabbis' teaching, the Jewish writings which we still possess, composed between 200 B.C. and A.D. 100—the Apocrypha and Pseudepigrapha—bear witness to many elements akin to Jesus' thought. "Blessed is he in whose mouth is mercy and gentleness";[20] "The holy man is merciful to his reviler, and holds his peace";[21] "If anyone seeks to do evil unto you, do well unto him, and pray for him, and you will be redeemed of the Lord from all evil"[22]—such teaching was in the Jewish literature of Jesus' day. He carried the sin of adultery back into lustful desire, but so did the books of his time: "Except my wife I have not known any woman. I never committed fornication by the uplifting of my eyes";[23] "He that has a pure mind in love, does not lust after a woman with a view to fornication; for he has no defilement in his heart."[24] Jesus minimized ceremonial sacrifice in comparison with a devout and righteous life, but so did the contemporary writings: "All sacrifice is little for a sweet savor, and all the fat is very little for a whole burnt offering to Thee; but he that fears the Lord is great continually."[25]

Such selective attention to kindred elements between the teaching of Jesus and the best Jewish religion of his time undoubtedly oversimplifies the situation. Such kinship did exist, however, and the movement of thought and life which he started went victoriously on into the Christian era, not simply despite the scribes and Pharisees, but because at least some of them responded to him and believed. They too were eager for the spiritual renewal of Judaism. They too were praying not simply for the Messiah's coming but for a prophet who should cleanse his people and prepare their hearts for his arrival. They were often men of true piety and profound spiritual life, ready to respond to new insights and to discover new dimensions in their faith.

Nevertheless, as a party, the Pharisees rejected Jesus. They saw him treating with carelessness or with disdain many distinctive practices of Jewish religion. Nation after nation had been absorbed by Persian and Greek conquerors and, losing their separate identity, had perished. The Jews, however, had persisted unassimilated, and it was the Pharisees who had saved them. In the middle of the second century B.C. the revolt, led by the Maccabees, had won a military victory which brought release from Hellenistic Syrian oppressors. The peril in which Judaism stood, however, was deeper than any war could overcome or any change of political regime could guard against. The appeal of Greek culture was pervasive, penetrating, constant. Many Jews ceased being Jews and became Hellenists, in dress and daily customs, in habits of thought and of recreation, in love of the Greek gymnasium and theater, and even in religious practice. The Maccabees won the military battle, but the Pharisees won this more vital war.

To them religion, far more than an individual matter of belief and character, concerned the entire culture of the Jewish people. Orthodoxy with them was not, as is commonly the case with us, a matter simply or mainly of creed. Their religion determined not only how they believed or prayed, but how they dressed and washed and ate, how they observed the sabbath, fasted and kept aloof from all Gentile defilements. From circumcision and phylacteries to Kosher food, therefore, from tassels on their garments to scrupulous observance of the sabbath, the minutiae of the law were to them much more than minutiae. They were the distinguishing marks of a Jew, the indispensable guardians against assimilation. Without them the Jews too would gradually have been absorbed into the powerful, alluring culture of the Hellenistic world.

To study, honor and obey the law, and thus to preserve the distinctive integrity of the Jewish people was the central passion of the Pharisees. The word itself means "Separatists." They were not simply quibblers over legalistic trivialities. They were fighting for a cause they willingly would die for: to save their people from being assimilated by the Gentiles. To achieve that required more than a profound religious faith and a high ethic; it required outward signs and symbols, customs and observances whose practice would make a Jew stand out from all others, unmistakably a Jew.

Then Jesus came. Loyal Jew he might claim to be but he minimized and even treated with disdain ceremonial and legalistic customs which the scribes and Pharisees had pain-stakingly elaborated. He was undoing their work, breaking down the barriers that marked off Jews from all other people. He and his disciples did not keep the appointed fasts.[26] They

broke the sabbath laws.[27] They failed to observe the appointed
ritual washings before eating.[28] They disregarded the rules
concerning food, eating with Publicans and sinners at whose
tables no Kosher customs were respected.[29] Indeed, Jesus,
addressing "the multitude," even said, "There is nothing outside a man which by going into him can defile him; but the
things which come out of a man are what defile him."[30] Of
course the Pharisees were outraged! At one with Jesus in many
of his positive emphases, they were grieved at first, then frightened, then incensed by his failure to understand the necessity
to Judaism's future of those distinctive cultural and religious
customs which were to them the very commandments of God.
Let his ideas obtain ascendancy, let a profound faith in God
and a high ethic become the essence of religion and all else
relatively negligible, what would any longer distinguish a
godly and righteous Jew from a godly and righteous Gentile?
Far off and dimly they caught the foreshadowing of a possibility—which from their point of view they were justified in
fearing—that some day Jews might say, "Neither circumcision nor uncircumcision is of any avail, but faith working
through love."[31]

How far Jesus himself foresaw the implications of a universal
religion in the things he said and did against the ceremonial
and legalistic differentials of Judaism is open to argument. The
instinctive fear of the Pharisees, however, that he was breaking
down the distinguishing characteristics of Judaism, has been
justified by the event. This new teacher, centering his attention on the spiritual core of Israel's prophetic faith, making it
primarily a matter of personal loyalty to God and goodness,
and either pushing into a secondary place or quite canceling
the scribal rules and regulations, was a peril to Phariseeism's
major purpose. "The Judaism of that time," says a modern

Jewish scholar, "had no other aim than to save the tiny nation, the guardian of great ideals, from sinking into the broad sea of heathen culture."[32] How could that be done, if the distinctive ceremonial and legalistic customs of the Jews were not maintained? With a good conscience the Pharisees determined to suppress Jesus, as later Saul of Tarsus, a Pharisee, for the same reason, persecuted his followers.

The Pharisees, however, were only human, and in their case, as in all religions, this program of moral and ritual legalism, justified by a high motive though it was, could not escape deterioration. Religion makes sacred whatever it thinks important. A legal requirement, if it is only *that*, can be treated as a practical matter, easily adjusted, altered or annulled but, if religion adopts it, however minor it may be, it becomes sacred, the will of God, a holy and inviolable commandment of the Most High. It was not an ancient Pharisee but a New England Puritan who said that to hold a wedding banquet or any similar festivity on the Lord's day was "as great a sin as for a Father to take a knife and cut his child's throat."[33] It was not a Jewish rabbi in the first century but a Christian clergyman in the twentieth century who wrote that to eat breakfast before partaking of Holy Communion was a sin comparable with fornication.[34]

This is what "Phariseeism" has now popularly come to mean, and it is a degradation that has afflicted all religions. Behind it is a noble motive—to discover and to do the will of God. That motive was the driving power of the Pharisees in Jesus' day. As they saw themselves, they wanted above all else to learn God's will and to do all of it, in matters great and small. Still in *The Standard Prayer Book* of the synagogue, Rabbi Judah, the Patriarch, is quoted: "Be heedful of a light precept

[ 73 ]

as of a grave one, for thou knowest not the grant of reward for each precept." The consequence of this is obvious, not only in the Gospels but in the literature and continuing practice of orthodox Judaism. Major ethical obligations and legalistic trivialities were put upon a common level. Alike they were the will of God and alike mandatory. Who was man to distinguish in importance between requirements that God himself had laid down?

Then Jesus came, not simply distinguishing between the religious and ethical profundities of Israel's faith and the legalistic minutiae of Pharisaic rules and regulations, but setting the two in contrast, and pouring derision on those who, tithing "mint and dill and cummin," neglected "the weightier matters of the law."[35] He even said that they were straining out gnats and swallowing camels.[36] These ritualistic and moralistic rules, however, were to the Pharisees not gnats but the holy will of God. Where would this teacher stop, thus picking and choosing among the divine commandments?

Once Jesus dined with certain scribes and Pharisees. Great matters were on his mind, and here was an opportunity to announce them. Then the dinner was held up because a ceremony of ritual cleansing had been neglected. "Why do your disciples not live according to the tradition of the elders, but eat with hands defiled?"[37] asked the Pharisees. To Jesus this religion of precise etiquette seemed trivial. Did not the Pharisees themselves say that the great commandments were to love God and one's neighbor as one's self? What right, then, had this ceremonial peccadillo to stride into the center of the picture when great matters were afoot? So, Mark tells us, Jesus indignantly condemned their triviality, accusing them of substituting "human tradition" for "God's commands."[38] To the Pharisees, however, these rules and regulations *were* "God's commands." "He who lightly esteems hand-washing," says the Talmud, "will perish from the earth."[39]

This conflict emerged again with reference to oaths. "When a man voweth a vow unto Jehovah, or sweareth an oath to bind his soul with a bond, he shall not break his word"[40]— with painstaking care the scribes had amplified that command, prescribed its applications in varied circumstances, "built a hedge around the law," as they described it, with detailed regulations guarding it from any possibility of being broken. Then Jesus swept their accumulated rules and precedents aside: "Do not swear at all. . . . Let what you say be simply 'Yes' or 'No'; anything more than this comes from evil."[41]

To a Pharisee such an attitude was utterly unrealistic. People did take oaths; to this day in the Near East vows are the common expression of strong feeling; in Jesus' time they were a stubborn fact, not to be brushed aside by the ideal of an oathless life, but to be practically dealt with. Moreover, the scribes had dealt with them—often sensibly. Their infinite finesse, however, elaborating rules about the phrasing of an oath if it was to be binding, had run out into absurdity. If a man swore by a great matter, such as the temple, without having the details of the temple, such as its golden adornment, clearly in mind, his vow was not binding, but if, when he swore by the temple, the gold was clearly in his thought, he was bound. To Jesus this was trivial nonsense: "You say, 'Swear by the sanctuary, and it means nothing; but swear by the gold of the sanctuary, and the oath is binding.' You are senseless and blind!"[42] As for a son who, by swearing an oath with technical correctness, avoided responsibility for financial aid to his parents, Jesus was indignant: "You say that if a man tells his father or mother, 'This money might have been at your service, but it is Korban' (that is, dedicated to God), he

[ 75 ]

is exempt, so you hold, from doing anything for his father or mother. That is repealing the word of God in the interests of the tradition which you keep up. And you do many things like that."[43]

In Christian circles today, the popular picture of the Pharisees is mainly composed of such trivial legalisms, especially concerning the observance of the sabbath. Plenty of evidence in the Talmud illustrates this aspect of Pharisaic formalism. A man might walk two thousand cubits on the sabbath, but no more. Some knots and not others could be tied or untied on the sabbath. Vinegar, if swallowed, could be used to relieve a sore throat, but it could not be gargled. No woman was to look in a mirror on the sabbath lest, seeing a gray hair, she might be tempted to pull it out. No fire could be kindled on the sabbath. In case death threatened, a physician could be summoned, but, "A fracture may not be attended to," says the Mishna; "If anyone has sprained his hand or foot, he may not pour cold water on it."[44] The schools of Hillel and Shammai, the two most famous rabbis in the generation immediately preceding Jesus, even discussed and disagreed about the question whether an egg that a hen had laid on the sabbath could be eaten.[45]

Such punctilious legalism did characterize Phariseeism, and on the basis of Jewish testimony itself it is evident that many a Pharisee was, in Mark Twain's phrase, "a good man in the worst sense of the word." Nevertheless, to allow this fact to monopolize attention is as unfair as it would be to see New England puritanism in terms only of its senseless scrupulosities. Both Pharisees and Puritans believed in a theocracy, God sovereign and his will the law alike of the individual and the community; this law they found infallibly revealed in sacred books; to determine the meaning and make possible the ob-

servance of this law in daily life, they developed official interpreters, the scribes in one case, the clergy in the other; these
interpreters faced the inescapable necessity of all legalism, to
define permitted and unpermitted conduct in varied circumstances, to establish precedents and to lay down corollary
rules deduced from major laws; and since these deduced
regulations were the official definition of God's will, scribes
and clergy had to be intolerant of all divergence from them.
So, in Boston, Captain Kemple, three years absent on a sea
voyage, returning on a Sunday, was greeted by his wife on
their front doorsill, and for kissing her there in public was put
in the stocks.

The similarity between Puritans and Pharisees is especially
notable with regard to the observance of the sabbath. "It has
truly and justly been observed," wrote Cotton Mather, "that
our whole religion fares according to our sabbaths."[46] So, in
the Puritan commonwealth to gather firewood on the sabbath
was a sin punished with the same severity meted out to theft
and adultery.[47] Indeed, one would think that Increase Mather
had deliberately chosen the Pharisees rather than Jesus for
spiritual guidance to hear him saying, after the great fire swept
Boston in 1711: "Has not God's holy day been profaned in
New England? Has it not been so in Boston this last summer?
Have not burdens been carried through the streets on the
sabbath day? Nay, have not bakers, carpenters and other
tradesmen been employed in servile works on the sabbath
day? When I saw this, my heart said, 'Will not the Lord for
this kindle a fire in Boston?'"[48]

Nevertheless, the Puritans were a sturdy breed, with much
more to be said of them than such quotations indicate. Few
groups in history, so small in numbers, ever made a more con-
structive contribution to the building of a nation. The same is

true of the Pharisees. The drift of religion toward petty ritualistic and moralistic legalism is universal. All religions exhibit it—Christianity not least of all—and to estimate the real quality and significance of any religious group one must have a wider perspective than its punctilious casuistry affords.

Moreover, there were countermovements among the Pharisees, as there were among the Puritans. Not all were compliant and satisfied with the prevalent casuistry. A Gentile, asking that he be told the whole law while standing on one foot, Shammai scorned; but Hillel answered: "What you would not have done to yourself, do not to another; that is the whole law, the rest is commentary."[49] Orthodox Judaism was no more unanimous than most religions are, and over three hundred dissenting opinions are reported in the Talmud between the schools of Hillel and Shammai.[50] In Jesus' day—when Shammai's influence was probably dominant—Jesus' protest against the rigorous legalism by which one could escape filial obligation by saying "Korban" was doubtless justified. The Jewish Mishna, however, which, while codified much later, may well reflect opinions present in the first century, is all on his side, holding that no vows can release a man from responsibility to support his parents.[51] The precarious basis of Pharisaic legalism was frankly noted by an early rabbi: "The [provisions for] release from vows float in the air, there is nothing to support them; the regulations about the sabbath, and offerings at festivals, and the misappropriation of sacred things are like mountains hanging by a hair, for they are very little Bible and many rules."[52]

Some teachers in Israel were not so blind as to miss seeing what they themselves called "the plagues of the Pharisees,"[53] and not so lacking in humor as to miss observing the ridiculousness of much Pharisaic scrupulosity. The Talmud caricatures one Pharisee who with sham humility drags his feet along the ground and stubs his toe; and makes fun of another who, walking with eyes half shut for fear of seeing a woman, bruises his head against a wall.[54] Moreover, the impression made by some sabbath laws of utter heartlessness in forbidding the relief of misery on the sabbath is far from representing the whole truth. Jesus' saying, "The sabbath was made for man, not man for the sabbath"[55] is paralleled by the rabbis. "The sabbath was given into your hand, and ye were not given into its hand," said R. Jonathan ben Joseph; "The sabbath is delivered to you, and ye are not delivered to the sabbath,"[56] said R. Shimeon ben Menassia.

Nevertheless, the fact remained that the Pharisees were thoroughgoing legalists and Jesus was not. "A body of Jews who profess to be more religious than the rest and to explain the laws more precisely," is Josephus' description of the Pharisees,[57] and they could not possibly tolerate Jesus. To be sure, they put the saving of life above the keeping of the sabbath laws. Says the Talmud, "The saving of human life sets aside the laws of the sabbath."[58] Jesus, however, went further. He defended his disciples for plucking corn on the sabbath because they were hungry;[59] he healed a withered hand on the sabbath, when no question of life and death was involved;[60] and he stated the principle of his conduct unmistakably, "Thus it is right to do a kindness on the sabbath."[61] Any strict Pharisee could see that such an idea, once gaining general acceptance, would ruin the whole superstructure of sabbath laws.

This point of conflict came plainly out when Jesus on the sabbath healed a woman who for eighteen years had been "bent double" so that she could not "raise herself." "The president of the synagogue," we read, "was annoyed at Jesus' healing on the sabbath, and he said to the crowd, 'There are six days for work to be done; come during them to get healed, instead of on the sabbath.' " [62] That Pharisee could with good logic have argued his case. No question of threatened death was involved. Had death threatened, a reasonable rule of the rabbis, formulated later but in principle quite probably recognized in Jesus' day, would have covered the case: "A man may profane one sabbath in order that he may observe many sabbaths." [63] A disability endured for eighteen years, however, could be borne one day more—there was no need of desecrating the holy day by that woman's healing. Jesus, however, was incensed by such an attitude. "You hypocrite," he said, "does not each of you untether his ox or ass from the stall on the sabbath and lead it away to drink? And this woman, a daughter of Abraham, bound by Satan for all these eighteen years, was she not to be freed from her bondage on the sabbath?" [64] Luke adds that "all his opponents were put to shame, but all the crowd rejoiced over all his splendid doings." It is evident, however, that his opponents were more than "put to shame"; they were affronted and outraged; their whole legalistic system was in danger so long as this man was abroad in the land.

Insult was added to injury, as the Pharisees saw it, when Jesus not only imperiled the peculiar customs that distinguished Jews from Gentiles and threatened their system of ritual observances, but defended his attitude by appeals to their sacred Scriptures. This was, in Shakespeare's phrase, hoisting them with their own petard, and they could not endure it.

Jesus, criticized because his disciples on the sabbath plucked, husked and ate corn in the fields, came back at his critics with an appeal to Scripture: "Have you not read what David did when he and his men were hungry, how he went into the house of God, and there they ate *the loaves of the Presence* which neither he nor his men were allowed to eat, but only the priests?"[65] It was bad enough to face the laxness of Jesus, but to confront a defense of it from their own sacred authorities was infuriating. He was using Scripture to demolish Scripture. When the question of divorce came up, he asked them what the Mosaic law was, and when they replied, "Moses permitted a man *to divorce her by writing out a separation notice,*" he answered, "He wrote you that command on account of the hardness of your hearts." He did not leave the matter there, however, as though his disregard of a Mosaic law were his own opinion merely. He appealed to Scripture, going back to God's intent concerning marriage when he first made man and woman:

"From the beginning, when God created the world
   Male and female, He created them:
   hence a man shall leave his
    father and mother,
   and the pair shall be one flesh.
So they are no longer two but one flesh. What God has joined, then, man must not separate."[66]

Such setting of Scripture against Scripture was disturbing. According to Matthew, on two occasions—once when he had eaten with publicans and sinners, breaking Kosher laws,[67] and once when his disciples had broken sabbath laws—Jesus appealed in self-defense to Hosea: "I desire goodness, and not sacrifice."[68] The Pharisees used that quotation too. Once Rabbi Johanan ben Zakkai, Jesus' contemporary, heard a friend lament over the ruins of Jerusalem, "Woe unto us, that this, the place where the iniquities of Israel were pardoned, is laid waste." But Rabbi Johanan said to him, "My son, be not distressed; we have another atonement as effective as this.

And what is that? It is deeds of lovingkindness; as it is said, 'For I desire mercy, and not sacrifice.' "[69] All the more, however, because that prophetic passage was holy writ to the Pharisees, Jesus' use of it was unendurable. He was aligning Hosea on his side against their sacred laws, using Hosea to break down the legal system on which depended the future of Judaism. Nothing more enrages the orthodox in any religion than this appeal to their own sacred writings against their orthodoxy.

Luke's Gospel strongly stresses the idea that Jesus turned to the Gentiles because the Jews rejected him, and this emphasis in the evangelist's thought may have affected his rendering of the incident at Nazareth, when Jesus returned there and preached in the synagogue. There is vivid verisimilitude in the narrative, however, especially with regard to Jesus' use of Scripture: "There were many widows in Israel in the days of Elijah, when the heaven was shut up three years and six months, when there came a great famine over all the land; and Elijah was sent to none of them but only to Zarephath, in the land of Sidon, to a woman who was a widow. And there were many lepers in Israel in the time of the prophet Elisha; and none of them was cleansed, but only Naaman the Syrian."[70] At that point "all in the synagogue were filled with wrath." To have their racial prejudice called in question was bad enough, but to have Elijah and Elisha marshaled on the critic's side, their sacred Scripture used to condemn the very exclusiveness that saved them from Gentile defilement, was intolerable. This was "new teaching" indeed, holy writ employed to unholy ends, the devil himself, as it were, quoting Scripture to his purpose.

Jesus used this same style of argument in dealing with the Sadducees. They could find no warrant for any hope of resurrection from the dead in their sacred canon, the Books of Moses, and so they held no hope. When they confronted Jesus, however, with their skeptical ridicule of the resurrected life, his answer came from their own Scriptures. He brushed aside as senseless their question—to which husband, in the resurrection, would a wife belong who had had seven husbands—and went to the pith of the matter in a passage from Exodus.[71] Centuries after Abraham, Isaac and Jacob had died, God said to Moses: "I am the God of Abraham, and the God of Isaac, and the God of Jacob." So, Jesus argued, on the basis of Mosaic authority itself, God claims the great dead as his living servants still. "He is not God of the dead, but of the living."[72] Whether this reply to the Sadducees from the Sadducean canon of Scripture convinced any we do not know, but that it incensed many we may be sure.

Even if the controversy thus arising between Jesus and the leaders of his people had remained in the theoretical realm, teaching against teaching, it would have been serious. The scribes, however, were used to controversy. They were at variance among themselves; Sadducees and Pharisees radically differed; argument and counterargument about the meaning of Scripture and the observance of the law were their familiar occupation.

In Jesus, however, they faced another phenomenon. Jesus was not primarily a teacher. He was a reformer. He came not only to *say* something but to *do* something—to call his nation to repentance, to cleanse the synagogue of its sterile conventionality and the temple of its abuses, to open the gates of salvation to folk who were forgotten or despised, to usher in a new age of righteousness. Whatever else was in his mind, this much was there, and it made of him not so much a rabbi,

founding a school, as an active reformer insisting on change.
It is easy now to conceive him as a religious philosopher and
to arrange his teaching in systematic order, but no contemporary could so have pictured him. He was actively proposing
revolutionary changes in the religious life and practice of his
people. His offense was not simply "new teaching"; what he
said they might with difficulty have endured, but what he did
was unendurable. He actually broke the sabbath, ate with the
unclean, defied the laws of purification, and called on the
people to live by his blasphemous innovations—"It was said
to the men of old . . . but I say to you . . ."[73] He was gathering
disciples, sending them out on missions, attracting a popular
following, launching a movement. This man intended insurrection against the cherished customs of his people, and he
said so: "No one puts new wine into old wineskins; if he does,
the wine will burst the skins, and the wine is lost, and so are
the skins: but new wine is for fresh skins."[74] From the day he
first defied the sabbath laws to the day he cleansed the temple
in Jerusalem he was a doer, not a speaker only.

This fact, indeed, often makes difficult the recovery of the
exact meaning of his teaching. As the Gospels present his doctrine, there is no system or order in it. All his teaching was
incidental to what he was doing with some individual or
group. A personal conversationalist, what he said was determined, not by the logical development of a thesis, but by the
needs of those whom he addressed. When scholars now abstract from his scattered sayings a religious philosophy, there
is always a wooden, stereotyped, unreal quality in their systematic classification of his doctrines. What actually happened
was that, facing self-righteous Pharisees, he told his parables
of the lost sheep, the lost coin and the lost son to show up the
evil of their attitude;[75] taking a little child in his arms, he

[ 84 ]

spoke his unforgettable words about what real greatness is;[76] confronted by a scribe with a much discussed question as to who one's neighbor is, he told the story of the good Samaritan;[77] when dining with Simon the Pharisee, the presence of a sinful woman called out his startling pronouncement on forgiveness.[78] All his teaching was thus incidental, casual, called out by something he was doing with some individual or group.

To be sure, Matthew's Gospel groups together narratives of Jesus' typical miracles, and, in another section, groups his typical teachings in what we call "The Sermon on the Mount." It is evident, however—as in the case of the Lord's Prayer which Luke assigns to a different setting[79]—that these various sayings were at first separate, and that the original background of circumstance which called them out had been forgotten. If we could know, for example, what occasion elicited his saying—so unlike him, as it is usually interpreted—about casting pearls before swine,[80] what light would be thrown on its meaning!

Such was the man the Pharisees confronted, out to do something radical and revolutionary in Israel. It was no theory they faced but a situation to which indifference was impossible.

In the lush days when faith in progress—even inevitable progress—was prevalent, Jesus was sometimes interpreted as a social reformer, striving by gradual processes to reconstruct society and bring in the divine utopia. That such a picture of him is unjustified modernization has long since been evident. He did not attack "social problems" in our modern sense. He did not conceive his mission as reconstructing the government, dethroning Caesar, changing the economic system, or even abolishing slavery by progressive means. He shared the hope which was real to his people's tradition—a divine intervention in history that would bring the kingdom in. The idea of evolu-

[ 85 ]

tionary progress was nowhere present in the ancient world, and not long-drawn-out amelioration but sudden catastrophic intervention was the vivid hope of the Jews in Jesus' generation. Nevertheless, to deny that Jesus was a social reformer and then to substitute the idea that he was a wistful, expectant dreamer, merely awaiting God's apocalyptic action, is to put one falsehood in the place of another. Not a social reformer in our modern sense, he was certainly a reformer. He would not give the *status quo* in Israel a moment's rest. At one point after another he attacked it—the economic evils of proud and greedy wealth, the social evils of class prejudice, the ruthless tyranny of rulers like "that fox," Herod, the blasphemy of commercialism in the temple courts, the unfairness to women of the current laws concerning divorce, and with tireless vigor and insistence the religious failures of Pharisaic legalism. Moreover, wherever the opportunity opened, he not only talked but acted. Apocalyptic hopes suggest to moderns a substitute for energetic action, but among the Jews they were far more commonly a stimulus to energetic action.

That Jesus himself was aware of this real point of conflict seems evident. He even told "the multitudes" to "practice and observe" whatever the scribes and Pharisees bade, as though with the major intent and meaning of their teaching he could make shift to get along. It was "what they do" that troubled him. Their self-righteousness and exhibitionism, their show of broad phylacteries, their outward piety and inward unworthiness, their punctilious scruples alongside their major sins, their withering scorn of outcast folk and moral failures, their misrepresentation of the grace of God and the spirit of humaneness which should be Israel's glory—these were the crux of his attack. The law he too wanted to see fulfilled but in them he saw it misused—

The meanest man I ever saw,
allus kep' inside o' the law.[81]

Such criticisms, leveled by Jesus against the Pharisees, are paralleled in Jewish literature. They apply not to all Pharisees, but to perverse members of the party. When Jesus charges that "they bind heavy burdens, hard to bear, and lay them on men's shoulders; but they themselves will not move them with their finger,"[82] he is confirmed by the Talmud, which calls a scribe who so interprets the law as to make its rules light for himself and burdensome for others a "subtle knave."[83] Jesus' picture of the Pharisee thanking God in the temple that he is "not like other men,"[84] has its counterpart in a rabbi's prayer, quoted in the Talmud, "I give thanks before thee, O Lord my God, that thou hast set my portion with those who sit in the house of study and not with those who sit at street-corners; for I and they rise early—I to words of Torah, but they to vain matters; I and they labor, but I labor and receive a reward, whereas they labor and receive no reward: I and they hasten—I to the life of the world to come, but they to the pit of destruction."[85] Such self-righteousness is a major temptation of legalism, and it was so understood by the better sort of Pharisee. Not even Jesus himself pled more earnestly for humility than did Hillel: "My abasement is my exaltation and my exaltation is my abasement."[86]

Such recognition of Pharisaic faults by Pharisees, while it brings into the foreground the nobler members of the party, also confirms the fact that Jesus was dealing with a real problem. As a teacher only, he might have been content to argue against scribal exegesis; as a reformer of Israel, he had to attack a way of living, entrenched in the most influential religious group among his people.

The radical cause of this difference between Jesus and the Pharisees runs deep. They were thinking primarily of saving Judaism in general and the nation in particular; Jesus was thinking primarily of saving individuals. To be sure, the Pharisees would have affirmed that the Jewish nation and religion could not be saved without devout and faithful individuals, and Jesus obviously was thinking of a transformed nation and world as the crown and consummation of transformed persons. The focus in each case, however, was distinctive. Both wanted right living, but the Pharisees, with the protection of Judaism and its people from pagan defilement in the center of attention, could think of its achievement mainly in terms of legalistic discipline, rules and regulations externally imposed; while Jesus, with individual persons central, thought in terms of inward transformation—

A good tree cannot bear bad fruit,
and a rotten tree cannot bear sound fruit.[87]

If one is aiming primarily at the defense of a people and a religion from the corruption of surrounding heathenism, the Pharisaic method is logical and defensible. Distinctive customs, rigidly defined, insisted on as the very will of God, and drilled into a devout and loyal nation, will protect, and did protect the Jews, from assimilation. If one, however, is digging the tunnel from the other end, seeing transformed persons as the only way to a transformed people, such a method is inadequate and self-defeating. Far from making bad people good, rules and regulations externally imposed—as religious history amply proves—commonly lead to mere external conformity, the outside meticulously correct while the inside is all wrong.

Here was the deepest source of conflict between Jesus and Jewish legalism—"You blind Pharisee! first cleanse the inside of the cup and of the plate, that the outside also may be clean"[88]—and the reason for this conflict lay in a radical difference of predominant aim. Legalism might save a nation but, by itself alone, it never saved a person. Persons, to be made good men and women, must be inwardly transformed, and because this was Jesus' central interest, his distinctive approach to the human problem, he rebelled against the whole Pharisaic system. Whether one takes Matthew's rendering, just quoted, where the contrast lies between cleansing the outside and the inside of a dish, or takes Luke's rendering—"You Pharisees clean the outside of cups and dishes, but inside you are full of greed and wickedness"[89]—where the contrast lies between the external cleansing of dishes and the internal cleansing of human souls, Jesus' essential meaning is the same. He was content with nothing less than transformed life within. What was first with the Pharisees—a people faithfully observing a mass of regulations—was not first with him: "first cleanse the inside of the cup and of the plate."

Far from inwardly redeeming persons to a good life, Jesus saw the Pharisaic method issuing in what he called hypocrisy. That word has come to mean conscious pretense, deliberate play-acting and insincerity, but this almost certainly was not Jesus' meaning. The Pharisees, as a whole, were obviously sincere, ready to lay life down for their law; but they were, said Jesus, "blind," self-complacent about their scrupulosities, depending on the techniques of legalism to do what only inward, personal regeneration can do. Whatever other quality Jesus' ethic and religion had, *inwardness* was at the heart of them. When Dr. Manson says, "For Jesus good living is spontaneous activity of a transformed character; for the scribes

THE MAN FROM NAZARETH

and Pharisees it is obedience to a discipline imposed from without,"[90] he states the gist of the matter. Those two approaches are not easily reconcilable. In this regard the Pharisees were right in thinking that they faced in Jesus a mortal enemy of their whole system.

This inwardness of Jesus' approach lights up one of the most difficult problems in our Gospels: the seeming contradiction between Jesus' professed intention, on one side, not to abolish but to fulfill the law, and, on the other, Jesus' sustained and vehement attack upon scribal legalism. When all the guesses concerning Matthew's special interest in the sanctity of Jewish law, and concerning the possible reflection in the Gospels of the early church's controversy between Judaistic and Hellenistic Christians, are taken full account of, that contradiction is too tenacious to be easily eliminated, and the question still remains: what if Jesus did say that he came not to abolish but to fulfill the law, and what if he meant it?

There are two ways of fulfilling the great commandments of Judaism. One the Pharisees tried. They drew out corollary rules from major laws, deduced specific regulations from general principles, created detailed precepts applying to endless concrete situations, and so built up their immense and complicated legal system. Jesus, however, used another method. If a man does not hate, he will not kill; if he does not lust, he will not commit adultery; if his word is "simply 'Yes' or 'No,'" he will not break his oath; if evil thoughts do not proceed out of his heart, he will do no evil; if he is a fig tree he will bear no thistles. Jesus did come to fulfill the law, but by a method that could not be reconciled with Pharisaic legalism.

A typical illustration of this difference is provided by the desire of both Jesus and the Pharisees to escape from the old law by which, in cases of personal injury, the victim could demand an eye from the aggressor if his own eye had been destroyed. While the Sadducees called for the law's literal observance, the Pharisaic substitution of financial compensation was almost certainly the general, if not the universal, practice. Nevertheless, the Pharisees were forced by their theory to retain and fulfill the law, and they did so in typical legalistic fashion. The victim could extract the aggressor's eye, they said, but only if it was exactly like his own in size and color; and since this condition is never present, the principle of retaliation was retained without its barbarous expression.[91] Jesus, however, went at that problem in another way by rejecting the law of retaliation altogether—undiscourageable goodwill even toward those who injure us, the vindictiveness that desires an eye for an eye conquered at its source in the heart of the injured man.

This does not mean that Jesus would have denied the function of custom, law and regulation. In any culture they are indispensable to personality, as a trellis is to guide the growth of a living vine. Jesus' concern, however, was centered on the living vine and, as he saw it, the vast elaboration of the Pharisaic trellis endangered the very growth it was intended to assist.

One suspects, therefore, that the seeming contradiction between what Jesus said about fulfilling the law and what he did about it is no real contradiction at all. He had pondered deeply the meaning of the law, as interpreted by the prophets, and with all the passionate devotion of a true Pharisee he wanted it fulfilled. But was it being fulfilled by this multiplication of rules and this insistence on their meticulous observance? Did not the fulfillment of the law demand another method altogether—inward transformation, spiritual rebirth, the cleansing of motive, the creation of a quality in life that prevented and forestalled the evils which the law prohibited? Not legalistic regulation but inward regeneration was the way he chose to the law's fulfillment, and he stated the contrast between the two with merciless clarity.

Inevitably, then, the scribes and Pharisees found him a dangerous enemy. As they saw themselves they were Judaism's hope, and he was putting them to scorn. So, in the end, that "strictest party of our religion," as Paul called the Pharisees,[92] turned against Jesus, convinced that he must be suppressed. They never dreamed that history, watching them in retrospect, would see them facing in the Man of Nazareth a personality too big for their acceptance and understanding.

## CHAPTER IV

# *As the Self-Complacent Saw Him*

A MAJOR tragedy of legalistic religion is that its rules can be observed and that, like Saul of Tarsus, its devotees can be, "as to righteousness under the law blameless."[1] Self-complacency always dogs the footsteps of legalism. The elder brother of the Prodigal Son incarnated Jesus' idea of Phariseeism at its worst; yet that elder brother said to his father: "Lo, these many years I have served you, and I never disobeyed your command."[2] Such self-complacent folk found Jesus a disturbing person.

A man of wealth and station once asked him, "Good Teacher, what must I do to inherit eternal life?" and when Jesus rehearsed certain major commandments, the man replied: "Teacher, all these I have observed from my youth."[3] Then Jesus called on him to sell whatever he had and give to the poor, required of him, that is, an excess of goodness which no one could reasonably expect. Jesus was aiming at that man's self-complacency, showing him dimensions in goodness which no rules and regulations could express, and facing which no man could be self-satisfied. That rich man's "countenance fell, and he went away sorrowful." While some, however, may thus have responded to Jesus' extravagant ethical demands

[ 93 ]

with sorrow, there must have been more who responded with resentment.

No record exists that Jesus asked any other individual to sell all his possessions for the sake of the poor. He habitually dealt with persons, one by one, sailing, as it were, around the island of each life until he saw where the real problem was, and then landing *there*. Zacchaeus called out Jesus' praise when he gave only half his goods to the poor and restored his extortions fourfold.[4] Jesus said nothing to Martha about selling her goods, but dealt with her personal problem of overanxiety about small details.[5] In the earliest Gospel one who wanted to do what Jesus required of the rich man—leave all and follow him—was not permitted by Jesus to do it, but was told instead: "Go home to your friends."[6] What Jesus said to an individual about his personal problem may not without due care be generalized as though applicable to everyone. Always, however, Jesus presented to any self-complacent person an ethical ideal that made blamelessness impossible.

What, then, did these morally self-satisfied folk see in Jesus—the rich man in love with his wealth, who had observed all the laws from his youth; men like the elder brother of the Prodigal, who had never transgressed a command; men like the Pharisee, who thanked God that he was not as the rest of men;[7] Simon the Pharisee, unaware of his need of forgiveness, finding himself unfavorably compared with a sinful woman, who, forgiven much, loved much?[8]

To such characters Jesus must have seemed what we would call "perfectionist," asking the impossible, presenting not observable rules but unattainable ideals. "You have heard that it was said to the men of old, 'You shall not kill; and whoever kills shall be liable to judgment.' But I say to you that every one who is angry with his brother shall be liable to judgment"[9]—no one ever lived up to *that*. Indeed, many ancient authorities read, "every one who is angry with his brother *without cause*"—obviously a later addition, written in by someone desiring to mitigate Jesus' unqualified ideal. Such unqualified idealism, however, was the very essence of Jesus' ethical demand. He went far beyond rules, plunged deep into the inner recesses of motive and emotion, and called for a quality of spirit beyond the reach of any man's volition. This distinctive characteristic of Jesus' teaching was his way of dealing with the actual situation which he faced. Self-complacency, inherent in any legalistic system, confronted him on every side, and he deliberately challenged it with an ethic that made self-righteousness impossible.

To be sure, Jesus did not altogether discard legalism, whether moral or ritual. When he condemned the Pharisees for tithing "mint and rue and every herb" and passing over "justice and the love of God," he did not eliminate the tithing: "These you ought to have done without neglecting the others."[10] He himself observed faithfully the more important customs of his people, and far from being a ruthless iconoclast, he told one whom he had healed, "Go and show yourself to the priest, and make an offering for your cleansing, as Moses commanded."[11]

As Jesus would not have discarded all legalism, so the Pharisees would have lifted the Psalmist's prayer for a clean heart and a right spirit.[12] They too remembered Jeremiah, "I will put my law in their inward parts, and in their heart will I write it."[13] Nevertheless, while Jesus and the legalists could each have granted much to the other's position, the practical situation meant controversy. Legalism, dominant, detailed, obsessing, was bringing its inevitable consequence—the self-righteousness of men who thought themselves blameless.

Attempted explanations of Jesus' idealism have gone far afield. He expected the speedy end of the age and the coming of God's victorious kingdom, some have said; his ethic was not intended to be livable in this present evil world; it was the ethic of a heavenly realm soon to come, or an "interim" morality conceivable today only because today would soon be replaced by an ideal tomorrow. The Pharisees, however, also believed in the coming messianic reign. They too were expecting an ideal tomorrow; yet, far from sharing Jesus' so-called "perfectionist" ethic, many of them were contented legalists. While undoubtedly their faith in the coming kingdom was less intense than his, and while they did not feel, as vividly as he did, its imminence, this difference in intensity and vividness should not blind us to the fact that Jesus and the Pharisees shared a basic hope of God's victorious intervention. The unique quality of Jesus' ethic, so sharply in contrast with Phariseeism, demands a deeper explanation than the eschatological expectation which he shared with them.

The essential demand of Jesus for inner rightness was in the Psalms and prophets before messianism became central in Israel's thought, and many noble sayings of the rabbis gave it voice after messianism became peripheral. Jesus' expectation of the speedy coming of the kingdom was neither the profound origin of his inward ethic nor the immediate motive of his insistence on it. The sources of his high ideals must be sought in the depths of his own personality and in his idea of God, rather than in a single category of contemporary thought like messianism. He was an idealist because he was that kind of person, and he would have been that kind of person in the twentieth century with its ideas of progress as well as in the first century with its apocalyptic hopes. Moreover, as the Gospel record stands, his presentation of unattainable ideals was, in part at least, called out by an immediate situation. He confronted self-satisfied moralists. *"Unless your righteousness exceeds that of the scribes and Pharisees"*—with this crucial need his ethical demands in the Sermon on the Mount were dealing.

You say your prayers, he said, but what about your inward life of prayer in secret where no man sees? You do not break your spoken vows, but what about sincerity? You do not commit adultery, but what about lust? You give alms, but what about love? You fast, but what about penitence? The impression made by these searching demands is not at all that of a man constructing a perfectionist ethic in view of a coming messianic reign, but of a man, practically in earnest, speaking to real people who needed these things said to them. Self-righteousness, pride, complacency with kept rules, were prevalent vices. Jesus saw no hope for his people until they confronted God's will in terms of a good life that made such pride impossible.

Legalism in religion is commonly presented as a heavy burden, obedience to whose many rules is difficult and wearisome. There is, however, another side to the matter. To live up to a perfect ideal is impossible, but a rule can be observed. For earnest religious people, seriously wishing to do God's will, there is positive relief in having duty precisely defined, saved thus from vagueness, brought down to earth, translated into detailed commandments which can be obeyed. To be "in the Spirit on the Lord's day,"[14] as the New Testament says, is an ideal that leaves so much to the imagination and inner quality of the individual that many would despair of knowing what it means, but strict sabbatarian regulations simplify the problem; they can be learned and obeyed.

The familiar idea, therefore, that the laws of the Pharisees were an onerous burden to faithful Jews misrepresents the total picture. It was rather their glory, as sons of Israel, to possess the law and, in small matters and large alike, thus to have God's will defined for them. They said that the law is like a garden, all of whose fruits and flowers are cultivated by the son because he loves his father. They said that while an inferior guest at a banquet may have only one dish or one cup of wine, whereas the sons of the house have access to the whole larder and the whole wine cellar, so Israel has the privilege of knowing and obeying all the divine precepts.[15] The best of the Pharisees, therefore, conceiving their multiplied commandments as garden flowers or varied courses at a banquet, were not, as commonly pictured, dour, glum, heavily burdened obeyers of meticulous rules, but often were radiant souls, carrying off their observance of the divine laws as happily as distinguished gentlemen at a royal court might carry off customary ceremonies, to observe which is their pride. As for the common people, wide areas of required observance, especially at the Jewish festivals, were doubtless as joyfully handled as Christmas customs are among Christians now.

Nevertheless, the nemesis of legalism is inescapable. It does become burdensome. A modern Jewish scholar writes, "The requirements of the Law, both moral and ritual, were far-reaching, intricate, manifold. They did not merely affect the great concerns of life, but fussed over the small; they left few things untouched, and their touch was mostly, though far from invariably, a heavy one."[16] Worse than this, however, was the temptation to self-righteousness, to observe laws and then thank God in consequence that one is not as the rest of men.

In the face of this temptation Jesus presented an ethical demand so inward, concerned so deeply with quality of thought, motive and emotion, that being "in every respect . . . tempted as we are,"[17] he said even about himself, "Why do you call me good? No one is good but God alone."[18]

The morally self-satisfied faced in Jesus a demand not only for inward rightness but for positiveness of life and character. It was this that left the "rich young ruler" baffled. An attractive personality—"Jesus looking upon him loved him"[19]—his goodness was negative. The commandments he had obeyed were prohibitions and his virtue was respectability. Jesus demanded of him devotion, enthusiasm, sacrificial loyalty. "So far, so good!" Jesus seemed to say about his conventional correctness, "but now, amount to something! Leave the nest of your comfortable living and give yourself to a cause greater than yourself! Follow me, and find your life not in what belongs to you but in what you belong to!"

That kind of goodness lies beyond the power of law to generate. Laws may help define its expression, but the thing itself is inwardly begotten, and no prohibitions can even touch the fringes of its meaning. Inherent in Jesus' character, illustrated in his mission, it was central also in his message. None could follow him without accepting as the essential constituent of discipleship a positive sacrificial loyalty that burned all bridges behind it. As for self-righteousness, based on the observance of prohibitions, that seemed to Jesus the caricature of goodness.

The morally self-satisfied, therefore, content in their re-respectability, found him an annoying person. Some of his sternest condemnations fell on people, not who did something wrong, but who did nothing. The priest and Levite, who went by on the other side and left the victim of the robbers unhelped, fell under his censure.[20] What had they done? Nothing whatever! The condemned in the judgment to whom the Lord said, "I was hungry and you gave me no food, I was thirsty and you gave me no drink, I was a stranger and you did not welcome me, naked and you did not clothe me, sick and in prison and you did not visit me,"[21] faced doom because they had done nothing. The rich man who had fared sumptuously every day, while Lazarus lay starving at his door, was condemned not for doing but for not doing. The son who roughly answered his father's command to "work in the vineyard" by saying, "I will not," but who then went, was praised by Jesus rather than the son who answered, "I go, sir," but who did not go.[22] Negativeness was the disdain of Jesus. Once he told a parable, alike whimsical and urgently serious, about an unclean spirit which, having left a man to roam abroad, came back again to find "the house empty, swept, and put in order"; then into this vacant, decent, respectable habitation that unclean spirit brought seven others, "and the last state of that man becomes worse than the first."[23]

It would be grossly unjust to the Pharisees to represent them as lacking in positive, devoted, sacrificial loyalty. It was they who had refused easy compromise with pagan culture and who labored tirelessly to save Judaism from corruption. They were in deadly earnest about their cause, traversing "sea and land to make a single proselyte."[24] Their furious resistance against any rupture of their laws or profanation of their holy places was the despair of the Romans. Not once but many times—as when Petronius proposed a statue to the emperor in the temple area—the answer of the Pharisees was resolute and final: They would all die rather than transgress the law.[25] Seldom in history has a more persistent, sacrificial devotion to a cause been seen than in the long struggle of the Pharisees to save Judaism.

Nevertheless, as Jesus watched the consequences, one factor in it was to him unendurable. This positive devotion was given to the support and maintenance of a legalistic system, too much concerned with prohibitory rules. It was, in too large measure, positiveness dedicated to negativeness. No religious cult altogether escapes this paradox; current Christianity furnishes plentiful illustrations. From being right within, which is very difficult, the emphasis shifts to doing right which is then defined in precepts; but doing right is most easily guarded by prohibitions against doing wrong. So in every religion intense loyalty has been massed around commandments concerning things forbidden. There is nothing peculiar to Phariseeism in the Pharisee who thanked God he was not as the rest of men largely because of what he had *not* done.[26]

Such self-righteousness, as Jesus saw it, was much too cheaply won. Anyone could have it by lowering the standard of goodness to prohibitory rules. From not doing, therefore, he turned his stress to doing, and from doing to being, in part at least because he saw self-righteousness, cheaply bought, as a major problem among his people.

What Jesus wanted was humility. He would have agreed with Rabbi Joshua ben Levi that it is the greatest of the virtues[27]—certainly that without it no genuine virtue is possible —and he came at it by making the criterion of moral excellence so deep, inward and positive that no one could be self-satisfied. What troubled him, as he watched some of the Pharisees, was their pride. They did their deeds to be seen of men, made their phylacteries ostentatiously broad and their tassels long, loved places of honor at feasts, the best seats in the synagogues, and salutations in the market place;[28] and, worst of all, they thought of themselves as "righteous persons who need no repentance."[29]

That the best of the rabbis talked just as Jesus did about pride and humility is sometimes urged as a reason for thinking his judgment on Pharisaic self-complacency unjustified. Upon the contrary, at this point such rabbis confirm Jesus. They too saw the peril of self-righteousness. God cannot live in the same world with the proud and arrogant man, they said.[30] It is not in the Gospels only that we meet "Some who trusted in themselves that they were righteous and despised others."[31] The rabbis bear witness to the same type of person.

If Jesus could not tolerate such folk, neither could they tolerate him. He disturbed their complacency, upset their equanimity, stole from them the occasion of their pride. What modern psychiatry teaches he discovered as a grim fact, that few possessions are dearer to men than those claims to superiority which set them above their fellows. How, then, could the morally respectable and self-satisfied endure one who said to them: "The tax collectors and the harlots go into the kingdom of God before you"?[32]

At no point did Jesus state his uncompromising ethical ideal in more difficult fashion than in his demand for all-inclusive undiscourageable love, even toward enemies. To this day the familiar passage in the Sermon on the Mount seems to the world at large and to honest Christians in particular unattainably perfectionist. What must it have seemed to galled, embittered Jews under the yoke of Rome in a Palestine seething with incipient revolt?

"You have heard the saying, 'An eye for an eye and a tooth for a tooth.' But I tell you, you are not to resist an injury:
>whoever strikes you on the right cheek,
>>turn the other to him as well;
>whoever wants to sue you for your shirt,
>>let him have your coat as well;
>whoever forces you to go one mile,
>>go two miles with him;
>give to the man who begs from you, and turn
>>not away from him who wants to borrow.

"You have heard the saying, 'You must love your neighbour and hate your enemy.' But I tell you, love your enemies and pray for those who persecute you, that you may be sons of your Father in heaven:
>he makes his sun rise on the evil and the
>>good, and sends rain on the just and
>>the unjust.
>For if you love only those who love you,
>>what reward do you get for that?
>do not the very taxgatherers do as much?
>and if you only salute your friends, what is
>>special about that?
>do not the very pagans do as much?
You must be perfect as your heavenly Father is perfect."[33]

From the uncompromising idealism of this passage some moderns seek escape by calling it the ethic of the coming kingdom, which men now are not expected to observe. To Jesus' contemporaries, however, no such refuge would have been possible. They were then and there facing the indignities which Jesus described—insulted, sued, compelled by Roman law to carry a soldier's burden for a mile, and in every way experiencing the humiliation of their country's occupancy by enemies. Jesus' injunctions were not relevant to any messianic age of heavenly perfection, when they would not be smitten, cheated and coerced by foes, but to the present time when these evils realistically confronted them.

To suppose that Jesus taught undiscourageable love only because he thought that tomorrow the messianic age would come is to miss his meaning, and fail to hear his message as his contemporaries heard it. For centuries the best thought of Judaism about the treatment of enemies had been developing toward Jesus' ideal. Said the Book of Proverbs:

> If thine enemy be hungry, give him
> bread to eat;
> And if he be thirsty, give him water
> to drink;[34]

and Job, asserting his innocence of wrong-doing, pleaded that he had never

> rejoiced at the destruction of him
> that hated me,
> Or lifted up myself when evil found him.[35]

No special form of eschatology is needed to explain such ideas. Jesus could tell a Jew not to resist a Roman soldier's requisition of coerced service, say some, only because so soon the Messiah would put an end to Rome. But Epictetus, the Roman stoic, said: "If there is a requisition and a soldier seizes your ass, let it go! Do not resist or complain, otherwise you will be first beaten, and lose the ass after all."[36] Granted that Jesus' similar demand was based on the nature of God and his mercy, rather than on prudential considerations such as Epictetus cites, nevertheless the messianic expectation is not needed to explain that difference.

If over four hundred years before Christ, Socrates, with no apocalypticism in his thinking, could say that if he had to choose between doing and suffering wrong, he would prefer to suffer rather than do it,[37] why must apocalpyticism be taken as the central and controlling motive of the similar quality in Jesus' ethic? The philosophic background of Buddhism's thinking is utterly different from that of Jesus and nothing remotely like Jewish apocalyptic is in it, but Buddhism says:

> Worse is he who, when reviled, reviles again.
>> Who, when reviled, does not revile again
>>> A two-fold victory wins.
> He seeks the good both of the other and himself.[38]

> We live happily indeed, not hating those who hate us.
> Among men who hate us, we dwell free from hatred.[39]

> If villainous bandits were to carve you limb from limb,
>> even then be it your task to preserve your hearts
>>> unmoved,
>> never to allow an ill word to pass your lips,
> but always to abide in compassion and goodwill
>> with no hate in your hearts.[40]

In Jesus' teaching about all-inclusive love he was talking to contemporaries who shared his messianic hopes but who differed with him concerning legalism. That he had in mind the insurrectionist party in Israel, afterward called Zealots, is highly probable. Not waiting for the Messiah's coming, they were already dreaming of violent revolt against Rome, which a few years after Jesus' death broke out in fury and ended in Jerusalem's destruction. Certainly what Jesus said was relevant to them. The Zealots, however, sprang from the left wing of the Pharisees and, as Matthew's record stands, it is of the Pharisees as a whole and of their legalism that Jesus primarily was thinking when he pleaded for all-inclusive love. Here, too, as when he appealed for inwardness and positiveness of life and character, he was announcing an ideal superior to common practices. The very wording of his plea reveals this motive. The ordinary levels of respectable behavior anyone can reach, he said—"Do not even the tax collectors do the same?" "Do not even the Gentiles do the same?" He was deliberately presenting a way of life so demanding that no legalism could define it, no unredeemed heart practice it, no saint perfectly fulfill it.

To be sure, the messianic hope must have affected Jesus' ethic by heightening the expression of his demands, intensifying his urgency, and thrusting into the background prudential counsels for getting on in this present world. When Jesus, however, pleaded for all-inclusive love, what the morally self-satisfied heard was not some corollary of messianism but the presentation of an ethical standard that made their self-righteousness impossible. This whole range of Jesus' teaching is best understood if the theme with which it started is kept steadily in mind: "Unless your righteousness exceeds that of the scribes and Pharisees."[41]

A common description of Jesus' teaching today is to call it an "absolute ethic," thus suggesting its irrelevance to immediate practical problems whether among his contemporaries or among us. In Hebrew, however, there is no such word as "absolute," and the whole range of theoretical abstractness which in our speech that word connotes is alien to Jesus and to the Jews of his time. We are continually warned against modernizing Jesus, attributing to him ideas and motives at home in our day but not in his; but no modernizing of Jesus is more flagrant than the ascription to him of the concepts which across the centuries have accumulated around the word "absolute." Among the books that Jesus almost certainly read was *The Testament of the Twelve Patriarchs*, written about 100 B.C. "Love one another from the heart," says this book, "and if any man

[ 106 ]

sin against you, speak peaceably to him, and in your soul hold not guile; and if he repent and confess, forgive him." Was this admonition ethical absolutism, moving only in the stratosphere above Israel's actual life, irrelevant to and unlivable in the present evil age when enemies were rampant? When Booker T. Washington, the Negro leader, enduring his humiliations, said, "I will not let any man reduce my soul to the level of hatred," was that an "absolute ethic," and not a way of life to be undertaken in the face of actual hostility?

Impressed by the unattainableness of Jesus' ideal of love un-limited, committed to the idea that it is an unlivable, absolute ethic, some interpreters stretch the evidence to make their point. The phrase, "Do not resist one who is evil," can be torn from its grammatical context and from its larger matrix in the speaker's life, and made to mean something not only impossible but undesirable. But Jesus himself did resist evil. All his ministry he fearlessly resisted evil. In this very text he was attacking evil—but, he would have insisted, *not with evil*. Paul understood his meaning: "Do not be overcome by evil, but overcome evil with good."[42] The problem he was dealing with is inherent in a wicked world—the temptation to become a monster when one fights a monster, to meet hate with hate, and violence with violence. Against such moral surrender Jesus protested.

A principle of interpretation is here involved of primary importance in the case of Jesus: *what is said must be understood in terms of the life of the one who said it*. To make nonresistance an "absolute" is to lift a single phrase completely out of the context of Jesus' life. Soft compliance with evil deeds and with un-repentant evil men was no characteristic of his. "Of the teachers of the past, whose sayings have been preserved," said Sir John Seeley, "Mohammed would be regarded by most as the type of unrelenting severity, and yet we may read the Koran from beginning to end, without finding words expressive of more vehement condemnation than those attributed to Christ." Indeed, on this point critics of Jesus have insisted that while he taught love to enemies he did not practice it. A modern Jewish scholar, Dr. C. G. Montefiore, grants the beauty of Jesus' demand that we love our enemies and the originality with which he expressed it, but then adds: "Yet how much more telling his injunction would have been if we had *a single story* about his doing good to, or praying for, a single Rabbi or Pharisee! One grain of practise is worth a pound of theory. ... But no such deed is ascribed to Jesus in the Gospels. Toward his enemies, toward those who did not believe in him, whether individuals, groups, or cities (Matthew 11:20–24), only denunciation and bitter words! The injunctions are beautiful, but how much more beautiful would have been a *fulfillment* of those injunctions by Jesus himself."[43]

To Christians such a charge is shocking. Nevertheless, the charge must be faced. In answer to it, we may doubt the authenticity of some of Jesus' wrathful words, and may ascribe them to the later church speaking out of its bitter Jewish-Christian controversy. We may say that this later controversy easily could have caused the remembrance of Jesus' harsh words and the forgetting of others, which critics like Dr. Montefiore wish were in the record. We may say that as Matthew grouped typical miracles in a connected passage and typical teachings in the Sermon on the Mount, so in his twenty-third chapter he grouped Jesus' criticisms of scribes and Pharisees, which originally were not so massed in a prolonged invective, but were individually called out by separate occasions when they were justified. We may say that while Jesus with prophetic indignation attacked Pharisaic evils, in his personal relationships with Pharisees, dining and conversing with them,

[ 108 ]

he met them with friendly goodwill. We may say that while he did condemn cities that rejected him, he also wept with pity over Jerusalem where he experienced his ultimate rejection.[44] We may say that even at the close of Matthew's twenty-third chapter, his mercy went out to the city that killed the prophets, "How often would I have gathered your children together as a hen gathers her brood under her wings, and you would not!"[45] Nevertheless, what we cannot do is to picture Jesus as one who did not resist evil.

The idea that Jesus taught nonresistance as an absolute ethic is part of the sentimentalizing of him which has characterized much modern Christianity. "Tenderness of heart," wrote Renan, "was in him transformed into an infinite sweetness, a vague poetry, and a universal charm."[46] If Jesus was anything like that, one wonders why they crucified him. He stirred some men to loyalty so intense that they willingly died for him and others to hatred so fierce that they would not rest until they killed him. Some called him a blasphemer, some a sorcerer in league with the devil, but apparently they never thought of him in terms of "infinite sweetness, vague poetry, universal charm." Money-changers driven from the temple courts, self-complacent moralists castigated by his stinging condemnation, faced another kind of man than that—a formidable personality who certainly did attack evil. What he meant by "Do not resist one who is evil,"[47] cannot be adequately understood apart from its setting in his life.

This principle, that Jesus' words must be interpreted in terms of his deeds, is illustrated in that most impractical of all passages ascribed to him where, saying, "Do not be anxious,"[48] he used the carefree attitude of flowers and birds as an illustration of what his disciples' unworried life should be. Such teaching can easily be interpreted as utterly unrealistic—until one sees it as autobiography. Jesus had plenty to be anxious about. Early in his ministry the cross loomed, and from then until he sweat blood in Gethsemane, anxiety about his disciples, his mission and his own fate was his familiar companion. His injunction against worry sprang from his own inner struggle, accentuated by his sensitiveness, made more acute because he cared so much for the cause he was willing to die for. Even in John's Gospel which minimizes the indications of Jesus' humanness and which, to that end, omits altogether his agony in Gethsemane, this anxious stress and strain in Jesus' life could not be utterly left out: "Now is my soul troubled. And what shall I say? 'Father, save me from this hour'? No, for this purpose I have come to this hour. Father, glorify thy name."[49] Set thus in the matrix of his own life his words about anxiety gain reality. This winning of freedom from fear was his problem. This admonition to live day by day, borrowing no trouble from tomorrow, doing one's best and leaving the consequence in God's hands, he had addressed to himself before he addressed it to his disciples. When one thinks of the many people who have said, "Don't worry," to an unimpressed world that soon forgot, one sees that Jesus' words about anxiety gained their first impact and won their permanence in mankind's memory because his confident, fearless life, lived under terrific tension, drove them home. When words like "Be not anxious" are spoken, it makes all the difference in the world what kind of person says them.

To set Jesus' teaching about love of enemies in the matrix of his life is similarly revealing. His contemporaries, like all the rest of mankind, were used to an average ethic based on reciprocity. If we can count on decency from others, we should be decent to them; we should extend goodwill to those from whom we have received or can expect it—so runs ordinary morality.

Far past *that* went Jesus' thinking. Be decent, he said, whether others are decent or not. Exercise goodwill whether they do or not. Never let your rightness depend upon another's conduct. Do not hate because you are hated, or revile because you are reviled. If two blows must be given prefer taking both to giving one. Never let vindictiveness be the motive or retaliation the standard of your conduct, else your conduct will be at the mercy of others' ill behavior. Keep your own criteria of character intact and independent. Love even when hated, bless even when cursed.

That, too, was Jesus' own problem, and his solution of it went far beyond legalistic rules that could be blamelessly observed. To call it an "interim ethic," however, or to deny its relevancy to this present evil age because it is "perfectionist" and "absolutist" is fantastic. Jesus' ethic was expressly meant for this tough world, where goodwill and fair play from others are often not to be counted on, and where, if because of that we justify our own ill will and inhumanity, there is no hope. For then mankind will go on, evil always met by evil, hatred met by hatred, violence arousing violence, injustice calling out injustice. From that vicious cycle the only escape lies in those who break through it, refusing to surrender their own criteria of conduct to the standards of their enemies. To be sure, Jesus based his plea for such superior living not on the future welfare of society conceived in terms of progress but on the eternal character of God; yet even when this ethic is assayed in hard-headed modern terms, its realism is evident. Until mankind can do better then meet hate with hate, it heads for catastrophe.

This realism in Jesus' teaching some try to deny by stressing the sentence with which, according to Matthew, he concludes it: "You, therefore, must be perfect, as your heavenly Father is perfect."[50] One wishes that the Aramaic word which Jesus used

[ 111 ]

were known. In Luke's account the phrase is not "be perfect," but "be merciful, even as your Father is merciful."[51] Dr. Torrey catches the logical conclusion of Jesus' argument and the probable meaning of the Aramaic words he used, when he translates Matthew's sentence thus: "Be therefore all-including (in your goodwill), even as your heavenly Father includes all."[52] The word "perfect" in our speech has come to mean blamelessness. That, however, was the very thing the proud claim to which Jesus was rebuking. The main point of his teaching concerning inward rightness, devoted character, and all inclusive love, was that such an ethic makes faultlessness and its attendant pride impossible. The Greek word translated "perfect" is variously rendered in the New Testament. "Solid food is for the mature";[53] "until we all attain . . . to mature manhood";[54] "Be babes in evil, but in thinking be mature"[55]— such is its common meaning. It connotes full spiritual growth. Of God only is it used in the complete sense. God's all-inclusive mercy is our ideal, said Jesus; to attain maturity so that our mercy too is all-inclusive should be our aim. That is not "perfectionism," as the word now is used to indicate an absolutist ethic inapplicable to realistic living, but it is a demand for a quality of spirit and a manner of life that rules out self-righteousness. When one puts oneself into the place of Jesus' contemporaries, what they saw in him was no ethical absolutist, but a teacher who with almost maddening directness was attacking one of the commonest evils of their time, insistently saying, in every way he could find to say it, often with the extravagant hyperbole characteristic of his speech, that real goodness must exceed the legalistic righteousness of the scribes and Pharisees.

All this explains Jesus' constant and weighty emphasis on repentance. He called on men not alone to change their behavior but, first of all, to change their minds, to recognize their deep, inward sin, to acknowledge their ingrained self-love, their unjustified pride, their unpayable debt of guilt,[56] and to seek pardon and rebirth. Moreover, he addressed this call for penitence not alone to obvious sinners, guilty of gross iniquity, out-and-out thievery and debauchery, but more especially to the conventionally respectable and self-satisfied.[57] It was they who needed most to see how stained with self-seeking their best goodness was, and with how thin a veneer their obedience to many laws covered their disobedience to God's divine intent for their characters.

The morally self-satisfied, therefore, had to reject Jesus. They might be drawn to him, as the "rich young ruler" was, but they could not follow him. They had to choose between their prized self-satisfaction and his idea of what the good life really is and, preferring the former, they easily could rationalize their choice: his demands were extravagant, no one could live up to them. Their legalistic habit was, starting with a great law, to seek its specific applications in the varied situations life presents, and so alike to define what the law's observance practically implied and to prove its observance practically possible. Let any one try *that* with these ideals of Jesus—turning the other cheek, refusing to resist an injury, surrendering coat and cloak together rather than go to law to protect one's rights, offering to bear a soldier's burden two miles when required to bear it one—and endless concrete situations were imaginable where the literal application of such injunctions would be impossible for the individual and dangerous to the community. This was no ethic for a man of common sense or for a nation whose self-preservation was important to the world. Far better seemed their type of religion, practical, livable, defined in laws that men could learn and observe, and which, when observed,

made one a good Jew and a good man. So Li Hung Chang,
centuries later, comparing Confucianism with Christianity,
sincerely stated his preference for the former because Jesus'
ideals were too lofty to be practical.

This conflict between Jesus and the legalists in the ethical
realm involved an underlying conflict of temperament. Whatever else Jesus was, he was exuberant. He loved nature, and
when the Galilean hills were clothed with flowers, he felt that
"Solomon in all his glory was not arrayed like one of these."[58]
He loved children, and even on a busy day "was indignant"
because the disciples tried to keep them from him.[59] He had
little use for the solemn fast days of his people, called his company of friends a bridal party, exempt from fasting,[60] and even
when his disciples did fast, bade them, "Do not look dismal."[61]
He described his gospel as an invitation to a royal banquet,[62]
and when his message was accepted by even a single sinner, he
said that the very angels in heaven rejoiced.[63] There is no
mistaking Jesus' temperament—vital, dynamic, exuberant—
the very kind of temperament that legalistic precisionists least
of all could understand.

This superabundant vitality naturally expressed itself in the
ethical and religious realm in ways infuriating to precise minds.
Jesus' teaching—even in our present Gospels, from which more
flagrant contradictions may well have been omitted—is full of
paradox and seeming inconsistency. He said that we were not
to practice our piety before men in order to be seen by them;[64]
but he also said that we were to put our lamps not under a
bushel but on a stand, and to let our light so shine before men
that they might see our good works.[65] He called to him the
heavy-laden, promising them an easy yoke, a light burden, and
rest for their souls;[66] but he also said that if any man would

[ 114 ]

come after him, he must deny himself, and take up his cross.[67] He said that we were not to be "anxious about tomorrow";[68] but then he told the parable in which foolish maidens, providing no oil with their lamps, were condemned because they had not been anxious enough about tomorrow.[69] He said that his disciples were to "do good . . . expecting nothing in return"; but in the same sentence, as in many another passage, he promised, "your reward will be great."[70] He said, "Blessed are the peacemakers"[71] but he also said, "Do you think that I have come to give peace on earth? No, I tell you, but rather division."[72] He pictured the fatherly God sending his merciful sun and rain on good and evil men alike;[73] but he also said about God, "I will warn you whom to fear: fear him who, after he has killed, has power to cast into hell; yes, I tell you, fear him!"[74] He claimed that he did not come to abolish the law;[75] and yet he cried, "It was said to the men of old . . . But I say to you."[76]

To be sure, the modern reader, considering the way Jesus' sayings were addressed, now to this individual or group and now to that, sees in such contrasting statements not inconsistency but many-sidedness. Some men do need to be warned against pious exhibitionism, and others against hiding their light under a bushel. Jesus saw truth and duty from many angles—his discipleship refreshing, liberating, exhilarating and yet costly and sacrificial too: forethought for the morrow both dangerous and indispensable, goodness for the sake of reward selfish, and yet in God's world goodness without ultimate reward unthinkable; peacemaking both divine and sometimes impossible; God both merciful and stern; the law eternal in its profundities but transient in its forms. To contemporary legalists, however, devoted to clarity and consistency, Jesus must have been difficult to understand. The typical rabbinical mind was scholastic; Jesus' mind was anything but that. The rabbis sought precise definitions of duty; Jesus threw out metaphors and similes in the direction of high ideals.

One feels this temperamental conflict when Jesus is compared with a great rabbi, such as Akiba ben Joseph. Born about A.D. 40 and dying a martyr's death when he was in his nineties, he was a forceful character, whose influence on Judaism is comparable with the influence of his contemporary, the Apostle Paul, on Christianity. He too was vital, sincere, courageous, deeply devout and, within the limits of rabbinism, progressive and forward looking. All the more, modern minds, both Jewish and Christian, wonder at the concerns which habitually occupied his thought. If, said the law, a person was murdered on the highway and the assassin was not discovered, the nearest town must bring a calf as an atonement. If, however, the corpse was found halfway between two towns, where on the dead body should the measurement begin to determine which town must bring the calf? Rabbi Eliezar said one must measure from the navel, but Rabbi Akiba, with elaborate reasons based on man's creation in the image of God, argued that one must measure from the nose.[77]

All his life this really great rabbi dealt with such legalisms. When, with Rabbi Gamaliel and others, he went by ship on a mission to Rome, the question arose whether, since two thousand cubits were the limit of travel for a faithful Jew on the sabbath day, they had to count the distance the ship sailed, and whether or not in addition they could walk about the deck for exercise. Rabbi Gamaliel was sure that they could not. Once, coming into port and discovering that the improvised ladder by which they were to descend to the wharf had been made on the sabbath, they debated whether—since no Jew should profit by work done, even by a Gentile, on the holy day—they could use it. Rabbi Gamaliel resolved their scruples: "Since it was not made in our presence (and therefore was not specially intended for us), we may use it."[78]

That Jesus not only held ideas alien to such punctiliousness, but was essentially the kind of person who could not endure it, is obvious. The difference between him and the legalists was irreconcilable. Especially when he saw the legalists supposing that by such meticulous observance of scruples they gained merit with God, he rose in wrath. Dr. Arthur Marmorstein, himself a loyal Jew, in his volume, *The Doctrine of Merits in Old Rabbinical Literature*, sums up his research by saying that, while obedience to rabbinical regulations is not the only way to obtain merit in the sight of God, "the faithful observance of the law and ceremonies is not unimportant. . . . By performing the commandments man is entitled to a reward. . . . The laws and observances were given to obtain merits."[79]

Against this idea Jesus directed his parable about the servant who, having worked all day in the fields and then having prepared his lord's supper and served him, expects not even thanks. "So you also," said Jesus, "when you have done all that is commanded you, say, 'We are unworthy servants; we have only done what was our duty.' "[80] Here again, Jesus' demand for excess goodness appears. There is no such thing as being good enough, no service which justifies any man in saying, I have done enough; with all the commandments obeyed, no merit has been gained; real goodness lies beyond commandments in willingness to do more than anyone has a right to expect; when the first required mile has been finished, goodness lies in voluntarily going the second mile; the best of men desperately need to repent. Shakespeare caught the spirit of the kind of ethic Jesus stood for in his lines about Desdemona—

[ 117 ]

"She is of so free, so kind, so apt, so blessed a disposition, she holds it a vice in her goodness not to do more than she is requested."[81]

This quality of exuberance in Jesus' ethic must have puzzled the disciples—he told them that when they were hated, excommunicated, denounced and defamed, they were to "Rejoice in that day, and leap for joy"[82]—but it both puzzled and enraged the precisionists. According to rabbinic teaching one was bound to forgive one's brother three times.[83] Peter was being generous when he asked, "Lord, how often shall my brother sin against me, and I forgive him? As many as seven times?" Jesus, however, pushed the limit out toward infinity: "I do not say to you seven times, but seventy times seven."[84] To be sure, here as always, one must remember the rabbis who would not altogether have disagreed with Jesus. Said one of his contemporaries, Rabbi Johanan ben Zakkai, "If thou hast practiced Torah much, claim not merit to thyself, for thereunto wast thou created."[85] Nevertheless, the rabbi would still have regarded legalism as alone a safe morality for individuals and alone a sufficient defense of Judaism, and would have regarded Jesus' idealism as visionary, unrealistic, extravagant.

Easy as it is, however, to see why legalists—especially those who found in the successful performance of the law's demands their chief self-satisfaction—rejected Jesus, it is easy also to see now what lay beyond their vision then. Jesus' ethic inculcated a spirit, presented a goal; like a compass, it indicated a direction, moving in which through the jungle of this evil world, one often had to make detours. Not always was Jesus himself in a position to choose between courses of conduct, the one ideal and the other utterly wrong. He too had to find his way as best he could *toward* his ideals amid confusing choices between what was better on the whole and what was worse. He said, "Judge not, that you be not judged,"[86] but times came when he had not only to judge but to denounce. He said, "Do not be anxious," but this evil world plunged him into the agony of Gethsemane where he sweat blood. He said that his disciples should swear no oaths, but when the high priest put him under oath— "I adjure you by the living God"[87]—he nonetheless answered.

It is no wonder that his ethic has always been a stumbling block to legalists. Nevertheless, his ideals, which often cannot be taken literally, can be taken seriously. Legalistic rules and regulations are formulated to meet contingencies, and with changing circumstances pass away, but his ideals have gone before the best thinking and living of the race, like a pillar of cloud by day and of fire by night. They are the standard by which even the best conduct is judged and moral progress is measured; and, as the world faces today the consequence of mankind's neglect and defiance of them, Jesus' saying has in it a realistic relevance to practical affairs that his contemporary rejectors could not have dreamed: "Everyone who listens to these words of mine and acts upon them will be like a sensible man who built his house on rock."[88]

## CHAPTER V

## *As Religious and Moral Outcasts Saw Him*

TWO familiar groups in first century Palestine were the *haberim* and the *amme ha-arez*. The former were a fellowship of scrupulous Jews, pledged to ceremonial purity and to carefulness in tithing. The members of this fellowship may have been drawn mainly from among the more fortunate and better educated, but their distinction was not so much learning, economic comfort or social station as punctilious piety in the observance of tithing, dietary rules and ritual cleanliness.

*Amme ha-arez* means literally "people of the land," and by inference "the masses," but it came more specifically to signify religiously negligent Jews, who either did not know the scribal laws or who, knowing them, were indifferent to their observance. An *am ha-arez* was a nonpracticing Jew, who did not recite the formal prayers, omitted the ritual fringes from his garments and the donning of phylacteries at his devotions, who neglected tithing and ritual washing, or, having a son, failed to train him in scrupulous obedience to the law.[1] That the word meaning "the masses" should thus come to signify Jews ignorant or negligent of the scribal laws suggests that such folk for the most part may have come from the underprivileged classes —the poor, the uneducated, the toilers—engaged in trades that made ritual purity difficult, if not impossible, and, in any

[ 120 ]

case, too hard pressed to be scrupulous about ceremonial niceties. This is further suggested by the fact that, along with condemnation of the impiety of the *amme ha-arez*, rabbinical literature reveals contempt of them as illiterate, coarse, uncouth.

No such idea of the *amme ha-arez*, however, based solely on class lines, is adequate. A tax collector, or a priest by grace of secular influence, if careless of rabbinical laws, would be to the scrupulous an *am ha-arez*, although the tax collector would not be poor nor the priest socially depressed. As the word "heathen," originally meaning a peasant dwelling on a heath, came later to have almost exclusively an ideological and moral significance, so the phrase, "people of the land," outgrew its origin. Folk of all social classes could be *amme ha-arez*, as folk of all social classes could be heathen. Indeed, an *am ha-arez* could rise to the highest ranks of religious leadership, as did Rabbi Akiba ben Joseph. Born of a lowly family, a shepherd by occupation, he was an out-and-out *am ha-arez*, hating the rabbis, and refusing observance of their casuistry but, later changing his mind, he became a learned student and expositor of the law, and rose to first-rate eminence.

Between the *haberim* and these rebels against rabbinical casuistry no love was lost. Among the pledges taken by the *haberim* when joining their fellowship were vows never to be the guest of an *am ha-arez*, or to entertain one unless the unclean visitor left his cloak outside, never to sell him any products of the soil or buy from him anything that legally could be subject to impurity, never to travel in company with one, or perform purifications in his presence. "Do not be frequently in the company of an *am ha-arez*," ran the admonition, "for in the end he will give you something to eat from which the tithes have not been separated."[2]

Underneath these caste rules which made the *amme ha-arez* an outlawed group, ran hatred and contempt whose expressions are often shocking. One rabbi, describing the kind of girl a good Jew might marry, lists "The daughter of one of the great men," "The daughter of the president of a synagogue," "The daughter of a teacher of children," and then adds: "But let him not marry the daughters of the *amme ha-arez*, for they are loathsome, and their children are abominations, and of them the Scripture says, 'Cursed is he that lies with any manner of beast.' "[3] One rabbi denied all hope of resurrection to an *am ha-arez*;[4] another said, perhaps as a bitter joke, "It is lawful to stab an *am ha-arez* on a Day of Atonement";[5] and even Rabbi Hillel said, "No *am ha-arez* is truly religious."[6]

Such contempt on the part of the *haberim* for this outlawed group was naturally returned in kind. "The hatred of the *amme ha-arez* for the learned class," said one rabbi, "is greater than the hatred of the Gentiles against Israel, and the hatred of their wives exceeds theirs."[7] Were there any doubt of this, the personal testimony of Rabbi Akiba would dispel it. "When I was an *am ha-arez*," he remarked, "I used to say, 'I wish I had one of those scholars, and I would bite him like an ass.' His disciples said, 'You mean like a dog.' He replied, 'An ass's bite breaks the bone; a dog's does not.' "[8]

One of the earliest intimations we have in the Gospels concerning the kind of people attracted to Jesus is Mark's description of him as he "sat at table in his house," with "many tax collectors and sinners" sitting with him.[9] The tax collectors are familiar, one of the most detested groups in Palestine, but who were the "sinners"? To suppose them to be only moral derelicts is surely a mistake. Moral failure doubtless was represented among them, but they were in general nonpracticing Jews, ignorant or careless of the scribal laws, the scorn of the scrupulous, the outcast *amme ha-arez*, concerning whom one rabbi said that only because of them God's punishments fall upon the world.[10]

Few things are more indicative of the kind of person Jesus was than the fact that the *haberim* reacted against him, while these "sinners" responded to him. The Fourth Gospel sums up the contempt of scrupulous Jews for this aspect of Jesus' ministry: "Have any of the authorities or of the Pharisees believed in him?" they said, "But this crowd, who do not know the law, are accursed."[11] What did such outcast contemporaries of Jesus see in him as they sought his company?

Obviously they felt his sympathy. Accustomed to the contempt of the purists, they saw in Jesus a phenomenon they had never faced before—a religious teacher, speaking as "one who had authority, and not as their scribes,"[12] a loyal Jew affirming the great faiths of Israel and concerned for the redemption of his people, a powerful personality whose words and works alike could not be hid, yet who was one with them, who, far from despising them, made himself their champion and broke through one barricade after another of impeding ceremonial laws to get at them and claim their following. The later rabbis were carrying on an ancient tradition when they wrote, "The wise say, Let not a man associate with sinners even to bring them near to the Torah."[13] To that attitude the outcasts were accustomed. Not simply about Jesus' miracles of healing, therefore, but about this other miracle—a towering spokesman of Judaism, who understood, valued, and loved the *amme ha-arez*—it must have been true that "the crowds marveled, saying, 'Never was anything like this seen in Israel.' "[14]

In so far as the *amme ha-arez* were poor, depressed, underprivileged—as many of them doubtless were—Jesus' understanding sympathy went out to them. There, too, he was one with

[ 123 ]

them, and saw their problems from within. More fortunately situated legalistic precisionists could know little about the difficulties a poor man faced in his tithing, or about the sheer impossibility of observing meticulous rules concerning phylacteries and ceremonial washings amid the soil and drudgery of impoverished, laborious days. But Jesus knew. The early church fathers quote a saying of Jesus not in our Gospels: "Because of the weak was I weak, and because of the hungry did I hunger and because of the thirsty did I thirst." This unmistakable quality in Jesus was evident in his treatment of the *amme ha-arez.* He looked at them through no window of privilege; he was one with them. His sympathy with them sprang from intimate understanding of the reasons why many of them were not faithful Jews. What Shakespeare's apothecary who sold the poison said—"My poverty and not my will consents"— Jesus heard from many a guilty conscience among these outcasts. He resented the contempt the precisionists poured out on them, and to his understanding sympathy they responded.

In so far as these *amme ha-arez* were not only poor, but uneducated and ignorant, Jesus understood them. He himself faced as they faced the scorn of the educated: "How is it that this man has learning, when he has never studied?"[15] To be sure, ample evidence indicates that Jesus had studied long and deeply; some scholars even think that, while he spoke Aramaic, he was well versed also in Rabbinical Hebrew, the technical language of the schools.[16] He knew the Hebrew Scriptures— eighty-seven quotations from the Old Testament are attributed to him in our Gospels. Repeatedly he met the rabbis on their own terms and outargued them, and not only did his own disciples call him "Rabbi," but so did the scribes and Pharisees.[17] In his earlier ministry he taught in the synagogues, and the inference is most probable that the years between his boy-

[ 124 ]

hood's questioning of the rabbis in the temple and the beginning of his public ministry had been absorbed not in carpentry alone, but in profound study of his fathers' faith.

Nevertheless, from the viewpoint of the technical scholastics he was an untaught, unlearned man, and in that regard also one of the *amme ha-arez*.

The condescension of the learned rabbis toward the unlearned multitude was one of Israel's tragedies, for it was the misuse of one of the noblest elements in Judaism. The Pharisaic ideal was an educated people, loving the law, studying it, intelligent about it, observing it. Josephus wrote only a few years after Jesus' death: "Most of all we are mindful of the education of children . . . so that if anyone ask us concerning the laws, we can tell them all more easily than our own name. Having learned them straightway with our earliest perception, they become engraven in our souls."[18] The rabbis were fighting for the hope of Israel when they thus put education first among their priorities, saying, "The world is saved only by the breath of the school-children"; "Study is more meritorious than sacrifice"; "No one is poor except the man who is poor in knowledge."[19] The emphasis which the rabbis thus put on learning and the devotion with which they tried to spread knowledge of the law among their people were admirable.

Nevertheless, this emphasis when perverted led to pride of learning and contempt for the unlearned. The rabbis thought they had good reason for this contempt. These folk who did not and perhaps would not study the law, who through innate boorishness were incapable of knowledge or through willfulness refused it, were the peril of Israel; nothing too bad could be said about them.

It is not difficult, therefore, to put oneself into the place of

[ 125 ]

a sensitive *am ha-arez*. He knows that he is ignorant of the laws, despised for his illiteracy and boorishness, and regarded as a public menace. To such contempt he reacts with bitterness, but along with resentment go humiliation, a sense of inferiority ill-concealed by hatred, an inner, unacknowledged drift toward self-disdain. Then this *am ha-arez* confronts Jesus, who does not shrink from him, even eats with him, breaks the laws of Kosher food and ritual purity to get next to him, speaks up for him as a champion and appeals for his support. No wonder the scribes and Pharisees were outraged, unable to understand that outreaching sympathy which stirred the *amme ha-arez*, and which the centuries have not been able to forget: "When he saw the crowds, he had compassion for them, because they were harassed and helpless, like sheep without a shepherd."[20]

If Jesus' foes, calling him "a friend of tax collectors and sinners,"[21] had reason to despise the latter, with even better reason they hated the former. Piety and patriotism alike aroused wrath against these Jewish publicans who fleeced their own people to fill the Roman treasury. They were a contaminated class to be avoided; their evidence was not valid in court; a promise made to them was not binding; and even a charitable offering made by a tax gatherer to temple or synagogue was declared unacceptable.[22] The Gospels give clear evidence of their dishonesty, as when John the Baptist said to certain tax gatherers who came to be baptized, "Collect no more than is appointed you,"[23] or when penitent Zacchaeus took for granted the kind of sin he had been guilty of: "If I have defrauded any one of anything, I restore it fourfold."[24] One can understand Jesus' compassion for the poor, illiterate, depressed peasantry who did not keep the scribal laws, but how could he have been the friend of tax collectors?

One reason is evident: to Jesus contempt of a whole class of people was intolerable. He said "Judge not, that ye be not judged," but he himself passed scathing judgment on three things—cruelty, sham and contemptuousness. The last especially he could not stand—not even when directed against so ugly a group as the tax collectors. Luke introduces Jesus' story of the Pharisee and the publican, who prayed in the temple, with this revealing remark: "He also told this parable to some who trusted in themselves that they were righteous and despised others."[25] That aroused Jesus' indignation; no group, as a whole, should be thus gathered up and lumped together in indiscriminate disdain. Jesus scorned such scorn, contemned such contempt, and whenever he saw any group thus despised he instinctively came to their defense and help. If it be said that Jesus himself, as reported in the Gospels, visited upon the Pharisees as a whole just such indiscriminate denunciation, one answer is that they, at least, were not underdogs, outcast and scorned, as were the tax collectors. It was the outcast groups that called out his compassion.

Deeper than his contempt of contempt, however, in making him a friend of publicans, ran Jesus' invincible individualism. He saw men not as groups so much as persons. Some tax collectors were all their enemies said of them—greedy, dishonest, traitors to their people, the scum of the earth. Jesus was not in the least sentimental about them. They ganged up against their victims and co-operatively served their greedy interests— Jesus saw that. "If you love those who love you," he said, "what reward have you? Do not even the tax collectors do the same?"[26] But always his eyes were open to the individual publi-

[ 127 ]

can as a person, sure that here and there, at least, was one with the stuff in him out of which saints are made.

The Jewish records themselves consent to this, and tell of at least one tax gatherer, the father of a certain Rabbi Zevia, who used his office to lighten the burdens of his countrymen rather than to increase them.[27] That some publicans sought John's baptism of repentance shows clearly that not all of them were of one kind. It took Jesus, however, to make capital of this—to visit Zacchaeus, although "all murmured," with such effect that he could say, "Today salvation has come to this house, since he also is a son of Abraham;"[28] and even to find in Matthew, "sitting at the tax office," the makings of an apostle.[29]

Both the tax gatherers and the *amme ha-arez* in general saw in Jesus, therefore, one who refused to accept the current labels on their class and who insisted on coming at them as persons, one by one. Hillel was wrong when he said that no *am ha-arez* could be truly religious, and Jesus proved it. In Jesus' day no more loyal Jews were in Palestine than some of these plain people whom the rabbis despised. They believed in Israel's God, respected "the weightier matters of the law, justice and mercy and faithfulness,"[30] hoped with all their hearts for the coming kingdom and, though in ways Jesus would not approve were ready, as the event showed, to sell their lives dearly to make it come. Jesus was not going it blind when he saw values in these reprobated groups and, as for them, here one individual and there another responded to him, saw in him what the rabbis could not see, and justified his thanks to God "for hiding all this from the wise and learned and revealing it to the simple-minded."[31] In no small measure the victory of the early Christian movement was due to this appeal of Jesus to the masses, as over against the scorn of the Pharisees. Indeed, Dr. Kaufmann Kohler, a Jewish scholar, says: "There can be no doubt that it was this contemptuous and hostile attitude of the Pharisaic schools toward the masses that was the chief cause of the triumphant power of the Christian church."[32]

So distinctive was Jesus' attitude that his foes eagerly seized on it and, along with calling him "a glutton and a drunkard," because he was not an ascetic like John the Baptist, they nicknamed him "a friend of tax collectors and sinners."[33] To make matters worse, from their point of view, he did not check this outgoing friendship at the point where technical ceremonial negligence and disobedience passed over into moral wrongdoing. It was bad enough, they thought, to appoint—let us suppose—an honest publican, like Matthew, to the inner circle of his disciples, and to champion the *amme ha-arez* in general against the precisionists, but he went far beyond this, exhibiting what seemed to them a shocking care and compassion for flagrantly disreputable characters.

Indeed, he went so far that some records of his mercy toward real sinners apparently embarrassed the writers of our Gospels. How else can one explain the treatment accorded the story of the woman taken in adultery? In our versions John's Gospel contains it,[34] but with a single exception, on which its inclusion in our Bible is based—the Bezan Codex—it is omitted by all the oldest Greek manuscripts. In later manuscripts it is found sometimes at the end of John's Gospel, sometimes after Luke 21:38, and some manuscripts place the story in the margin or on extra leaves. Here was a wandering narrative which, since Papias apparently knew it,[35] went back in all probability to early oral transmission. It rings true to the spirit and method of Jesus; it has all the inner marks of authenticity; it is not the kind of story a later generation would have made up; and the surmise seems justified that we nearly lost it from the written record because not only were the Jews shocked by Jesus' leniency toward an adulteress, but the Christian writers themselves were afraid of its effect. They feared, as St. Augustine said, that because of it "an excuse for sinning might be given to women."[36]

Dangerous or not, the story stands, too typical of Jesus' conflict with the scribes and Pharisees to be left out. When they confronted him with the adulteress their primary concern was to catch him, "that they might have some charge to bring against him," showing up the looseness and leniency of his attitude even toward gross sinners whom the law condemned to stoning. His answer confounded them—"Let him who is without sin among you be the first to throw a stone at her"— and when, "one by one, beginning with the eldest," they had gone out, his treatment of the woman, all too abbreviated in our condensed record, sent her out too, forgiven for the past and challenged to a new future. The sins of the flesh are bad— such is Jesus' typical attitude—but the sins of the spirit are worse: harsh legalism, contemptuous condemnation without trying to understand its victim, concentration on the law's letter with no care for the personality involved and for what may yet by God's grace be done in her, pride without pity, judgment without mercy.

Not simply tax collectors and technical sinners, therefore, but the morally defeated and disreputable saw in Jesus a new phenomenon—a religious leader who when he faced their sin thought first not of condemnation but of cure. "Why do you eat and drink with tax collectors and sinners?" asked the scribes and Pharisees; "And Jesus answered them, 'Those who are well have no need of a physician, but those who are sick; I have not come to call the righteous, but sinners to repent-

[ 130 ]

ance.' "[37] No analogy could better express the attitude of Jesus—a physician. A man in sound health is no physician's chief concern; but show a doctor a sick man, with maladies complicated and difficult, and his every faculty is called into play. That extraordinary attitude toward sinners was characteristic of Jesus. Outcast, hurt, despised and disreputable folk called out his intense interest and sympathy. "Ninety-nine righteous persons who need no repentance" aroused him not half so much. No wonder that legalistic precisionists could not understand him!

When legalists of the stricter sort faced a disreputable sinner their instinctive reaction was to assume the function of judges. They established, as it were, a courtroom, announced the law and its prescribed penalties, presented the charge and began a trial. Jesus' instinctive reaction was that of a physician: the sinner is sick, he needs not so much a Doctor of Laws as a Doctor of Medicine, cure is the one aim above all others to be sought. One is tempted at this point to detour and note how far ahead of his time Jesus was, and with what difficulty modern penology, acknowledging his attitude to be right, struggles in practice to catch up with him. As for his contemporaries the gospel record bears witness to the resentment with which some of them, the grateful welcome with which others of them, and the surprise with which all of them met this characteristic attitude of Jesus—a physician, out to cure the sick. As the Fourth Gospel sums it up in words ascribed to the Master himself: "I did not come to judge the world but to save the world."[38]

While, however, this contrast between the attitude of the legalists and the attitude of Jesus is true, it must not be so sharply stated that on one side is judgment with no mercy and on the other mercy with no judgment. Every Pharisee, how-

ever strict, would have affirmed the mercy of God in the forgiveness of sinners. The Old Testament is rich in statements of
God's waiting pardon for the penitent; where could one find a
more moving expression of it than the Thirty-second Psalm?
Rabbinical literature abounds in passages celebrating the divine forgiveness. "There is no man who is not God's debtor,"
wrote one rabbi, "but God is gracious and pitiful and forgives
previous sins. It is like a man who borrowed money and forgot
to pay it back. After a time he came to the creditor and said,
I know that I owe you money. The other replied: Why re-
mind me of the old debt? It has long ago vanished from my
mind. So with God. Men sin against him; he sees that they do
not repent, and that they go on sinning; yet if at last they repent, he remits them their previous sins, and if they come before him in repentance, and mention the previous sins, he
says, Remember not your previous sins."[39] What Jesus faced
in his contemporary Judaism, therefore, was no theoretical
denial of God's forgiving mercy toward sinners. One suspects
that in everything he said and did in his attitude toward the
morally defeated and unworthy he thought of himself as the
spokesman of the gospel of divine grace that belonged at the
very heart of the Jewish faith. As one rabbinical passage puts
it, with an inclusiveness that Jesus himself could not have sur-
passed, "God holds no creature as unworthy, but opens the
door to all at every hour; he who would enter can enter."[40]

As thus the rabbis taught God's mercy as well as his judgment, so Jesus taught God's judgment as well as his mercy. He
pictured the terrific consequences of moral iniquity in terms as
stern as any rabbi could have used; his descriptions of Gehenna, "the eternal fire prepared for the devil and his angels,"[41]
still make moderns shrink; and when one hears him say that
some sinners should have great stones tied about their necks

[ 132 ]

and be cast into the midst of the sea,[42] one feels the depth of indignation against evildoers from which such condemnation must have come. To be sure, just how literally Jesus thought of Gehenna is uncertain. The word means Valley of Hinnom—in Hebrew, Gehinnom—the vale outside Jerusalem where the city's refuse was burned. In the second century B.C., the word first appears as descriptive of the place of punishment into which the unrighteous dead were cast. In Jesus' day, Jewish thinking about the nature of man's post-mortem future and, in particular, about Sheol, paradise, Gehenna, was in flux, full of crosscurrents and inconsistencies. Certainly to translate "Gehenna" as meaning "hell," and then to conceive hell with all the connotations which Christian theology has put into it, is to oversimplify and modernize with a vengeance the ancient Jewish portrayal of the future world. Says one rabbinical statement: "The wicked of Israel in their bodies, and the wicked of the nations of the world in their bodies go down to Gehenna and are punished in it for twelve months. After twelve months their souls become extinct, and their bodies are burned up, and hell casts them out, and they turn to ashes."[43] It may be, therefore, that in similar fashion—true to the analogy of what went on in the Valley of Hinnom outside Jerusalem—Jesus meant to picture the "fire" as "eternal," but not the refuse which was being consumed. Nevertheless, however one may interpret his use of "Gehenna," Jesus' judgment on sin and on sinners was fearfully stern. Even in his conversation with Zacchaeus or with the woman taken in adultery—could we have the full account—one feels sure that no easygoing softness toward the sins involved characterized his dealing. No physician minimizes illness, says it does not matter, treats it lightly.

The question, therefore, rises: where was the difference between Jesus and his rabbinical opponents with regard to the treatment of sinners? To that question three answers are suggested by the available evidence.

The first seems clear: in characteristic Phariseeism, while God was willing to forgive, the initiative was left to the sinner. He, being a sinner, was under condemnation; if he would repent, God would pardon him—but that was up to him. "He who would enter, can enter." Jesus, on the contrary, sought out sinners, took the initiative himself, practiced a positive, outreaching, sacrificial saviorhood. The lost sheep is not to be left wandering in the wilderness to find the shepherd, if he can; it is the shepherd who seeks the sheep, not the sheep the shepherd. Such is the divine compassion, as Jesus proclaims and practices it. Even the analogy of the physician becomes inadequate here, for in Jesus' practice it is not the sick who seek the physician, but the physician who seeks the sick, as though, long before its time, the positive, aggressive advance of medicine into the community were presaged.

Concerning this positive, outgoing quest of Jesus for the despised and sinful—"The Son of man came to seek and to save that which was lost"[44]—Dr. Montefiore comments as follows: "That a teacher should go about and associate with such persons, and attempt to help and 'cure' them by familiar and friendly intercourse with them, was, I imagine, an unheard of procedure. That the physician of the soul should seek out the 'sick' was a new phenomenon. According to the rabbis, the visiting of the *bodily* sick was an obligation and a duty of the first order. But the seeking out of the *morally* sick was not put upon the same footing, nor, so far as we can gather, was it practised. Here Jesus appears to be 'original.' "[45]

Certainly the outcast groups in Israel felt in him an originality that made him unique. A powerful personality, concerning whom even the crowds were saying that he was Elijah, Jeremiah or one of the prophets,[46] was doing what they had never seen a religious leader of their people do—searching the mountains for one lost sheep, sweeping the house for one lost coin.[47]

Beneath this outreaching search of Jesus for the despised and outcast was a profound religious conviction that went beyond the customary thinking of the rabbis: God himself cared for these lost souls; he valued them, had compassion on them, sought after them; "There is joy before the angels of God over one sinner who repents."[48] The picture of God on a judgment seat, meting out rewards to the righteous and penalties to the wicked, was as familiar in Jesus' teaching as in the teaching of the rabbis, but Jesus, accepting such truth as he saw in this traditional analogy, went much further. His God never stayed on the judgment seat. The father of the Prodigal was moved with compassion for the lost son;[49] the king was moved with compassion for the hopelessly insolvent debtor.[50]

Religious and moral outcasts, drawn close enough to Jesus to get his message, felt not simply his human sympathy and care, but heard a message about God that must have startled them. Heaven itself was more concerned over one of them than over ninety-nine law-abiding, pious, scrupulous sons of Israel. That was shocking to the precisionists; it must have been arresting to the despised. Of all his sheep, the shepherd cares most for "the one that has strayed," said Jesus. "And if he happens to find it, I tell you he rejoices over it more than over the ninety-nine that never went astray. So it is not the will of your Father in heaven that a single one of these little ones should be lost."[51]

A new day in mankind's spiritual history began when that

[ 135 ]

was said. To be sure, the soil and rootage of Jesus' conviction about God's care for men were in his Jewish heritage. "Dear (to God) is man," said Rabbi Akiba, "in that he was created in the (divine) image."[52] The God of Israel was not simply a Judge, nor yet Father of the nation only, but Father of individual souls, and the value of the soul was the presupposition of many a noble passage in the writings of the rabbis. Why, for example, should witnesses in a trial where capital punishment might be the penalty beware of giving false evidence? Because, said the rabbis, one person is infinitely valuable: "For this reason a single man only (Adam) was created: to teach that if one destroys a single person, the Scripture imputes it to him as if he had destroyed the whole world, and if he saves the life of a single person, as though he had saved the whole world."[53] Had Jesus himself said that, we should now be taking it as the very theme of his ministry.

Nevertheless, when sinners were concerned, as the rabbis saw it, judgment was God's predominant function. Both law and gospel were present in rabbinical Judaism and in Jesus, but the difference in emphasis is unmistakable. Law's business is to define sins, announce penalties and pronounce judgment, and Jewish legalism, facing sinners, bore down heavily upon this emphasis. Jesus did not by any means neglect it, but his stress was on gospel—the outreaching mercy of God for sinners, divine grace acting not as judge but as physician.

Along with these two factors which differentiated Jesus' attitude from the rabbis'—his positive outreaching saviorhood and his conviction concerning God's searching love for sinners—went a third. Jesus believed in the savableness of sinners with extraordinary warmth and hopefulness. The lost sheep and the lost coin could be found; the Prodigal Son could come

[ 136 ]

home; Zacchaeus could become a true "son of Abraham," and the adulteress could "sin no more." This confident faith in their possibilities must have astonished derelicts and outcasts. Accustomed to condemnation they faced in Jesus not alone sympathy but hope. Potentially they were valuable, although seven devils had to be cast out of Mary Magdalene, and in a tax collector Matthew's discipleship had to be discovered and set free.

Jesus was no sentimentalist about human nature; many, he said, take the broad road leading to destruction, and few the narrow road leading unto life.[54] That certainly is not easy-going optimism. Nonetheless, he came at individual men and women, disdained of others and self-disdained, with the undiscourageable assurance that here might be one more transformed character. Even the rich can become sons of the kingdom, though it be like a camel going through a needle's eye, since "all things are possible with God."[55]

The "Parable of the Prodigal Son" should be called the "Parable of the Two Sons," for the story's major impact falls not alone on the Prodigal but on his elder brother. "Now the tax collectors and sinners were all drawing near to him. And the Pharisees and the scribes murmured, saying, 'This man receives sinners and eats with them!'"[56] Thus a double audience confronted Jesus; he had both groups in front of him—scrupulous legalists on one side and publicans, *amme ha-arez*, downright sinners on the other—and he put them both into his parable.

He pictured the lawless, careless, negligent and profligate in terms of the Prodigal. That is what *you* are like, he said, deserters from your father's house. Participants in the rich heritage of Israel, you have squandered your "share of the property." With spendthrift "loose living" you have wasted your in-

[ 137 ]

heritance, and have landed in the defilement of a swine pasture.

We popularly stress this parable's tenderness toward sinners, but the picture of the Prodigal, as representing the outcast group in Israel, was far from tender. The strictest Pharisee might well have felt satisfaction with it—all the scathing things he had ever said about the *amme ha-arez* incorporated in this picture of a faithless profligate, false to his heritage, and landing in such pollution that "he would gladly have fed on the pods that the swine ate; and no one gave him anything." As for that listening group of sinners, facing this rude portrait of themselves, their first impression must have been not the speaker's tenderness but his sternness. Their friend he may have been, but his friendliness was not sentimental. He, too, could see them at their worst, renegades and apostates, without hope unless they recognized their lost estate and turned homeward saying, "Father, I have sinned against heaven and before you; I am no longer worthy to be called your son."

At this point in the parable the Pharisees and scribes must have been well satisfied.

Then Jesus portrayed *them* in terms of the elder son—a good son, as Jesus pictured him, meticulously obedient, so that he could say to his father, "I never disobeyed your command." Moreover, the father appreciated him, loved him, and was grateful to him: "Son, you are always with me, and all that is mine is yours."

The idea that Jesus uniformly and indiscriminately denounced the scribes and Pharisees, with no appreciation of their virtues, leaves this parable out of account. Here their virtues are acknowledged; their fidelity, their conscientiousness, their obedience, their indefatigable labor. The Prodigal's portrait is harshly drawn, but the Pharisee's portrait depicts a

[ 138 ]

man of honor and respectability, proud of his heritage, and tireless in his labors for it.

Then Jesus put his finger on the one quality in that elder brother which spoiled everything. When the younger son was in the far country, with the father day and night compassionately awaiting his return, the elder son was all condemnation without mercy, hard as nails and pitiless as pride could make him. When the younger son came home, crushed and penitent, and the father's welcome made the whole household "merry," he angrily refused to go in, though "his father came out and entreated him." In scorn he would not even acknowledge his brotherhood with the returning sinner, but brushed him off with a phrase that recognized neither penitence, forgiveness nor regeneration as possible: "this son of yours . . . who has devoured your living with harlots."

This was the main point of conflict between Jesus and the religious leaders of his people. Their many virtues he gratefully acknowledged, but still they seemed to him to be spoiling the hope of Israel. They did not seek the salvation of sinners. They despised the despicable instead of interpreting sin in terms of need and need as a call for compassion. Outreaching, sacrificial concern for the wayward and the lost was not in them. The situation, as Jesus pictured it at the parable's end, was tragic—the Prodigal restored to the father's house, while the elder son was angry, unforgiving, alienated from the very household he was so loyal to, and deaf to the father's plea: "It was fitting to make merry and be glad, for this your brother was dead, and is alive; he was lost, and is found."

As religious and moral outcasts saw Jesus, he was their friend, but he was far from being an easy friend to deal with. He faced them with high standards of ethical living—higher than any that scribal laws could require. He spared no condemnation of their sin, glossed over no iniquity, but along with stern requirements and judgments went a gospel. Law's business is to define sin and announce penalties, but the whole area beyond law's function—the saving of men—Jesus made peculiarly his own. Their infinite value in God's sight, their possibilities of renovation, their essential worth calling for sacrificial saviorhood—this was his specialty, and as Dr. Montefiore, speaking from the standpoint of Judaism, says, it was a "new note in religious history."

## CHAPTER VI

## As Women and Children Saw Him

JESUS' home in Nazareth was full of children—"his brothers James and Joseph and Simon and Judas" and "all his sisters"[1]—and Jesus' understanding and appreciation of children are evident. He recalled hungry children, asking for bread or fish.[2] He knew children's capricious moods, happy or sulky at their games.[3] He remembered neighbors disturbing the family at midnight, when all the children were peaceably in bed.[4] When his disciples jealously asked who among them was to be greatest, he set a child before them, saying, "Whoever humbles himself like this child, he is the greatest in the kingdom of heaven."[5] He identified himself with children, declaring that to welcome "one such child" is to welcome him.[6] According to Matthew, when children in the temple shouted "Hosanna" at the sight of him and indignant priests protested, he quoted the Psalmist:

> Out of the mouths of babes and sucklings
> thou hast brought perfect praise.[7]

As for his personal affection toward children, Matthew, Mark and Luke all recall how the disciples, trying to prevent parents from bringing their babes for his blessing, were rebuked: "Let the children come unto me; do not hinder them."[8]

The profound influence of family life on Jesus' thinking is evident. His words, according to the Fourth Gospel, "I am not alone, for the Father is with me,"[9] express an experience with God amply illustrated in the synoptic narratives, as when in Gethsemane Jesus addressed God with the intimacy of a Jewish child at home, "Abba."[10] Concerning Jesus' earthly father, Joseph, we know little; presumably he died in Jesus' youth; after the family's journey to Jerusalem, when Jesus was twelve years old, we do not hear of him. He must have left behind him, however, an admirable memory, for to the growing boy, Jesus, God became "Father" with an intimacy and depth of meaning that make his use of the term unique. As for his fellow men, they were his brothers. The humblest, neediest man he could imagine was "one of the least of these my brethren."[11]

Even when the break came between Jesus and his family, he retained the ideas and terminology of the home as descriptive of his divine and human relationships. For the break did come when his mother and his brothers, thinking it madness that he should so dangerously plunge into his public ministry, came to get him and bring him home. "Your mother and your brothers are outside, asking for you," he was told. "And he answered, 'Who are my mother and my brothers?' And looking around on those who sat about him, he said, 'Here are my mother and my brothers! Whoever does the will of God is my brother, and sister, and mother.' "[12] Thus forced by his mission to give up the narrower home circle, where his ideas of God and man had been nourished, he still kept the ideas themselves, extending family relationships to a wider group, and revealing by implication his ideal for mankind—a good home become universal.

One evidence of this profound influence of family life on

Jesus is seen in his attitude toward women. "He is a great champion of womanhood," writes Dr. Montefiore.[13] In all the Gospels this is evident but especially in Luke. In six important passages Luke alone records Jesus' sympathetic care for, and friendly dealing with, women. Only he reports the raising from the dead at Nain of a young man, "the only son of his mother, and she was a widow."[14] Only he narrates the scene in the home of Simon the Pharisee, where Jesus compares a sinful woman with righteous Simon to the latter's discredit.[15] Only he records the Master's conversation with Mary and Martha about the "one thing . . . needful,"[16] or the healing on the sabbath of the crippled woman, "who had had a spirit of infirmity for eighteen years,"[17] or the words addressed by Jesus to the "women who bewailed and lamented him," as he went to Calvary: "Daughters of Jerusalem, do not weep for me, but weep for yourselves and for your children."[18] In some ways most important of all stands Luke's passage about those who accompanied Jesus on one of his preaching missions: "And the twelve were with him, and also some women who had been healed of evil spirits and infirmities: Mary, called Magdalene, from whom seven demons had gone out, and Joanna, the wife of Chuza, Herod's steward, and Susanna, and many others, who provided for them out of their means."[19]

Here is detailed information, with names given, suggesting that these women were well-known members of the first church, whom Luke might have met during his stay in Jerusalem or Caesarea. Moreover, the major intent of Luke's passage is confirmed by Mark, who records that at the crucifixion, "There were also women looking on from afar, among whom were Mary Magdalene, and Mary the mother of James the younger and of Joses, and Salome, who, when he was in Galilee, followed him, and ministered to him; and also many

[ 143 ]

other women who came up with him to Jerusalem."[20] Such
specific facts as these are not likely to have been invented by
the later church. No motive can be readily suggested to explain
interest in these names of women who followed Jesus, save as
they came down from early eyewitnesses as part of the original
tradition. Moreover, they are notable facts, suggesting Jesus'
break with oriental ideas of woman's subordination, and revealing his companionship with women on an equal basis with
men. "The relation of Jesus to women," says Dr. Montefiore,
"seems unlike what would have been usual for a rabbi. He
seems to have definitely broken with orientalism in this
particular."[21]

Here, at any rate, is a group of Jesus' contemporaries—the
women—whose response to him should be worth studying.

That they found in him sensitive sympathy and understanding is clear. In view of the Gospels' brevity and the
sparse selection of material from all that Jesus must have said
and done, his references to the humble goings-on in a household and to women's tasks in particular are remarkable. Even
when he thought of the world's end and the Messiah's advent
he thought of "two women grinding together; one will be
taken and the other left."[22] Even when telling a parable about
an unclean spirit returning to the empty house from which he
had been exiled, Jesus added, as though with a woman's insight, "When he comes he finds it swept and put in order."[23]
If God's love for a sinner is like a shepherd searching the
mountains for a sheep, it is also like a woman lighting a lamp
and sweeping the house until she finds a coin which she has
lost, possibly from her headdress.[24] The ovens heated by field-
grass where women cooked,[25] the bread-making where women
hid leaven "in three measures of meal, till it was all leavened,"[26]

even the moths that must be kept from the family's garments and the rust which ruined household utensils,[27] were his familiar figures of speech. When called upon to defend the radical novelty of his teaching and practice, such as his dislike of fasting, he dealt with it in terms of refusal to put new wine into old wineskins, or to sew "a piece of unshrunk cloth on an old garment," for "the patch tears away from it, the new from the old, and a worse tear is made."[28] Jesus' imagination was filled with the homely details of housekeeping. The duties with which he had seen his mother and sisters dealing in Nazareth, even to buying five sparrows for two pennies,[29] he had watched and helped at with sympathetic care.

Beyond such intimate insight into woman's work in a humble Palestinian household, Jesus was plainly aware of the injustice women suffered, which called for rectification and redress. There is no mistaking the compassion and indignation with which he spoke of widow's wrongs, and if his mother was a widow, as seems practically certain, one reason for Jesus' sensitiveness concerning them may be sought in that fact. Woman's estate in the oriental world was one of subordination even at the best. Paul, a Hellenistic Jew, leaves no doubt of that. He clung to old discriminations—such as the veiling of women, to which he had been accustomed in Tarsus—despite his acceptance of the doctrine which Jesus had inspired, "there is neither male nor female; for you are all one in Christ Jesus."[30] Even if one concludes, after studying the evidence, that in the first century one would prefer being a Jewess to being a Greek woman, it still remains true that it was a man's world then, that woman's place was subservient, often humiliating, cramped by a long tradition of organized inferiority, and that the situation of widows was especially difficult.

When Jesus drew a picture of an unjust judge who "had no

reverence for God and no respect even for man," it is no accident that the victim before him, pleading for redress in the
inhospitable court, was a widow. "She used to go and appeal
to him," Jesus said—a picture of repeated rebuffs and denials
—and, in the end, she won reluctant consideration from the
judge, not because he cared to be just or thought a widow's
wrongs important, but only because "this widow is bothering
me, I will see justice done to her—not to have her for ever
coming and pestering me."[31] One wonders whether behind
that parable was an occurrence of like sort in Jesus' experience
in Nazareth.

Watching "the rich putting their gifts into the treasury,"
"he saw a poor widow put in two copper coins," and his exclamation that she had "put in more than all of them," suggests memories of his mother.[32] When he returned to Nazareth
to preach, he recalled how Elijah was sent "to Zarephath, in
the land of Sidon, to a woman who was a widow."[33] Even
when widows had property he indignantly saw them being
fleeced by unscrupulous scribes and priests, who played upon
their pious generosity; they "devour widows' houses and for a
pretense make long prayers."[34]

To be sure, the wrongs suffered by women in general and by
widows in particular were not the sympathetic concern of
Jesus only. If he valued a poor widow's gift, so did the scribe
according to whom a certain priest, scornful of a woman's
small offering of flour, was rebuked in a dream: "Despise her
not; it is as though she offered her life."[35] Jewish civil law tried
by numerous regulations to protect widows from harsh
wrongs;[36] and if Jesus condemned religious leaders, using their
influence to "prey upon the property of widows,"[37] so did the
best of the scribes: "He who robs widows and orphans is as
though he robbed God himself."[38]

[ 146 ]

These very laws and exhortations, however, emphasize the presence of the wrongs against which Jesus protested. To be sure, romantic love was prized, as in the Song of Songs; some women, from Esther to Judith, rose to positions of powerful leadership; and the praises of a good wife were sung in one of the most eloquent and lovely passages in the Hebrew scriptures.[39] Nevertheless, there was another side to the matter. Woman in that ancient world was valued altogether with reference to man; he was first and central; woman's value was rated by her meaning and service to him. She was not a person in her own right, as he was. She was at his disposal, to be regulated, suppressed, coddled or discarded as might most please him. In the current books of Jesus' time there is warm appreciation of womanhood. If a wife be beautiful and of "a gentle tongue," then

> He that acquireth a wife hath the highest possession,
> A helpmeet to him and a pillar of support.[40]

But there are other passages also whose presence in the sacred books reveals an attitude ingrained in that whole ancient world.

> A daughter is to a father a deceptive treasure,
>    And the care of her putteth away sleep;
> In her youth lest she commit adultery,
>    And when she is married lest she be hated, . . .
> Keep a strict watch over a headstrong daughter
>    Lest she make thee a laughing-stock.
> In the place where she abideth let there be no lattice,
>    And in the house where she sleepeth no entry round about.
> Let her not display her beauty before any man,
>    And in the house of women let her not gossip;

For from the garment cometh forth the moth,
  And from a woman a woman's wickedness.
Better the wickedness of a man than the goodness of a woman.[41]

Against such an attitude Jesus' ministry was a sustained protest. He treated women as he treated men—as persons sacred in their own right, as souls loved of God and full of undisclosed possibilities. He never condescended to women, but habitually showed them deference, and to the surprise of the attendant audience more than once came to their spirited defense.

His rebuke of those who look "at a woman lustfully"[42] is a case in point. We commonly rob the passage of its full significance, as though it were concerned only with the licentious passions of men. But to look upon a woman lustfully is to regard her as a chattel, a thing to serve man's sensual desire, not a person but a physical instrument of transient pleasure. Inwardly it is the very opposite of love, and socially it is the root of woman's many and long-continued indignities. Against this whole degrading view of womanhood Jesus protested. He stands out from the low standards of his time and of all times in his estimate of woman as a personality, to be so regarded and treated, to be loved for her whole self, and not looked on merely as a means of satisfying man's sexual desire.

Even today in the prayer book of the orthodox Jewish synagogue we read: "Blessed art thou, O Lord our God! King of the universe, who hast not made me a woman." However one may explain the persistence of this prayer, it illustrates the ancient tradition out of which we all came. The women who followed Jesus, however, saw in him another attitude. Even today the modern reader of the Gospels commonly fails to notice it. The difference between Mary and Martha,[43] for example, we modernize; it lies, we say, in the contrast between the busy service of the practically-minded and the quiet intake of the receptive, listening soul. Martha was "distracted with much service" in preparing a meal for Jesus; Mary was absorbed in the more important matter of gaining insight into Jesus' message. This interpretation is true enough, but when Jesus said of Mary, she "has chosen the good portion which shall not be taken away from her," he meant more than that. Jesus was treating Mary as a full-orbed personality. To her, as a child of God, he was opening up the treasures of his spirit. In the presence of his gospel there was no male or female, but all were one, and probably Mary had never in her life before been so dealt with, so treated with intellectual and spiritual respect by any religious teacher. Jesus wanted Martha too to respond to his approach, and be less contented than she was with the traditional pattern of woman's status. Said one rabbi, "Better that the words of the law should be burned than delivered to women."[44] Against the whole philosophy of life involved in such a saying Jesus was in rebellion and his attitude toward womanhood which was revealed in his treatment of Mary was habitually characteristic of him.

Indeed, the record represents him as coming to woman's defense in situations where his defense needs to be defended. Mark, Matthew, and John[45] all relate the story of the grateful woman who anointed him with costly spikenard. "This angered some of those present," we read. "What was the use of wasting perfume like this? This perfume might have been sold for over 300 shillings, and the poor might have got that. So they upbraided her." Surely, their upbraiding had justification—a shilling was a day's wages then—and Jesus was the last of men either to forget the poor or to welcome extravagant adulation of himself with costly perfume. But there stood the woman who with good intent, out of a grateful heart, had done this generous, impulsive deed. He would not leave her shamefaced, humiliated, her costly reverence misunderstood, her devout motive forgotten, her sacrificial gift condemned. "Let her alone," he said. "Why are you annoying her? She has done a beautiful thing to me. The poor you always have beside you, and you can be kind to them whenever you want; but you will not always have me."[46] So he stood up for her, and if he really said the rest of what is reported—"wherever the gospel is preached all over the world, men will speak of what she has done in memory of her"—that has been fulfilled. Such championship of womanhood, distinctive of Jesus, was quite uncharacteristic of the world he lived in.

How Jesus came to the defense even of a woman taken in adultery we have seen.[47] The men who would have stoned her were grounded in an old tradition: woman was man's temptress, the creature who first in Eden had led man to sin, and their righteous wrath, backed by the Mosaic law, was ready to do away with any adulteress—as though in adultery man could ever be the mere victim, as though he is not always the equal participant, if not the probable aggressor. So Jesus turned on the men: "Let him who is without sin among you be the first to throw a stone at her." He was announcing there the single standard for men and women in the morality of sex. Once more he was denying man's right to lord it over woman with an assumed superiority not grounded in facts. As for the sinful woman, Jesus' final words to her opened the door to a transformed life: "Neither do I condemn you; go and do not sin again."

As the early records of the church, both in the New Testament and afterwards, bear witness, women were among its most ardent and effective members, and this response of womanhood to Christ and his message goes back to his own ministry. Simon, the Pharisee, seeing Jesus anointed by a sinful woman was sure he could not be a prophet; else he would have known the uncleanness of the one who touched him.[48] But here again Jesus became the woman's defender. Almost certainly she had met Jesus before, else why should she have been so grateful to him? Through him she had found forgiveness, cleansing, reinstatement as a child of God, power to amend her life and, forgiven much, she loved much. In Simon's house that day the parable of the prodigal daughter was enacted, with Simon in the part of the elder brother. Unconscious of sin, feeling little or no need of pardon, he was cold, complacent, all condescension and contempt, while the prodigal daughter, come to herself again, was penitent, thankful, adoring. To her, not to Simon, Jesus' benediction was given: "Your faith has saved you; go in peace."

While the story of Jesus' meeting with the woman of Samaria is told in John's Gospel only,[49] one thing is certain: whoever first told that story had been at the well of Sychar. Still "the well is deep," one of the deepest in Palestine. Still "this mountain," Gerizim, close at hand, rises from the plateau. Still, one has a far view across the plain and can "see how the fields are already white for harvest." In Jesus' day, however, the woman of Samaria, who had had five husbands and now was living with a man not her husband, would never have been addressed by a Jewish rabbi. When Jesus' disciples returned, we read, "They marveled that he was talking with a woman." But Jesus had no regard for such barriers, and once more he immortalized a woman who, but for him, would have lived and died in unrespected obscurity.

Such was the teacher to whom the women who followed Jesus responded. He was to them more than a teacher—a champion of womanhood in a time when a champion was needed.

[ 151 ]

If the Samaritans interpreted the Mosaic law, which was their Scripture too, as the Jews did, that woman, who had had five husbands,[50] had not divorced them—they had divorced her. Divorce among the Jews, in Jesus' day, was altogether in the power of the husband. To be sure, paganized Jewesses, Salome and Herodias, both of the Herodian house, divorced their husbands, but among law-abiding Jews such a scandal would have been impossible. In Jesus' day the legal continuance of any Jewish marriage depended solely on the husband's caprice. According to the law he could discard his wife at will —"write her a bill of divorcement" and "send her out of his house," if he "found some unseemly thing in her."[51] The schools of Shammai and Hillel did indeed differ as to what the "unseemly thing" might be. Shammai had interpreted it to mean unchastity, but Hillel had said it might be anything which displeased the husband, even spoiling his food, and Rabbi Akiba added that a husband might divorce his wife for the sole reason that he found another woman more comely than she.[52]

The consequent hardship on women, even under modern conditions, would have been bad enough, but in Jesus' day it was worse. Women then were regarded in effect, as by ancient tradition they had been regarded in fact, as the possession of men. A woman from her birth belonged to some man, first as daughter, then as wife. She had her status in society because she did belong to some man, and to be cast off by him, divorced, left ownerless and unattached was lamentable. Cruel as the Mosaic law may seem, therefore, making the husband judge, jury and executioner in dismissing his wife, a valuable social advance over primitive custom was involved in it: it forced the man to give her a "bill of divorcement," establishing for her a kind of legal status and freeing her to marry another.

Nevertheless, the injustice to women involved in the divorce system of Jesus' day was monstrous, and it is fair to let a Jewish scholar state the case: "The religious position of women and the law of divorce form the least attractive feature of the rabbinical system. . . . The unerring ethical instinct of Jesus led him to put his finger upon the weak spots and sore places of the established religion. Of all such weak spots and sore places this was the weakest and sorest."[53]

Apparently the Pharisees heard that Jesus had protested against this wrong to women, and "in order to test him," Mark tells us, they asked him, " 'Is it lawful for a man to divorce his wife?' He answered them, 'What did Moses command you?' They said, 'Moses permitted a man to write a certificate of divorce, and to put her away.' But Jesus said to them, 'For your hardness of heart he wrote you this commandment. But from the beginning of creation, 'God made them male and female.' 'For this reason a man shall leave his father and mother and be joined to his wife, and the two shall become one.' So they are no longer two but one. What therefore God has joined together, let not man put asunder."[54]

The difficulties involved in this total condemnation of divorce were evident from the first. Paul knew what Jesus had said and reported it in unmitigated form to the Corinthian church: "To the married I give charge, not I but the Lord, that the wife should not separate from her husband (but if she does, let her remain single or else be reconciled to her husband)—and that the husband should not divorce his wife."[55] By the time Matthew's Gospel was written, however, compromise had begun, and Jesus is quoted as making one exception, "whoever divorces his wife, except for unchastity, and marries another, commits adultery."[56] Indeed, the question which the Pharisees asked Jesus is so phrased by Matthew—

[ 153 ]

"Is it lawful to divorce one's wife for any cause?"—that some have thought it a demand for a decision by Jesus between the schools of Shammai and Hillel. Was Shammai right that unchastity alone was ground for divorce or was Hillel right that there were many other grounds? If such was the question, Jesus sided with Shammai. That was not Jesus' way, however —to get at important matters by defining legalistic applications and by backing one rabbinical school against another. Far more congenial with Jesus' method is it to take Paul and Mark, the earliest witnesses, as reporting what he really said, announcing without qualification that the monogamous family is right and that broken families, divorces and tandem remarriages are wrong. This he said sweepingly, without compromise or exception, basing his judgment concerning an ideal home on God's original intent in marriage.

The first disciples, according to Matthew, felt at once the impracticality of any such sweeping pronouncement—even if an exception was made in the case of unchastity—and the impossibility of enforcing it. "The disciples said to him, 'If such is the case of a man with his wife, it is not expedient to marry.' But he said to them, 'Not all men can receive this precept, but only those to whom it is given. . . . He who is able to receive this, let him receive it.'"[57] This lifts Jesus' words on divorce out of the legalistic category altogether and puts them where they belong—not a regulation to be enforced by public law courts, but the ideal of what marriage ought to be, and would be if men and women were truly his disciples. Only transformed persons can or will exercise the sexual self-control that makes true marriage possible. Only they will wish to have or can have the one kind of home which fulfills the divine intention: a household where two people love each other so much that they do not care to love anyone else in the same way, and who throw around each other and their growing children the security and affection of an indissoluble family.

Had Jesus foreseen the long evolutionary extension of society in a changing world, he would doubtless have foreseen, what indeed he never denied, the need of law codes and law courts to enforce as high a standard as at any given time was practically possible. But he still would have kept his major message unimpaired. He stood for the highest ideal of the family ever presented to mankind. He sought to re-create men and women, so right within that they were capable of having such homes. He was calling for the very best which, by God's grace, could be attained in a family.

Jesus' approach to the problem of marriage and divorce was not, however, simply a matter of his characteristic idealism. He was deeply concerned over the wrong done to woman by the existing system. Mark, writing his Gospel in Rome, where women could initiate divorce, added to Jesus' words the phrase, "if she divorces her husband,"[58] but that phrase must be Mark's, not Jesus', for among the Jews no such possibility existed. That many mitigations of the estate of divorced women had been introduced into the rabbinical regulations, some making arrangements for alimony, is true. It took ingenuity to do it, but Rabbi Jacob bar Aha deduced from a verse in Isaiah the law, "Do not withdraw help from thy divorced wife."[59] Nor, of course, was Jesus the first to deplore broken families. Had not Malachi written: "Therefore take heed to your spirit, and let none deal treacherously against the wife of his youth. For I hate putting away, saith Jehovah, the God of Israel"?[60] Nevertheless, the divorce system in the Judaism of Jesus' day was a "sore spot." Rights are not readily surrendered and men were clinging tenaciously to their traditional power over their women.

[ 155 ]

At this point Jesus became outspokenly and controversially woman's champion. The women who followed him must have recognized the new note he was striking, and they responded to his friendship with loyal gratitude.

Jesus' conviction concerning the value of marriage and the home lights up the meaning of other sayings of his about the necessity of loving the kingdom of God more than the family. "If any one comes to me and does not hate his own father and mother and wife and children and brothers and sisters, yes, and even his own life, he cannot be my disciple"[61]—this saying, reported by Luke, has shocked many by its seeming harshness. Far from being harsh, however, it comes near to being the highest tribute Jesus paid the home. He was speaking of the supreme self-sacrifice. Only one cause could rightly demand it, the kingdom of God, but that could demand the most costly self-surrender. As to the nature of this supreme sacrifice Jesus had no doubt—to break with one's family and give up one's life. These two he put together as the most costly price which devotion to the kingdom might require. In Hebrew the word "hate" was used to mean "love less,"[62] a fact which Matthew makes evident in his rendition of Jesus' saying: "He who loves father or mother more than me is not worthy of me; he who loves son or daughter more than me is not worthy of me."[63] Both come to the same issue, however: the severest self-sacrifice that can be demanded of man is to turn his back on his home folk. This is not depreciation of the family's value but its exaltation.

That this way of stating the most difficult kind of self-sacrifice came from Jesus' experience with his own family seems clear. Near the beginning of his ministry, when, having appointed the twelve disciples, he had launched his public mission on the shores of the Sea of Galilee, and was drawing around him such crowds "that they could not even eat," we read in Mark's Gospel that "when his friends heard it, they went out to seize him, for they said, 'He is beside himself.' "[64] Who were these "friends" who thought Jesus was deranged? The Greek phrase means "those who belonged to him," and Dr. Moffatt translates it "his family." The context strongly supports this rendering, for Mark reports that it was "his mother and his brothers" who came to get him, and, standing outside, unable to reach him because of the crowd, tried to call him out to them. That call from his home folk presented Jesus with one of the most crucial tests of his vocation. He refused to go out to them, and turning to his listeners said: "Here are my mother and my brothers! Whoever does the will of God is my brother, and sister, and mother."[65]

Certainly this break between Jesus and his family was part of the tradition of the church, for John's Gospel says, "even his brothers did not believe in him,"[66] and that it was a constant factor in Jesus' own thinking seems evident. When he talked with Peter about those who specially deserved and would receive a rich reward, he singled out "one who has left house or brothers or sisters or mother or father or children or lands, for my sake and for the gospel."[67] When he saw the disruptive effect of his teaching, dividing families and alienating his followers from their own households, he exclaimed: "Do you think that I have come to give peace on earth? No, I tell you, but rather division; for henceforth in one house there will be five divided, three against two and two against three; they will be divided, father against son and son against father, mother against daughter and daughter against her mother, mother-in-law against her daughter-in-law and daughter-in-law against her mother-in-law."[68] Matthew adds that Jesus

[ 157 ]

quoted a saying of Micah, uttered in one of the prophet's downcast hours, "a man's foes will be those of his own household."[69] This was Jesus' heaviest cross before he went to Calvary.

What this alienation from his family meant to Jesus such passages poignantly suggest, but what it meant to his mother, how she felt about him during his perilous ministry with its tragic ending, one can only surmise. In the synoptic Gospels she never appears again. In John's Gospel she stands so close to the cross that Jesus can speak to her, commending her to the care of "the disciple whom he loved."[70] The difficulty in accepting this late account as historical lies in the fact that Mark and Matthew give the names of women—Matthew says "many women"—who stood "beholding from afar" the crucifixion of their Lord, and the name of Jesus' mother is not among them, as it surely would have been had the earlier writers ever heard of her presence there.[71] Of only one thing can we be certain: Jesus' mission involved a tragedy in the personal relationships of the home in Nazareth.

The effect of this fact on the credibility of the story of Jesus' virgin birth is obvious. There is no evidence in the Gospels, apart from the birth stories themselves, that any member of Jesus' family or any of his first disciples ever thought of him as virgin born. Mark, who gathered from Peter the facts of Jesus' life, does not mention it. In Matthew and Luke, where the birth stories appear, are two genealogies, so inconsistent that they cannot possibly be reconciled, both of which in tracing Jesus' lineage come down to Joseph, not to Mary. These genealogies are inconceivable except on the supposition that when they were prepared Joseph was thought to be Jesus' father. Indeed, in the Monastery of St. Catherine on the traditional Mount Sinai is an ancient Syriac translation of Matthew's

[ 158 ]

Gospel, rendering, so scholars feel assured, an older manuscript of Matthew than any which we now possess, and ending the genealogy with its only logical conclusion: "Joseph begat Jesus." As for Luke, he quotes the genealogy he has before him, but destroys its meaning as a record of Jesus' lineage by his parenthesis: "Jesus . . . being the son (as was supposed) of Joseph."[72]

The category of virgin birth was alien to Jewish thinking. The passage in Isaiah,[73] in which the church, at the time Matthew and Luke were written, found prophecy of Mary's virginity—"Behold, a virgin shall conceive, and bear a son"—was taken not from the original Hebrew but from the mistaken rendering in the Septuagint, the Greek translation of the Old Testament, which even Paul and much more the later church commonly used. The original Hebrew says not "virgin," but "young woman." It was the Greek world in which virgin births were a common way of explaining unusual personalities. So Plato was said to be virgin born, and Alexander the Great, and Aesculapius, and Pythagoras and Simon Magus and Apollonius of Tyana, and many more. In the second century, when Justin Martyr stated the case, he even put Jesus' birth, for argument's sake, in the same category with such legends: "When we declare that the Word, who is the first-born of God, came into being without sexual intercourse . . . we do not report anything different from your view about those called sons of Zeus."[74]

If, then, it was in the later Hellenistic area of the church that the story of the virgin birth arose, this would explain why the early records of Jesus' first contemporaries reveal no slightest sign that they ever thought of him as physically begotten by the special act of God. Had they so thought of him, those closest to him, his "friends," his "family," would never

[ 159 ]

have said that he was "beside himself" in undertaking his mission. As his first, immediate contemporaries saw him, therefore, he was not yet being explained by the category of virgin birth, and one of the strongest indications of this is the alienation between himself and his mother. One hopes that the alienation was temporary. One welcomes the account in Acts that, immediately after the ascension, the first disciples gathered in "the upper room ... together with the women and Mary the mother of Jesus, and with his brothers."[75] One is glad of Paul's direct testimony that in Jerusalem he conferred with "James the Lord's brother," who along with Peter was in the leadership of the apostles.[76] Whatever happened in the thinking of the family in Nazareth during his earthly ministry, Jesus' mother and at least one of his brothers were at the heart of the first church.

The prominence of women among Jesus' first devoted and loyal contemporaries is notable. They were drawn to him alike by their needs and by his masterful personality and message. They came for healing, for forgiveness, for power to lead a new life, and for his benediction on their children. The timid woman who touched the hem of his garment, and when found out "came in fear and trembling" to thank him;[77] the aggressive Canaanite woman, who would not be put off by the fact that she was not of Jewish race and faith;[78] the women who provided for him out of their means;[79] and the mothers whose children he took "in his arms and blessed, ... laying his hands upon them,"[80] are typical. There is no explaining how that first precarious movement of thought and life which Jesus started, with so much against it and, humanly speaking, so little for it, moved out into its world-transforming influence, without taking into account the response of womanhood to

Jesus. When they were sunk in sin, he forgave them; when they were humiliated, he stood up for them; when they suffered social wrongs, he defended them; when they had abilities to offer, he used them; and when they became sentimental and effusive in their devotion to him, he stopped them: "A woman in the crowd raised her voice and said to him, 'Blessed is the womb that bore you, and the breasts that you sucked!' But he said, 'Blessed rather are those who hear the word of God and keep it!' "[81]

Writes Dorothy Sayers, from the vantage-point of 1947: "Perhaps it is no wonder that the women were first at the Cradle and the last at the Cross. They had never known a man like this Man—there never has been such another."[82]

## CHAPTER VII

# As His First Disciples Saw Him

THE inner group of Jesus' followers numbered twelve, and we commonly assume that we know who they were. The Gospels, however, are not unanimous about the names of the disciples. Matthew, in our first Gospel, is apparently identical with "Levi the son of Alphaeus" in Mark's Gospel.[1] Thaddaeus appears in Matthew's list and Mark's, but in Luke's list, both in the Gospel and in Acts, his place is taken by "Judas the son of James."[2] The reason for this discrepancy is unknown; it may be that the personnel of the twelve was inconstant, that subtractions and additions occurred during Jesus' ministry, as after his death Matthias took the place of Judas Iscariot.

That there was an inner circle of specially chosen and commissioned disciples is clear, however, and from them must have come the earliest recollections of Jesus. The genuineness of their reminiscences is made evident, in part, by their reports about their own behavior. The later church idealized the "twelve apostles." When in the Book of Revelation the celestial city is pictured coming down out of heaven, it had twelve foundations, "and on them the twelve names of the twelve apostles of the Lamb."[3] In the Gospels, however, far from being idealized, the twelve are portrayed as acting in ways the later church would never have made up and might well have wished to forget.

Once, when Jesus and the twelve were inhospitably received by a Samaritan village, James and John vindictively wanted to call down fire from heaven to consume the villagers, but Jesus "rebuked them," and, as some ancient manuscripts add, "he said, You do not know what manner of spirit you are of."[4] Once, when Jesus brushed aside the scribal regulations concerning diet, the disciples were as bewildered as the rest, so that Jesus said to Peter, "Are you also still without understanding?"[5] Once, James and John, with scandalous egotism, tried to secure from Jesus a promise that they should have first places in the day of his glory, so that "when the ten heard it, they began to be indignant."[6] Once, all the twelve fell to disputing about precedence, and Jesus, setting a little child in the midst of them, read them a lesson in humility.[7] According to Luke, even as they sat together at the last supper, "A dispute also arose among them, which of them was to be regarded as the greatest."[8] As for the suffering, sacrificial Christ, they so failed to understand that idea and Peter so vehemently protested against it that Jesus said to him, "Get behind me, Satan! You are a hindrance to me; for you are not on the side of God, but of men."[9] And when the final crisis came Judas' betrayal, Peter's denial, and the frightened flight of the whole band, are plainly set down without extenuation or excuse.

The church, a generation after Jesus had gone, when the glorious twelve were idealized, would never have invented such stories; they bear the mark of genuine recollection from the first disciples. Difficult though they found it to understand and follow him, however, they were still closest to him, knew

[ 163 ]

him best, entered most intimately into his thinking and experience, and what they saw in him is of paramount importance.

That they warmly felt the impact of his friendship is clear. Only in John's Gospel are the words put on Jesus' lips, "No longer do I call you servants . . . I have called you friends;"[10] but, as is often the case with the Fourth Gospel, those words make explicit what is implicit in the earlier records.

The Gospels help us little in understanding the personal experiences of the first disciples as, one by one, they surrendered to the fascination of their Master. Mark's story condenses the event until it seems incredibly abrupt. Jesus "saw Simon and Andrew the brother of Simon casting a net in the sea; for they were fishermen. And Jesus said to them, 'Follow me and I will make you become fishers of men.' And immediately they left their nets and followed him;"[11] "He saw Levi the son of Alphaeus sitting at the tax office, and he said to him, 'Follow me.' And he rose and followed him."[12] Obviously that cannot be the whole story. The Fourth Gospel explicitly says that Andrew and Simon Peter had met Jesus first in the circle around John the Baptist.[13] They and the others had certainly met him somewhere; there must have been a history behind their swift acceptance of his call.

Mark's first chapter[14] apparently records the events of a notable day in Jesus' early ministry. One is tempted to imagine Simon Peter, years afterward in Rome, telling Mark about it. Jesus calls Simon and Andrew and the sons of Zebedee from their nets and they follow him; he speaks in the synagogue the following morning with such effect that all are "astonished" at his "authority"; he heals a possessed man so that the "amazed" people question among themselves, "What is this? A new

[ 164 ]

teaching! With authority he commands even the unclean spirits, and they obey him"; he enters Simon Peter's home and cures Peter's wife's mother of a fever; in the evening "the whole city" gathers about the doors and he heals many of their sick; early the next morning he goes out to a "lonely place," followed by "Simon and those who were with him," and thence—escaping the crowds, concerning which they tell him, "Every one is searching for you"—they start on a preaching tour through Galilee. This passage has been called "the memory of the greatest day in Peter's life. It was the day when his discipleship had begun."[15]

Even if imagination goes beyond the facts in such an interpretation, one suspects that the general impression is true. Those first disciples were swept off their feet, fascinated by a personality whom they could not resist, convinced that something new, unique, prophetic, was happening in Israel, carried out of themselves by a mission, only dimly understood, but incarnate in one whose call was a command.

So began a friendship with vast historic consequences. A few, at least, of its informal intimacies are remembered in the Gospels, despite the fact that when the Gospels were written informal intimacies with the Lord were not easily conceivable. The disciples critically questioned the method of Jesus' teaching in parables;[16] anxiously asked him if he understood how offensive his sayings were to the Pharisees;[17] insisted on being told what some of his difficult teachings meant—"Explain this parable to us at anyrate";[18] and once, at least, "Peter took him, and began to rebuke him."[19] They were a company of friends. He had many followers, but "He appointed twelve to be with him."[20] They were his cabinet, his counselors, his companions. When life became too hurried and hectic, he took

[ 165 ]

them away "to a lonely place," where they could "rest a while."[21] He carried their personal needs upon his heart, and what he said to Peter was doubtless typical, "I have prayed for you."[22] Even when Judas in the Garden gave him the traitor's kiss, Jesus said, "Friend, why are you here?"[23]

In understanding the motives which led the twelve to leave all and follow him, it is important to stress the fact that they joined his company during the early days of Jesus' popularity. Thinking of Jesus as despised and rejected, some picture the disciples as making a hazardous, sacrificial decision in espousing his cause. Far from being despised and rejected, however, Jesus was riding a rising tide of public favor when he called them. He was having no difficulty in securing followers. One man "begged him that he might be with him. But he refused, and said to him, 'Go home to your friends.' "[24] To another who insisted, "I will follow you wherever you go," Jesus gave a forbidding answer, describing his homeless, vagrant ministry.[25] Another who said, "I will follow you, Lord; but let me first say farewell to those at my home," found his offer declined and was frankly told that he was not "fit."[26] Many were eager to join Jesus' inner circle. The mass movement in his favor, his forceful personality, his authoritative message, his stirring deeds, constrained them. But Jesus was searching for his picked men, looking for the best reliability he could find, the hardiest characters, the most understanding minds. And then he chose the twelve. All night long, among the hills, "he continued in prayer to God," and then in the morning "he called his disciples, and chose from them twelve."[27] It was the greatest honor that had ever come to them.

To be sure, their motives were mixed. Self-seeking was there, and the crude emotions that stirred the crowd's wonderment and awe—but something deeper too. He had captured them.

They loved him. He had now honored them with his intimate confidence and trust. They were his men.

This deep personal attachment is the one factor which persisted throughout the many changes of thought and circumstance which followed, surviving crisis and hairbreadth escapes, and at last building the church. When the twelve first became Jesus' inner circle of friends they did not understand him. They were drawn to him in part because they could *not* understand him; his mystery, his strange, inscrutable authority and power, whose sources were beyond their comprehension, baffled and fascinated them. They had at first no profound discernment of his message and mission, no clear insight into who he was. A mixed lot—a tax collecter, fishermen, characters as diverse as Peter and Judas—they certainly had no common creed and probably never dreamed that they would one day believe Jesus to be the Messiah. Their faith was personal— they were drawn to *him*. The one constant factor which held them together even through the tragedy of Calvary was this personal devotion. *What* they believed they often did not know, but as the Second Letter to Timothy put it long afterward, they did know *whom* they believed.[28] The Christian movement began in friendship.

That in the end Jesus nourished this friendship with almost desperate eagerness seems evident. Apparently he planned his first appeal to Israel as a whole and was encouraged by the popular response to hope for a widespread reformation under his leadership. Then opposition grew; his powerful foes made public failure certain and his own death probable; the crowd's interest and loyalty were genuine but shallow, based on misunderstanding of his real meaning, and conditioned on terms which he could not accept. Only his disciples were left to rely

[ 167 ]

upon. He must train them—upon that everything depended. Over the slender bridge of their understanding and fidelity his message must move, if it was to survive at all.

One suspects that his parable of the sower[29] was in part autobiographical. Three-fourths of the seed he sowed was wasted. It fell on trodden paths and was devoured by birds; it fell on thin soil and, springing quickly up, soon withered; it fell among thorns and was choked. Such was his disillusionment concerning his appeal to Israel as a whole. Only a little of the seed he sowed had any chance. That bit of good ground —his twelve disciples and the few more who were like them— was his only hope. If they failed to be fruitful soil, bringing forth a hundredfold, or even sixty or thirtyfold, all was lost.

As Jesus' ministry went on, three groups of auditors appeared whom he consciously distinguished from one another and addressed in specific ways. Mark's seventh chapter makes this clear. Answering a question of the Pharisees and scribes— "Why do your disciples not live according to the tradition of the elders, but eat with hands defiled?"—Jesus spoke first to his opponents. His words were caustic, biting, a scathing polemic against their casuistry. Then, turning from his opponents, Jesus called "the people" to him, "the crowd," "the multitude," and addressed them: "Hear me, all of you, and understand." When, however, his opponents and the crowd had gone and he was alone within doors with his disciples, he centered his attention upon them. "Do you not see?" he said, and with elaborate care, doubtless inadequately represented in our condensed accounts, proceeded with what became the main preoccupation of his ministry, the training of the twelve. As Mark tells us, "Privately to his own disciples he explained everything."[30]

His foes, the crowd, the inner group of his disciples—these

three he faced: the first increasingly with condemnation; the second with concern, sympathy, and deep desire to win their understanding; the third with poignant affection, eager hope, solicitously praying for them, as he did for Peter, that their faith might not fail.

They were a fallible group and he knew it, but he called them "the light of the world" and "the salt of the earth."[31] The modern reader of the Gospels often wonders at Jesus' faith in God the Father, despite his life's tragedy, but that is easier to understand than his faith in those disciples. He demanded of them a quality of life far above the average. The modern reader commonly fails to distinguish in the Gospels the passages Jesus addressed specifically to the disciples—not to the crowd or to his foes—and, in reading them, fails to emphasize the pronouns that must have had most emphatic meaning when the disciples first listened to him. Jesus, speaking privately to the twelve, pictured the rulers of the Gentiles lording it over them and said: "But it shall not be so among *you*; but whoever would be great among *you* must be your servant."[32] He pictured the self-seeking arrogance of the contemporary clergy and said to his disciples: "But *you* are not to be called rabbi, for *you* have one teacher, and *you* are all brethren."[33]

He insistently required of his disciples this excess and surplus of goodness. Many a time they must have heard that recurrent theme—not so among *you*. In his solicitude for them, thus challenged to superior and costly living, to what motives did he not appeal? He pictured their rewards, if not in this world, then in the next.[34] Conversing alone with them, he put his confidence in victory into flaming figures: "I saw Satan fall like lightning from heaven."[35] Privately, when they were discouraged by their smallness, he comforted them: "Fear not, little flock, for

it is your Father's good pleasure to give you the kingdom."[36]
Scholars are correct in noting that the parables of the mustard
seed becoming a tree[37] and of yeast leavening the whole lump[38]
do not teach gradual growth from small beginnings to great
conclusions. That concept of progress slowly achieved was not
then in the minds of men. Those parables are studies in contrast—apparently insignificant littleness versus great consum-
mations—and they were relevant to the disciples' need. Were
they to carry on, they had to believe that what is vital, though
small, can have large consequence.

So Jesus poured his heart out on those disciples. Their faith
in him was engendered by his faith in them; their gratitude to
him was matched by his thankfulness for them. Sitting at table
in the upper room, "He said to them, 'I have earnestly desired
to eat this passover with you before I suffer,' "[39] and as the
meal ended, and farewell drew near, his grateful affection over-
flowed: "You are those who have continued with me in my
trials."[40] John's Gospel expands this farewell scene and ampli-
fies the words of Jesus to his friends but, in view of what the
earlier Gospels tell us, there is verisimilitude in their tone and
spirit: "I have manifested thy name to the men whom thou
gavest me out of the world; thine they were, and thou gavest
them to me. . . . I am praying for them; I am not praying for
the world but for those whom thou hast given me. . . . Holy
Father, keep them in thy name."[41]

In training the twelve Jesus tried especially to do two things:
to prepare them for opposition, rejection, sacrifice, and to share
with them adequate resources of inner power to see them
through. Jesus' reported predictions concerning the disciples'
future exhibit a striking contrast, not to say contradiction. On

one side, according to the record, he foresaw the speedy coming of the messianic age; within their own day,[42] suddenly like
the flood in Noah's time or like a thief in the night[43] would be
the glorious arrival of the Son of Man. On the other side, the
disciples would face, he said, ostracism, persecution, death;
they would be delivered up to councils, beaten in synagogues,
brought to trial, delivered to death by their own families and
"hated by all."[44]

However we may arrange the time schedule which was in
Jesus' mind concerning these contrasting events—about which
he is reported to have said that only God knew the "day and
hour"[45]—he certainly foresaw the sacrificial testing of his
followers. His call to them was stern, ominous, forbidding,
"blood, sweat and tears." If they were to follow him, they had
to deny themselves and take up their cross;[46] they must be
ready to disown their own families, if need be, when loyalties
clashed;[47] they must even be prepared to count themselves
"blessed" when men reviled them, persecuted them, and
uttered all kinds of evil against them.[48]

At this point we face one of the typical problems raised by
modern scholarship. Imagine Mark in Rome, around A.D. 70,
formulating his Gospel. He is certainly interested in the facts of
Jesus' historic ministry, but he is also anxiously concerned
about the contemporary church. Persecution has fallen on it.
Nero's deadly work is still fresh in memory; Paul and probably
Peter have died as martyrs; Christians are ostracized, hated,
persecuted, vile falsehoods about them popularly believed, and
mob violence a constant threat. How can Mark write his
Gospel without wishing to interject into it anything and everything that will encourage the struggling Christian community?
So, say the critics, not the historic Jesus but the harassed

[ 171 ]

church a long generation after him, is the real source of the stress which the Gospels lay on predicted suffering and persecution.

The measure of truth in this ought freely to be granted. That the circumstances of the churches when the Gospels were written affected the selection of material from the oral and written tradition which preceded them seems obvious. Moreover one can, at times, see persuasive evidence of the deliberate adaptation of such material to the pressing problems of the churches. Luke, for example, records a brief saying of Jesus: "If your brother sins, rebuke him, and if he repents, forgive him."[49] In Matthew, however, this saying is expanded into a regulation for the government of conduct in a church: "If your brother sins against you, go and tell him his fault, between you and him alone. If he listens to you, you have gained your brother. But if he does not listen, take one or two others along with you, that every word may be confirmed by the evidence of two or three witnesses. If he refuses to listen to them, tell it to the church; and if he refuses to listen even to the church, let him be to you as a Gentile and a tax collector."[50] Jesus himself could not have said that—before there was a church. That is clearly an expansion of something Jesus said to meet a need which the author of the Gospel saw in some early Christian community—early, as the reference to Gentiles and tax collectors shows.

No historian succeeds in being completely objective, even when he tries. As for the writers of the Gospels, they were not trying. They wrote, not as though a Ph.D. were the end in view, but to strengthen the churches which they loved. The persecuted church, therefore, must have directed their attention to anything Jesus ever said about persecution and must

[ 172 ]

have led to the natural expansion and application of it to contemporary needs.

It is no accident, therefore, that not only is the Passion story the most emphasized feature of the Gospels, but that along with it the inevitable sufferings of the early church are stressed: "The cup that I drink you will drink; and with the baptism with which I am baptized, you will be baptized."[51] Nevertheless, to suppose that this cancels the historical validity of Jesus' warnings to his disciples, that they must count the cost, bear the cross, renounce all that they had,[52] is surely unwarranted. There was plenty of reason in the immediate situation which Jesus and his first disciples faced for such forewarning. They had joined his company when public favor brought the wondering crowds around him. Their heads were full of self-seeking dreams concerning first places in his kingdom. They were thinking of the prizes, not the costs. At no point were they less prepared for what awaited them. They needed to be told that hatred and persecution were to be their lot, flogged in the synagogues and dragged before governors.[53]

The core of such passages, therefore, whatever expansions and applications may have come later, was surely part of Jesus' training of the twelve. He was a stern taskmaster. They tried to see their discipleship to him as all glory and honor, but he insisted on destroying their illusions. They promised to follow him when he was a popular leader with multitudes about him, and the hardest lesson they had to learn was that, even if he was the Messiah, he was the suffering Messiah, and that they must suffer with him.

Facing the twelve thus with heavy demands, Jesus sought also to supply them with deep resources. At this point it is most important to note to what audience Jesus addressed any saying we wish to interpret. So approached, the Gospels reveal that Jesus' most profound and inward teaching about God's fatherhood, his intimate care for individuals and his available help through prayer was addressed to the disciples alone.

"In the morning, a great while before day," Mark tells us, "he rose and went out to a lonely place, and there he prayed. And Simon and those who were with him followed him."[54] So, from the beginning, the disciples saw Jesus in his most intimate hours, when his relationship with God meant not output but intake, and what they thus saw became one of the most indispensable factors in their training. As good Jews they had always prayed, but in Jesus' practice of prayer they saw something new, unique. Here was prayer with transforming consequence, not a form but a force. It was evident that when he prayed, he did not "heap up empty phrases as the Gentiles do."[55]

> Lord, what a change within us one short hour,
> Spent in thy presence can avail to make—

*that* experience they saw illustrated in Jesus in ways which awoke their wonder and their emulation. What Luke says, in describing the transfiguration, they must have witnessed more than once: "As he was praying, the appearance of his countenance was altered."[56]

In general, Jesus in his teaching of the twelve is represented as taking the initiative, challenging their prejudices, instructing their ignorance, urging upon them his ideas and ideals. In the matter of prayer, however, it was they who took the initiative. Having seen what prayer meant to Jesus they craved a share in the experience. That was the only thing the disciples are pictured in the Gospels as asking Jesus to instruct them

[ 174 ]

about: "He was praying in a certain place, and when he ceased, one of his disciples said to him, 'Lord, teach us to pray.' "[57]

According to Luke, who alone records them, two of Jesus' most puzzling parables—when pleading for patience in prayer, he likens God to an apathetic neighbor in bed with his children, not wishing to be disturbed,[58] and to an unrighteous judge who regards a widow's appeal only because, as he said, she "bothers me," and "will wear me out by her continual coming"[59]—were told to the disciples alone. Granting the uncertainty which commonly attends the Gospels' circumstantial setting of Jesus' sayings, there is persuasive likelihood in Luke's ascription of these special parables to an occasion when he was alone with the twelve. With the inner group of his friends he could be intimate, frank, whimsical. To them he could say that God sometimes seems like a sleepy neighbor saying, "Do not bother me; the door is now shut, and my children are with me in bed; I cannot get up and give you anything." Prayer was no swift, easy way of getting what Jesus wanted, no magical guarantee against trouble. Did he not pray all night before selecting his disciples?—and then he picked out Judas. Did he not cry in Gethsemane, "Remove this cup from me"?—but it could not be removed. To Jesus prayer was a long-term, patient search—asking, seeking, knocking—undergirded by an undiscourageable faith, prepared to surmount denial and disappointment: "If you then, who are evil, know how to give good gifts to your children, how much more will the heavenly Father give the Holy Spirit to those who ask him?"[60]

Such insight, which the disciples were given into Jesus' experience in prayer, was not for the crowd. With the disciples alone he shared his most intimate feelings concerning God's fatherly care: "Are not five sparrows sold for two pennies?

[ 175 ]

And not one of them is forgotten before God. Why, even the hairs of your head are all numbered. Fear not; you are of more value than many sparrows."[61] He was trying to prepare his inner group of followers for the trials that awaited them, to make their resources adequate for the coming stress and strain. As one watches him, reserving for the chosen few his profoundest thoughts about prayer and about the God who responds to it, Plato's saying—despite the vast difference between Plato's aristocratic bias and Jesus' love of common folk —is lighted up: "To find the maker and father of this universe is a hard task; and when you have found him, it is impossible to speak of him before all people."[62]

So to the twelve Jesus unbosomed himself, sharing with them alike his experience of, and his thoughts about, the divine resources that would sustain both him and them. "Now it happened," we read, "that as he was praying alone the disciples were with him."[63] Thus by contagion they caught more than they understood, and when he talked about those spiritual depths which any words are insufficient to reveal, it was to them he spoke. One suspects that, in its original setting, the passage on prayer in the Sermon on the Mount was spoken when he and his disciples were alone: "When you pray, go into your room and shut the door and pray to your Father who is in secret; and your Father who sees in secret will reward you."[64]

Whether Jesus thought of himself as the Messiah, and if so, what he meant by it, is a moot question concerning whose answer scholars probably will never agree. Penetrating the self-consciousness of Jesus is a difficult undertaking. Even to the first disciples he was often inscrutable, and to us the problem of his messianic claim, whether he made it and if so what meaning he put into it, is soluble only by conjecture. But whatever Jesus may have thought about himself, what the disciples thought about him is clear—he was the Messiah. That was the climax of their faith in him.

Had they been not Jews but Greeks, they would not have called him that. Being Jews, however, they had no other category except messiahship in which to frame a transcendent personality. They faced on one side Jesus himself, unique, original, divinely ordained and commissioned, and on the other side the inherited ideas of the Messiah with their long-accumulated and diverse meanings. The fitting of those two together was inevitably confusing and still in our Gospels it presents an all but insoluble problem.

The final outcome, however, is not dubious: they believed with flaming faith that he was the Christ. Mark's Gospel from beginning to end reveals this central conviction of the first disciples and of the early church. Jesus' marvelous deeds display his messianic power; his teachings manifest his messianic authority. John the Baptist bears witness to him, "After me comes he who is mightier than I";[65] and at his baptism a divine voice salutes him, "Thou art my beloved Son."[66] The demons know him, calling him, "the Holy One of God";[67] whenever the unclean spirits behold him, they fall down before him and cry out, "You are the Son of God."[68] At last, the disciples, slow of understanding, see the truth and Peter says, "You are the Christ."[69] At the transfiguration, a voice from the cloud says, "This is my beloved Son."[70] And after the resurrection all misgiving is ended and he is known to be the Messiah indeed, crucified, risen and coming again. This without doubt is the ardent faith that from first to last illumines Mark's Gospel.

Nevertheless, while this faith saturates the whole narrative, it is not allowed to obscure Jesus' own attitude. When the demons acclaim him he says, "Be silent";[71] "And he strictly ordered them not to make him known."[72] Even when Peter makes his decisive profession, Mark says, "He charged them to tell no one about him";[73] Luke says, "He charged and commanded them to tell this to no one";[74] Matthew says, "He strictly charged the disciples to tell no one that he was the Christ."[75] Not until the high priest at Jesus' trial asked him, "Are you the Christ, the Son of the Blessed?" and Jesus answered, "I am,"[76] did he, according to Mark's record, publicly affirm his messiahship. Considering the fact that the Christhood of Jesus was the church's first creed, and that when the Gospels were written the church's strong conviction would naturally urge the writers to discover or surmise the earliest possible date for Jesus' proclamation of it, this reluctance of Jesus to acknowledge his messiahship, this postponement of his claim to the final hours of his life, seems clearly historical.

How, then, did the first disciples come to their faith in him as the Christ, and what did they mean by it?

They seem first to have shared the crowd's interpretation and to have thought of him as a prophet. "A great prophet has arisen among us!"[77] said the people, "a prophet, like one of the prophets of old,"[78] and when Jesus asked his disciples who men were taking him to be, they answered, " 'John the Baptist'; and others, 'Elijah'; and others, 'One of the prophets.' "[79] Even at the end, when Jesus entered Jerusalem in triumph, "the crowds said, 'This is the prophet Jesus from Nazareth of Galilee' ";[80] and the chief priests and the Pharisees, planning to arrest him, "feared the multitudes, because they held him to be a prophet."[81] Moreover, this is what Jesus called himself—"A prophet is not without honor, except in his own country";[82] "Nevertheless I must go on my way today and tomorrow and the day following; for it cannot be that a prophet should perish away from Jerusalem."[83] With this interpretation of Jesus the disciples probably started.

That they soon went deeper and perceived in him a unique consciousness of special relationship with God seems evident. Scholars commonly hang the discussion of this profound inner experience of Jesus upon special phrases attributed to him, such as his use of "Abba," "my Father,"[84] or upon special texts, such as "All things have been delivered to me by my Father; and no one knows who the Son is except the Father, or who the Father is except the Son and any one to whom the Son chooses to reveal him."[85] Such a text, however, can be too easily attributed to the later church's conviction about him, read back—as many a similar passage in John's Gospel was read back[86]—into the consciousness of Jesus. Here, too, penetrating Jesus' self-consciousness is difficult, but the conviction of the first disciples seems clear, that while God in one sense is Father of all, and in a deeper sense Father of right-minded, merciful men—"Blessed are the peacemakers, for they shall be called the sons of God";[87] "Love your enemies . . . so that you may be sons of your Father who is in heaven"[88]—he was in a special sense Jesus' Father and Jesus his Son. The disciples' deepening companionship with him revealed to them a spirit whose profundities they could not fathom—unique resources in prayer, a moving sense of divine vocation and mission, an emphasis upon the intimate, inward, personal meanings of God's fatherhood such as they had never met before. The flaming faith that in some special sense Jesus was *the* Son of God, without which the first church is inconceivable, and which burns throughout our present Gospels and throughout the earliest known documents used in their composition, was surely no improvisation of a later generation. Sonship to God, in Jewish thought, was not a metaphysical category; it involved

[ 179 ]

no such thinking as Hellenistic Christianity later put into the Nicene Creed; it was a matter of spiritual quality and divine vocation, involving in its supreme exhibition a unique commission to fulfill it. *That* the first disciples clearly perceived in Jesus.

That somewhere in the course of their discipleship they began to think of him in specifically messianic terms is evident. The term "Messiah," however, in Jesus' day, connoted no such clearcut idea as we moderns commonly assume. The Messiah might be a man, rising from among the people—"A man shall arise . . . like the sun of righteousness";[89] "a man working righteousness and working mercy."[90] Or he might be a military leader fomenting revolt against Rome, and more than one such violent rebel was greeted as the Expected One. Peaceable or militant, such a Messiah was human—"Nor shall he do all these things by his own will, but in obedience to the good ordinance of the mighty God."[91] The Messiah might spring from the house of David[92]—that idea is prominent in our Gospels—but there was another tradition also, that he would come from the house of Levi.[93] In conceiving the Messiah's mission, nationalistic victory might be stressed— "he shall make war against Beliar, and execute an everlasting vengeance on our enemies,"[94] or in the center of attention might be the whole world's welfare—"Neither shall there be any sword throughout the land nor battle din. . . . No war shall there be any more,"[95] and "there shall be peace in all the earth."[96] The Messiah, however, in some circles, took on superhuman aspects. He was pre-existent, at least in the sense that his name was known to God from all eternity. So Moses is represented in saying of himself: "He designed and devised me, and he prepared me before the foundation of the world, that I should be a mediator of his covenant."[97] In time, how-

ever, this Vicegerent of God was pictured by some as person-
ally present in the heavens, ready to come in glory at God's
appointed time to usher in the kingdom.[98]

Such contrasting ideas were in the air in Jesus' day. The
rabbis themselves had trouble harmonizing them. How could
Zechariah's picture of the Messiah—"Behold, thy king cometh
unto thee . . . lowly, and riding upon an ass"[99]—be reconciled
with Daniel's picture: "Behold, there came with the clouds of
heaven one like unto a son of man"?[100] As late as the third
century A.D., one rabbi was still tussling with that question,
saying that if Israel were worthy, Daniel's picture would come
true, but if unworthy, Zechariah's.[101]

When Jesus' disciples, therefore, first moved up through
thinking of him as a prophet, and as in some special sense the
Son of God, to thinking of him as the Messiah, what did they
have in mind? Only one idea is constant through all the varied
concepts of messiahship: the Messiah in some supreme sense is
God's agent, his instrument and representative in saving Israel
and ushering in God's kingdom. Messiahship is a category of
vocation and mission. It is not primarily metaphysical but
instrumental. The Messiah, human or superhuman, is a doer
of deeds, a divinely appointed agent of salvation to his people.

So much, at least, the disciples saw in Jesus when first they
called him the Christ. In the end they believed him to be the
superhuman Son of Man ascended into heaven and waiting to
come again in glory, but by what stages they reached that goal
and what confused conceptions they held in the beginning it is
not easy to be sure.

The contemporary confusion of thought concerning the nature of the Messiah suggests a natural explanation of Jesus'
own recorded attitude. How could he declare himself openly
even if he thought he was the Messiah? To many that decla-

[ 181 ]

ration would suggest ideas utterly alien to Jesus' concept of his mission. Even when Peter called him Christ, he turned at once to expounding an idea of his vocation which horrified the twelve. If he had reason to fear even their misunderstanding of what Christhood meant to him, how much more must he have feared the misconceptions of the multitude!

As for the twelve, the Gospels record the emergence among them of an unprecedented idea of the Christ which later took possession of the church: he was the suffering servant of the Lord whom the Isaiah of the Exile had described.[102] Despite diligent research and the stretching of exegesis to its limit, there is no convincing evidence that the idea of a martyred Messiah was extant in Judaism in Jesus' day.[103] The traditional synagogue teaching, as embodied in the Targum, did on at least four occasions identify the Messiah with Isaiah's servant of the Lord, but by a triumph of evasive exegesis the sufferings in every case were taken from the Messiah and assigned either to Israel or to the heathen.[104] To be sure, the concept of vicarious suffering was in Judaism. Israel had had many sacrificial saviors in its history. The aged Eleazar, in the Fourth Book of Maccabees, prays amid his torments—"Thou knowest, O God, that when I might be saved, I am dying in fiery tortures on account of thy law. Be gracious to thy people, being satisfied with our punishment in their behalf. Make my blood a sacrifice for their purification, and take my life as a substitute for theirs."[105] Such saving martyrdom, however, ran counter to all the prevailing Jewish ideas of the Messiah, and the identification of Christ in the New Testament with Isaiah's suffering servant was a startling innovation.

Philip, presenting the gospel to the Ethiopian eunuch, started with Isaiah's fifty-third chapter, and "beginning with this scripture he told him the good news of Jesus."[106] Peter,

[ 182 ]

interpreting Christian suffering, quoted from the Septuagint version of the same chapter,[107] and the Letter to the Hebrews interprets Christ's cross in terms of it.[108] There is no doubt, therefore, that the early church identified the Messiah with Isaiah's servant of the Lord, nor is there valid reason for questioning the evidence of the Gospels that this identification went back to Jesus and his first disciples. When he announced his mission in Nazareth's synagogue, he read from Isaiah's sixty-first chapter,[109] and when he answered the messages of John the Baptist he alluded to it.[110] Only one direct quotation from the fifty-third chapter is attributed to Jesus—"I tell you that this scripture must be fulfilled in me, 'And he was reckoned with transgressors' "[111]—but there are other indications that the suffering servant was influentially present in his thought. Isaiah had said that God's "righteous servant" would "justify many" and that he "bare the sin of many";[112] Jesus said that he came "to give his life as a ransom for many."[113] "How is it written of the Son of man, that he should suffer many things and be treated with contempt?"[114] said Jesus to his disciples, after the Transfiguration. "The Son of man goes, as it is written of him,"[115] he said at the Last Supper. Where else was such a suffering redeemer written about save in Isaiah's prophecies?

Whatever may have been in Jesus' mind, there can be no doubt that, in the end, the disciples' concept of messiahship moved out into this new dimension. They saw him, as their people had never seen him, as a sacrificial savior, his blood "poured out for many."[116] Nevertheless, they combined this idea of a martyred Messiah with the apocalyptic picture of a superhuman Son of Man, awaiting in heaven the appointed hour for his victorious return. Mark's Gospel frankly reveals the difficulty this juncture of ideas presented to them: "He

[ 183 ]

was teaching his disciples, saying to them, 'The Son of man will be delivered into the hands of men, and they will kill him; and when he is killed, after three days he will rise.' But they did not understand the saying, and they were afraid to ask him."[117] This passage almost certainly reveals a retrospective, postresurrection view of the first disciples' thinking, but it reveals also the fact that not at first did they incorporate into their concept of Jesus' messiahship the figure of the heavenly Son of Man. That was the climax of their developing idea of Christ, and it could hardly have come to full flower until their dismay at the crucifixion had been turned into victory by their conviction that he was alive again.[118]

So Jesus' first disciples, laboring to interpret him in such inherited categories as they possessed, saw him: God's prophet, God's Son, God's suffering servant, and God's coming victorious Son of Man.

The inward struggle in the disciples' minds, involved in their endeavor to fit Jesus into their inherited mental frameworks, especially their conflicting ideas of messiahship, came to a tragic exhibition in Judas' treachery. Why Judas betrayed Jesus is still a matter of difficult conjecture. Mark and Luke picture him offering his treacherous services to the chief priests with no motive recorded; it is the priests who suggest the monetary reward, promising "to give him money." Matthew, however, changes the picture, represents Judas as saying, "What will you give me if I deliver him to you?" and under the influence of a passage in Zechariah, which he mistakenly ascribes to Jeremiah,[119] names the price that Judas received.[120] Mark's Gospel and Luke's say nothing about Judas' death; Matthew says that in remorse he returned the chief priests' bribe and "went and hanged himself," and that with the returned money the priests bought a "potter's field, to bury strangers in."[121] The Book of Acts, however, reports that Judas himself "bought a field with the reward of his wickedness; and falling headlong he burst open in the middle and all his bowels gushed out."[122]

The mercenary motive for Judas' treachery is, therefore, dubious. If, as Matthew intimates, that was the controlling motive, why did Judas, as Matthew also says, at once return the money and commit suicide? There must have been something deeper going on in Judas' mind, and conjectures as to what that something was have, with general consent, centered on the conflicting notions of messiahship which must have puzzled all the disciples.

One conjecture is that for a time Judas did believe Jesus to be the Messiah—the militant Messiah of Jewish hopes. If Peter rebelled against the idea of a suffering and dying Christ, Judas may have rebelled more. He had expected Jesus to declare himself with power and, backed by superhuman authority, to seize the reins of government and usher in the glorious new era. But what could he make of this Christ, who taught humility and love for enemies and said that the Son of Man must suffer and die? Even in Jerusalem, where the triumphant revelation of Jesus' power was most to be expected, nothing but weakness and humiliation were evident. Judas had waited long enough. Doubt crept in. He had been made a fool of by this Galilean, and by as much as he had believed with ardent hope in Jesus' messiahship, by so much he now resented and was determined to destroy the one who had let him down. Such is one conjecture.

Another is that Judas did not lose faith in Jesus as the Christ. He had wagered his life on that and he clung to it to the bitter end. But if Jesus was the Messiah, he must declare himself and

[ 185 ]

manifest his glory. Now was the time, and this the place, Jerusalem, where, only a few days before, the crowds had welcomed him with palm branches and hosannas. Somehow the issue must be forced. If Jesus were faced with a dilemma, crowded into a corner where he had to choose between shameful death and the disclosure of his messianic glory, then the world would see the revelation of the victorious Son of Man. That forced issue must be arranged, and Judas would see to it. Was some such motive behind Judas' betrayal?

That such conjectures are sheer guessing is obvious, but far and away the most probable explanation of Judas' treachery connects his deed with some form of disillusionment concerning Jesus' messiahship. Moreover, while in the end Judas alone deliberately betrayed his Lord, Peter denied him and the others fled. They all were very human in their perplexities and doubts, and none of them came easily by the confident faith in Christ which later shone in the Gospels. Is there not an authentic recollection of their disappointment and bewilderment in Luke's postresurrection story of the two disciples going to Emmaus: "But we had hoped that he was the one to redeem Israel"?[123] Judas' betrayal is a window through which one sees some of the inner struggles of the twelve about Jesus' messiahship, which the later records inevitably toned down.

Nevertheless, with their complete assurance that Jesus had triumphed over death, their faith came back again. He was not dead—they were still his contemporaries—and with deepened meaning, they saw him as God's prophet, God's Son, the sacrificial Savior, and the Son of Man who soon would come in glory to bring God's kingdom in.

The modern mind has endless doubts and questions concerning the ancient frameworks of thought by means of which the first followers of Jesus interpreted him. Even when modern doubts are given full swing, however, the personality in whose interpretation they were used still remains, demanding explanation. Those who lived most intimately with him stood most in awe of him, with mingled love and adoration acknowledged in him a divine authority, felt in him the very presence of their God, gave him the supreme name they knew to express transcendent greatness, Messiah, and after Calvary they were victoriously confirmed in their adoration of him by their faith in his resurrection and their experience of his living presence. That is the astounding fact with which the Christian church began.

## CHAPTER VIII

# As Militant Nationalists Saw Him

TO THE casual reader our Gospels seem only slightly concerned about the political conditions in Palestine which Jesus faced. When the Gospels were written those conditions had passed away. The violent revolt against Rome had ended —or, possibly in the case of Mark, was soon to end—in Jerusalem's capture by Titus in A.D. 70. Judaism, as a political state, was ruined; the militant Zealots were decimated; the seething problems which had obsessed Palestine while Jesus lived were history. Moreover, the Gospels, written in cities of the Empire, such as Rome or Antioch, were not concerned with recording the story of Jewish politics, but were altogether intent on presenting Christ as the world's Savior. Whatever Jesus may have said about the bygone political controversies of his time and country naturally became irrelevant to the succeeding generation of Christians, and could be easily forgotten or, if remembered, could be misunderstood and referred to contexts different from the original setting. The wonder is not that the Gospels reveal so little about Jesus' attitude toward current political problems but that they reveal so much.

That Jesus took no attitude toward the public problems of his people seems incredible. We commonly think of the Jews, in their dealing with Jesus, as exclusively concerned with religion and, conceiving religion in modern fashion as altogether a matter of theology, worship, prayer, humane deeds and pious observances, we lose sight of an incalculably influential factor in the ancient scene. Jewish religion and Jewish patriotism were inextricably intermeshed. No people have ever exhibited a more passionate and sustained patriotism than the Jews and their religion was the inspiration of it. Assyria, Babylon, Persia, Greece and Rome had successively conquered and enslaved them, but still the cry of the Psalmist persisted:

> If I forget thee, O Jerusalem,
> Let my right hand forget her skill.
> Let my tongue cleave to the roof of my mouth,
> If I remember thee not;
> If I prefer not Jerusalem
> Above my chief joy.[1]

In Jesus' day in Palestine nationalistic patriotism was rampant. From the time of the Maccabees, throwing off the yoke of the Syrian Greeks, the conquerors might seize the land and work their brutal will on the bodies of the people, but they could not quell the Jewish spirit. One rebellious outburst after another had kept even the Romans uneasy on their seat of power. The predominant public problem in Jesus' day concerned the attitude which the Jews should take toward Roman rule. Should they, like the Sadducees, temporize and, for the time being, collaborate with Rome, or, like many of the Pharisees, should they wait, hating Rome but looking for the Messiah's coming to redeem the nation and crush its enemies, or should they revolt and trust in God to give victory to the right? We may call such questions political but to the Jews they were basically religious. Jewish religion was specifically organized to

[ 189 ]

protect the national life and culture from breakdown and assimilation, and Jewish patriotism was centrally dedicated to
preserve the great heritage of Judaism's faith.

As for the militant patriots who believed in armed revolt, it
is a question of small moment whether or not, in Jesus' day,
they were called "Zealots." Josephus dates the use of the name
from John of Gischala who, about A.D. 66, helped launch the
fatal revolt which ended in Jerusalem's downfall. Josephus
himself, however, records how Judas of Gamala, in A.D. 6, re-
belling against the census of Quirinus, founded a "Fourth
Philosophy" among the Jews—along with the Sadducees,
Pharisees, and Essenes—and his description of its followers
with their passionate love of liberty, their determination to
acknowledge no ruler except God, and their fanatical fearlessness whether in killing or dying, makes it evident that they
were Zealots in fact, if not in name. From their time, says
Josephus, "the nation began to grow mad with this dis-
temper."[2]

Jesus, therefore, grew up in a turbulent nation, boiling with
political unrest. Half of it was governed by a Roman Procurator, the other half by a prince of the hated family of Herod.
Even in Jerusalem, where the Sadducean priests kept the people as steady as they could, assassinations and riots were frequent, and the farther away from Jerusalem one went, the
more openly insurrection threatened. Both John of Gischala
and Judas of Gamala were Galileans, and in Galilee the militant, revolutionary movement had both its rise and its greatest
strength. "The Galileans," wrote Josephus, "are inured to war
from their infancy."[3] Into such an environment Jesus was
born, and in his childhood some of the most vivid stories told
in Nazareth's lounging places must have been memories of

tumult and bloodshed. Herod the Great, who "stole along to his throne like a fox, ruled like a tiger, and died like a dog," was still fresh in the recollections of Galilee, and many a tale of his wars there and of the furious resistance of the people must have been current in Nazareth. It was in the Galilean hill country, with its many natural caverns, Josephus tells us, that "there was one old man who was caught within one of these caves, with seven children and a wife; these prayed him to give them leave to go out, and yield themselves up to the enemy; but he stood at the cave's mouth, and always slew that child of his that went out, till he had destroyed them every one, and after that he slew his wife, and cast their dead bodies down the precipice, and himself after them, and so underwent death rather than slavery."[4]

Such were the vivid memories of Galilee from the generation preceding Jesus and, as for his own childhood, when Judas of Gamala first raised the standard of rebellion, about the time of Jesus' birth or just afterward, he marched on Sepphoris, a few miles north of Nazareth, seized the arsenal there and for a brief time triumphed, until Varus, the Roman general, defeated him, burned Sepphoris to the ground, and sold its ininhabitants into slavery.[5]

To suppose that Jesus had nothing to say about a situation so urgent and fearful, took no attitude toward it, lived in an ivory tower and taught a religion irrelevant to his people's most critical public debates and decisions, seems most improbable. For there was little, if any, mitigation of the furious unrest during his lifetime. Driven underground it might be, but if Mommsen is right in saying that the real date for the beginning of the Jewish-Roman war may well be put as early as A.D. 44,[6] then hardly more than a decade after Jesus' death the strug-

[ 191 ]

gle commenced. Meanwhile, what Josephus called "the madness of desperate men" was throughout Jesus' ministry preparing for the fray.

What Jesus thought about these nationalistic patriots is important to the understanding of him, and we can perhaps get at that matter best by inquiring what they must have thought of him.

That some of them thought he might become their leader in armed resistance against Rome seems evident. This was their main need—a rousing personality who would precipitate the general unrest into definite insurrection. From Judas of Gamala and Theudas[7] to Bar Cochba, concerning whom even Rabbi Akiba said, "This is the Messianic King,"[8] the revolutionists repeatedly rallied around vigorous, militant chieftains. We need not depend alone on the Fourth Gospel's statement that the crowd "were about to come and take him by force to make him king,"[9] to support the supposition that rebellious patriots thought Jesus might be the long-sought leader of their revolt.

How else can the third temptation of Jesus be explained except in terms of this possibility? "Again, the devil took him to a very high mountain, and showed him all the kingdoms of the world and the glory of them; and he said to him, 'All these I will give you, if you will fall down and worship me.'"[10] However the story of this temptation came into our records, the least probable explanation is that it was made up by the later church. The Christ in whom that church believed, by his atoning death and victorious resurrection, had become mankind's Savior. What motive could possibly have led his followers then to imagine him as tempted to worship the devil—that is, to use satanic means—to win the kingdoms of the world? In

[ 192 ]

Jesus' own lifetime, however, temptation to use bloody insurrection for the kingdom's sake was the most crucial public problem of his people.

If, as seems probable, Jesus' inner struggle concerning the nature and method of his ministry was told by him to his disciples, he let them see that he had faced the possibility of becoming a militant, revolutionary leader. He might have decided on such a messiahship as Judas Maccabaeus chose, trying to fulfill the expectations of the violent insurrectionists, who were impatiently awaiting the call of some popular leader to revolt. The pressure was on him, and it must have grown as, during the early months of his ministry, the multitudes flocked about him. When the rumor ran among the crowds that perhaps this was he who should redeem Israel, the militant spirits there were thinking, not of an apocalyptic Son of Man from heaven, but of the rebel against Rome who would lead them to triumph in a messianic war.

This expectation apparently came to its fiery climax when Jesus, having entered Jerusalem amid shouting crowds, cleansed the temple—an overt act of sedition against both priestly authority and Roman rule. The iron was hot; would he not strike then? Luke retains a recollection of that mounting hope: as Jesus drew "near to Jerusalem . . . they supposed that the kingdom of God was to appear immediately."[11] Amid Jerusalem's confusion that final week, diverse motives with reference to Jesus swayed the city. The Pharisees were indignant at him, mainly for religious reasons; the Sadducean priesthood was angry at his disturbance of public order, fearful that the uproar he was causing would bring Rome's wrath upon them; but the militant insurrectionists must have been there too, eagerly watching him and hoping that the longed for revolution was about to start. In their desire for his bellig-

[ 193 ]

erent leadership they could easily have misunderstood his real spirit and meaning. Did not the disciples themselves have difficulty in understanding him?

It may even be that a Zealot—"Simon who was called the Zealot" is Luke's description of him[12]—was one of the disciples. Both the Greek word, however, which Luke uses and its Aramaic equivalent in Matthew's Gospel, "Cananaean,"[13] mean "hot," "fervid," and if Josephus is right in saying that this appellation's use to describe a party in Israel began later, it may signify in Simon's case simply "zealous."[14] The meaning of "Iscariot," attached to the betrayer's name, is also dubious. It may indicate that his home town was Kerioth in Judea, or it may come from "sicarii"—"dagger-men"—a group who, as Josephus tells us, from the days of Herod the Great had practiced assassination and worked for bloody revolt. Whether or not, however, Simon had been a Zealot and Judas a dagger-man—as Matthew had been a tax collector—the disciples certainly did not find it easy to understand Jesus' nonmilitant idea of messiahship.

James and John, "sons of thunder,"[15] wanted to call down fire from heaven on inhospitable Samaritans,[16] and conspired to get seats on the right and the left of the king in the day of his triumph.[17] Peter's revolt against Jesus' idea of a suffering and dying Messiah was so vehement that the temptation which Jesus had faced in the militant expectations of his people revived, and turning on Peter he cried: "Get behind me, Satan! For you are not on the side of God, but of men."[18] Even at the Last Supper his disciples offered him two swords for self-defense,[19] and in Gethsemane one of them, drawing a sword, cut off the ear of the high priest's slave.[20] If the disciples could so misunderstand their Master's spirit and intent, the belligerent nationalists could utterly miss it. "I came to cast fire upon the earth; and would that it were already kindled!"[21]—if such a saying of Jesus were known to the insurrectionists, what they would have made of it is clear.

When our Gospels were written, the Zealots were defeated and dead. Their last desperate stand on the bleak heights of Masada was over and, unlike the Pharisees, they were no longer a problem to the Christian church of the next generation. The evidence concerning them in our records, therefore, is incidental, and its meaning must be gleaned by inference. Nevertheless, that they were a dominant factor in the situation which Jesus faced is undoubted history. Windisch is justified in saying, "The most important characteristic of his messiahship, speaking negatively, is to be found in his refusal to wage the messianic war."[22]

That the militant party turned against him at last with the bitterness of disappointed hopes seems clear. That last week in Jerusalem Jesus failed them. He cleansed the temple but, so Mark reports, he said it was because the temple was meant to be "a house of prayer for all the nations."[23] He described the payment of Roman taxes as giving to Caesar what was Caesar's. When he was arrested, he surrendered with no display of messianic power. There was no violent insurrection in him. One wonders whether some disillusioned revolutionists did not swell the cry in Pilate's court for the release of Barrabbas instead of Jesus. Barabbas was one of "the rebels in prison, who had committed murder in the insurrection."[24] The Greek word used of him in the Gospels corresponds with the word Josephus repeatedly uses of the Zealots. Barabbas was a violent rebel and if, as Mark reports, the high priests, who least of all desired revolt, wished his release, how much more would the Zealots in the crowd have cried for his liberation, and for the execution of Jesus who had let them down!

That Jesus foresaw the peril of Jewish insurrection and a Roman war and that the prospect filled him with foreboding seems evident. Luke puts it explicitly:

And when he drew near and saw the city he wept over it, saying, "Would that even today you knew the things that make for peace! But now they are hid from your eyes. For the days shall come upon you, when your enemies will cast up a bank about you and surround you, and hem you in on every side, and dash you to the ground, you and your children within you, and they will not leave one stone upon another in you; because you did not know the time of your visitation."[25]

Skeptical critics may say that since the doom here foretold already had fallen on Jerusalem when Luke's Gospel was written, such a passage probably came from the early church's conviction that Jesus must have foreseen it. Such skepticism, however, faces too much contrary evidence to make it easily credible. According to Mark, Jesus said of Jerusalem's "wonderful buildings," "There will not be left here one stone upon another, that will not be thrown down,"[26] and in the early written source which scholars call "Q," and which both Matthew and Luke used, Jesus' words were recorded: "O Jerusalem, Jerusalem, killing the prophets and stoning those who are sent to you! How often would I have gathered your children together as a hen gathers her brood under her wings, and you would not! Behold, your house is forsaken and desolate."[27]

This ominous outlook of Jesus on his nation's future is expressed too frequently to be dubious. To be sure, he also foretold the end of the age, the Son of Man's coming and the last judgment, and his words about Jerusalem's destruction in a Roman war are, in our records, so confused with his words about the final arrival of the Son of Man that scholars argue endlessly about disentangling them. Nevertheless, two future events—Jerusalem's fall in war and the Son of Man's coming —are plainly indicated in the Gospels.

The church of the evangelists' time was interested not so much in the fall of Jerusalem as in the hope of the coming Messiah, and the natural result of this would be the modification of his words about Zion's military fate to fit the last judgment. This seems clearly to have happened in Mark's so-called "Little Apocalypse."[28] That this was a written document which Mark incorporated in his Gospel is suggested by the phrase, "let the reader understand."[29] That it represents a collection of predictions attributed to Jesus, modified to suit known history when the Gospel was written—note the warning not to expect the Messiah's coming too soon—is probable. It starts with the disciples' question as to when the temple will be destroyed and it includes a description of the Son of Man's coming at the end of the age. In the midst of it, however, is a passage which, fitting the temple's destruction, does not fit the catastrophic arrival of the messianic age at all.

But when you see the desolating sacrilege set up where it ought not to be (let the reader understand), then let those who are in Judea flee to the mountains; let him who is on the housetop not go down, nor enter his house, to take anything away; and let him who is in the field not turn back to take his mantle. And alas for those who are with child and for those who give suck in those days! Pray that it may not happen in winter. For in those days there will be such tribulation as has not been from the beginning of the creation which God created until now, and never will be.[30]

This passage plainly concerns Jerusalem's downfall; and the details of danger and possible escape of which Jesus speaks, while vividly applicable to the military sacking of the city, are utterly inapplicable to the Messiah's coming. Had the apocalyptic arrival of the heavenly Son of Man been in Jesus' mind, what possible difference could it make whether or not that world-transforming event came in the winter, or how could Judeans escape it, as Jesus counseled, by fleeing to the mountains, or what relevance has his advice to escape without stopping even to pick up a garment? This passage is most reasonably explained as being a saying of Jesus about the fateful end of the coming Jewish-Roman war—a saying reset by the Gospel writers in the pattern of the later church's expectation of the woes attendant on the coming of the Son of Man from heaven.

Luke makes this reference unmistakable. Instead of the vaguer phrase "desolating sacrilege," he says, "But when you see Jerusalem surrounded by armies, then know that its desolation has come near,"[31] and, writing with the knowledge of the prediction's fulfillment, he concludes, "They will fall by the edge of the sword, and be led captive among all nations; and Jerusalem will be trodden down by the Gentiles, until the times of the Gentiles are fulfilled."[32]

Such definite forebodings concerning the threatened Jewish-Roman war light up the possible meaning of other premonitions of national doom in Jesus' thought. When he was told "of the Galileans whose blood Pilate had mingled with their sacrifices," and of the "eighteen upon whom the tower in Siloam fell," he answered, "Unless you repent you will all likewise perish."[33] One wonders whether the implication is not that they will perish in similar fashion at the hands of the Romans and under the falling towers of their city. He foresaw a storm and then "scorching heat" coming on his nation, and he rebuked the crowd who could predict the weather but who were too blind to "interpret the present time."[34] He told the nation's rulers that they were like faithless tenants of a vine-

[ 198 ]

yard who, having refused the owner his due and having slain his servants and his son, would themselves be destroyed and the vineyard given to others.[35] He said that upon that generation would fall the accumulated punishment for "all the righteous blood shed on earth, from the blood of innocent Abel to the blood of Zechariah the son of Barachiah, whom you murdered between the sanctuary and the altar."[36] Such was his habitual mood until, carrying his cross to Calvary, he said to the lamenting women:

Daughters of Jerusalem, do not weep for me, but weep for yourselves and for your children. For behold, the days are coming when they will say, "Blessed are the barren, and the wombs that never bore, and the breasts that never gave suck!" Then they will begin to say to the mountains, "Fall on us"; and to the hills "Cover us." For if they do this when the wood is green, what will happen when it is dry?[37]

We cannot step inside the Master's mind and see all the factors that contributed to this sense of impending national doom, but is it not reasonable to conjecture, in the light of Jesus' ethic, that he saw in his people's rejection of him, their rejection of their own national salvation? The alternative which they were choosing was the messianic war. It was brewing fearfully throughout his lifetime. When he spoke of inevitable "wars and rumors of wars,"[38] he was dealing with realistic forebodings. Sayings such as, "All who take the sword will perish by the sword,"[39] were relevant to his nation's most crucial public problem.

How the militant revolutionists must have felt toward one who thus saw the nation's future in terms of doom is evident. He was a defeatist, dashing their dearest hopes with his chill predictions. His religious faith itself was suspect, since he could so picture God surrendering his people to ruin, when they rose bravely up to defend his holy cause. What Jesus said that last week about the payment of taxes to Caesar was to the Zealots rank heresy, as well as rank lack of patriotism. Far from being, as it is often interpreted, a clever piece of repartee, evading the question asked him—"Is it lawful to pay taxes to Caesar, or not? Should we pay them, or should we not?"[40]—his answer met squarely the contention of the Zealots. They held that God alone was their rightful king; that there could not be two kings, God and Caesar; that a choice must be made, and that to pay taxes to Caesar was infidelity to God. When Jesus, therefore, said that they could pay Caesar's coin to Caesar and still give God his due, he was attacking a central article of their faith.

Worst of all, from the viewpoint of the militant patriots, was Jesus' prediction of the temple's destruction. That was heresy, indeed, too rank for priests and Pharisees, as well as for insurrectionists. They did not forget such blasphemy and at the hearing before the high priest this charge of doom pronounced against the temple was flung at him.[41] Garbled their quotations might be, but Jesus' intent was understood. He foresaw the messianic war ending in the temple's ruin.

Beyond such passages, still retained in our Gospels, despite the fact that living interest in the Jewish politics of Jesus' day had vanished from the churches out of which the Gospels came, it is reasonable to suppose that other words of Jesus, concerning the public problems of his time, must have been forgotten. One floating sentence, attached by Matthew to one context and by Luke to another, suggests what may have happened. "From the days of John the Baptist until now the kingdom of heaven has suffered violence, and men of violence take it by force"[42]—so Matthew quotes Jesus; and Luke renders it, "The law and the prophets were until John; since then the good news of the kingdom of God is preached, and every one enters it violently."[43] As the saying stands, little can be made of it, unless one sees it as an attack on violent men who sought to seize the kingdom by force as the revolutionaries did—an attack which, lacking relevance as the situation which called it out passed into bygone history, lost its context and became confused.

In any case the complete alienation between Jesus and the insurrectionists is plain, and what they must have thought of him is evident: not patriotic enough, not nationalistic enough, not belligerent enough!

The difference between Jesus and the insurrectionists, however, sprang from deeper sources than contemporary politics. His ethic was essentially incompatible with the spirit and strategy of the Zealots. That the teaching in the Sermon on the Mount concerning love of enemies was primarily directed against the legalism of the Pharisees we have seen.[44] As with prayer, fasting, philanthropic giving and a chaste life, so with reference to the treatment of foes, Jesus insisted on a righteousness exceeding that of the scribes and Pharisees. When, however, Jesus applied this principle of superlegalistic goodness to the treatment of enemies, he moved into a realm where not only the Pharisees but the militant revolutionists also, with their threatened war against Rome, were involved. That Jesus had them in mind seems evident.

When he said, "If any one forces you to go one mile, go with him two miles,"[45] he was almost certainly referring to the right of Roman officers to coerce labor. When he said, "Blessed are the peacemakers,"[46] how could he have been speaking in a vacuum with no reference to the most critical

[ 201 ]

public problem of his time? The cry of Jesus at the end, "Would that even today you knew the things that make for peace!"[47] was in his heart at the beginning. His love-ethic was shaped not only by his ideas of God, not only by his belief in undiscourageable goodwill in personal relationships, but also by his resolute opposition to the threatened messianic war.

Jesus was far from being alone in such opposition. For quite prudential reasons the Sadducean party had decided to collaborate with Rome; the Essenes were thoroughgoing pacifists, refusing even to manufacture munitions of war; and the greater portion of the Pharisees were counseling peace until God acted and the Messiah came. Notable in the leadership of the peace party was Rabbi Johanan ben Zakkai. Born some years before Jesus, he survived by a decade the fall of Jerusalem in A.D. 70. "Never did he waver," writes a Jewish scholar, "even for a moment, in his opposition to the rebellion, which he felt was destined to bring destruction on the people, the sanctuary, and the land. The romantic nationalism which was moving men to unheard-of deeds of heroism and self-sacrifice appeared to him altogether evil and irrational."[48] He too foresaw that Rome would conquer Judea, and of the temple, if war came, he said, "I know of thee that thou shalt be destroyed."[49] Even when Vespasian began the siege of Jerusalem in the winter of A.D. 68, he counseled submission. One wonders if Jesus and Johanan ben Zakkai ever met. They would have had much in common. Johanan even said, "Benevolence on the part of a nation has the atoning power of a sin-offering."[50]

Both the peace party and the war party in Israel had behind them powerful factors in the tradition of their people. On one side was the universalism of the Isaiah of the Exile, announcing Israel's mission to be "a light to the Gentiles" and God's "salvation unto the end of the earth."[51] Out of such universalism, filled with prophetic hope of a day when "nation shall not lift up sword against nation, neither shall they learn war any more,"[52] came reliance on nonviolence as the will of God. The Second Book of Enoch, written sometime between 30 B.C. and A.D. 70, says:

Endure for the sake of the Lord every wound, every injury, every evil word and attack. If ill-requitals befall you, return them not either to neighbor or enemy, because the Lord will return them for you and be your avenger on the day of the great judgment, that there be no avenging here among men.[53]

Jewish tradition, however, contained also a heritage of violence utterly contrary to such peaceful policies. The imprecatory psalms bear witness to it; the inevitable hatreds engendered against cruel conquerors strengthened it; and by the time books such as The Assumption of Moses (A.D. 7–29) and Second Esdras (A.D. 75–100) were written, it is plain what the Zealots had made of it. Says the former:

For the Most High will arise, the Eternal God alone, and he will appear to punish the Gentiles, and he will destroy all their idols. Then thou, O Israel, shalt be happy and thou shalt mount upon the neck and wings of the Eagle [i.e., the Roman eagle,] and they shall be ended and God will exalt thee. . . . And thou shalt look from on high and see thine enemies in Gehenna and thou shalt recognize them and rejoice. And thou shalt give thanks and confess thy Creator.[54]

Says the latter:

All this have I spoken before thee, O Lord, because thou hast said that for our sakes thou madest this world. As for the other nations, which also came from Adam, thou hast said that they are nothing, and are like unto spittle—and thou hast likened the abundance of them unto a drop that falleth from a vessel. And now, O Lord, these nations which are reputed as nothing, be lords over us, and devour us. But now thy people, whom thou hast called thy first-born, are given unto their hands. If the world now be made for our sakes, why do we not possess for an inheritance our world? How long shall it endure?[55]

As to which of these two traditions claimed Jesus' allegiance there can be no doubt. One of the clearest distinctions in his teaching is that drawn between enduring pain and death, and causing them. The first he resolutely undertook; the second he just as resolutely refused. That there was a hard-headed, realistic motive in this refusal, so far as the threatened Jewish-Roman war was concerned, is explicit in the Gospels. His love-ethic, applied to his nation's enemies, was not altogether abstract, theologically engendered, and aloof from actual conditions. The evidence is clear that, like the peace party in general, he foresaw the tragic doom which war would bring upon his people. There was, however, in Jesus' thinking, along with this horizontal concern with present problems, a vertical conviction which carried his love-ethic up into the nature of God himself. Successful or unsuccessful, belligerent violence was essentially wrong, and all its attendant motives of vindictiveness and hatred were of the devil. As one reads the Sermon on the Mount, this seems unmistakable.

That the Gospels should have been searched to discover loopholes of escape from so difficult an ethic was inevitable. No text, for example, has been more wildly used than Jesus' saying, "Do not think that I have come to bring peace on earth; I have not come to bring peace, but a sword." The idea that Jesus meant "sword" literally, is at once shut out by the context: "For I have come to set a man against his father, and a daughter against her mother, and a daughter-in-law against her mother-in-law; and a man's foes will be those of his own household."[56] Jesus was speaking not of war or of violence in any form but of the conflict caused in families when allegiance to him confronted hostility against him. This tragedy of divided households was beginning in Jesus' lifetime, and his comment on it was the sort of saying the later church would wish retained in the record, so applicable was it to what Christians faced everywhere in the pagan world. Indeed the metaphorical meaning of "sword" in this passage is vouched for by Luke, who drops the metaphor: "Do you think that I have come to give peace on earth? No, I tell you, but rather division."[57]

A more difficult passage is Luke's description of an incident at the last supper:

And he said to them, "When I sent you out with no purse or bag or sandals, did you lack anything?" They said, "Nothing." He said to them, "But now, let him who has a purse take it, and likewise a bag. And let him who has no sword sell his mantle and buy one. For I tell you that this scripture must be fulfilled in me, 'And he was reckoned with transgressors'; for what is written about me has its fulfillment." And they said, "Look, Lord, here are two swords." And he said to them, "It is enough".[58]

Jesus' general meaning is obvious: the days of happy ministry in his fellowship are over; his death and the disciples' persecution are at hand; no longer can they count on popular appreciation and the easy supply of their needs; they face hostility and want. He phrased this message with characteristic picturesqueness. They were going now to need purses, wallets, swords. The question is whether he meant "swords" literally. The disciples, thinking that he did, said: "Here are two

[ 205 ]

swords"; to which Jesus retorted, as Moffatt translates it, "Enough! Enough!" or, as Goodspeed renders it, "Enough of this!" That is to say, this passage illustrates what the Gospels as a whole make clear, that, to his ministry's very end, the disciples, believing him to be the Messiah, could not get out of their heads the militant idea of the messiahship's meaning, and once more Jesus brushed it aside.

The alternative to this interpretation is to suppose that Jesus literally counseled his disciples to buy swords and fight. But, in Luke's Gospel a few verses after this incident, when one of the disciples used his sword on the slave of the high priest, Jesus rebuked him, saying, "No more of this!"[59] and Matthew, narrating the same act of violence, records that Jesus said, "Put your sword back into its place; for all who take the sword will perish by the sword."[60] The supposition that Jesus' exclamation, "It is enough!" meant that two swords were sufficient to start insurrection is fantastic in itself, as well as being a complete denial of the whole tenor of his teaching. Far from being, therefore, an admonition to militancy, this passage illustrates the very opposite—the dullness of the disciples, namely, who under the pressure of current messianic hopes could not grasp Jesus' idea of his mission. So, at any rate, the later church understood the situation: "Jesus answered, 'My kingship is not of this world; if my kingship were of this world, my servants would fight, that I might not be handed over to the Jews; but my kingship is not from the world!' "[61]

If those closest to Jesus thus misinterpreted him, the militant nationalists even more easily could have done so. Jesus could be fierce sometimes as well as gentle. His similes and parables were sometimes violent. A king in one parable cried, "As for these enemies of mine, who did not want me to reign over them, bring them here and slay them before me";[62] and another, en-

raged, sent his troops and burned a city.[63] Jesus drew a lesson
for his followers from a king who, going to war, sat down first
and counted the cost,[64] and he pointed up a truth in terms of a
robber plundering a strong man's house after having bound
the strong man.[65] Jesus would have been easier for his contemporaries to understand, had he been, as in modern times he
has commonly been pictured, a sentimentalist. He was anything but that. His statements about the severity of God's punishments were terrific and, in human relationships, he sometimes found in violent and crooked men admirable qualities
that no merely "idyllic and sweet nature," as Renan described
Jesus, would have found there. He drew a lesson from an unscrupulous steward, who stole his employer's money to make
friends with, and he commented: "The sons of this world are
wiser in their own generation than the sons of light."[66] He
drew another lesson from a domineering slaveowner who
worked his servants to the limit, and then did not thank them.[67]
He drew lessons from shrewd investors of capital.[68] Obviously
this does not mean that he approved financial dishonesty in the
steward, ungrateful tyranny in the slaveowner, or the inequi-
ties of economic greed; and if from binding a strong man and
plundering his house, he could draw a lesson without approving burglary, it is clear that he could picture a wise king count-
ing the cost of a military campaign, without approving war.

Nevertheless, Jesus was the kind of character that militant
nationalists might easily have been drawn to. He had soldierly
qualities in him. He met a Roman centurion once and each
recognized kinship with the other. Jesus acclaimed the centurion's faith, and the centurion, feeling Jesus' "authority,"
said that he too was a man "with soldiers under me; and I say
to one, 'Go,' and he goes, and to another, 'Come,' and he
comes, and to my slave, 'Do this,' and he does it."[69] No wonder

the insurrectionists hoped that Jesus might be the leader of their revolt!

As for us moderns, Mahatma Gandhi should help us to understand Jesus. Gandhi's powerful leadership swayed millions of followers and upon his will time and again hung the success or failure of Great Britain's imperial policies. He had courage and daring, a fearlessness of danger and death, that any soldier might envy. Yet with indefatigable persistence he held to his nonviolent course, refusing militant revolt, and depending solely on the might and pressure of spiritual forces. Of all the paradoxical combinations of opposing qualities in Jesus' character—self-fulfillment and self-denial, explosive enthusiam and serenity, fierce indignation and compassionate gentleness, consciousness of divine mission and profound humility—none is more amazing than this conjunction of qualities that make a great soldier with those that make a great pacifist.

One favorite method of evading the full force and meaning of Jesus' love-ethic is to say that he meant it to apply not to national policy but only to personal relationships. All the available evidence, however, contradicts that. Indeed, in the realm of personal relationships the problem concerning Jesus' probable application of his love-ethic becomes most difficult. What if, in his presence, one of the little children whom he took in his arms and blessed were viciously attacked? Would he have stood passively by, offering no forceful resistance? The supposition that by restricting the application of Jesus' ethic to personal relationships one makes it easier to practice is insupportable. As for the evidence in the Gospels, one thing is certain: he did apply his ethic to national policy. He was out and out against the Zealots and all their ways. He was their "lost leader," and in the end they hated him.

The issue turned out to be one of the strangest paradoxes in history: Jesus who so stood out against insurrection was crucified as an insurrectionist. Many motives entered into the hostility which beset him that last week in Jerusalem. Early in his ministry, so Mark tells us, when crowds thronged about him in Galilee, scribes came from Jerusalem to investigate, and their fear and dislike were summed up in the worst thing they could think of saying: "He is possessed by Beelzebub."[70] From that day to the end the hostility of the rulers in the capital accumulated against Jesus, but his liquidation could not be finally achieved on religious grounds. That the Jews had been completely deprived of the right to impose the death penalty is improbable, but apparently there were limitations on that right under Roman rule.[71] At any rate, Jesus' Jewish enemies did not wish to assume the responsibility of executing him, and the Gospels make plain the reason. He was too popular. They "feared the people." Let the Romans bear the burden of resentment against his liquidation! If the Romans would execute him as a disturber of the peace, that would gain the desired end at minimum cost.

Then Jesus entered Jerusalem amid clamoring crowds and cleansed the temple. In explaining the reason for this act, Christian writers have commonly pictured the situation in the temple courts as outrageous, with the money-changers and the merchants who sold sacrificial birds and beasts fleecing pious pilgrims—a monstrous system of graft whose profits enriched the priests. The fact is, however, that much can be said in defense of the general arrangements which had been set up. The coinage of that day was notoriously unregulated; the real value of the money which pilgrims carried varied with the lands they came from; there was good reason why the authorities in

Jerusalem had ruled that before it could be used for paying the tax or making purchases in the temple, all money must be exchanged by experts into the Tyrian currency which was comparatively reliable.[72] As for birds and beasts for sacrifice, it was a public convenience to have the market organized and made easily available within the temple compound.

Nevertheless, the situation was one which readily got out of hand. The opportunity for crooked dealing was too obvious. The rate of exchange could easily be rigged in the interest of profits; and since all birds and beasts for sacrifice had to be passed by an official censor it was simple to force buyers to purchase from official merchants, and then simple for them to demand a price above the general market. Soon after the time of Jesus, Rabbi Shimeon ben Gamaliel protested vigorously against excessive charges for sacrificial birds.[73] That this factor was, in part, a cause of Jesus' act is evident. All three synoptic Gospels quote his charge that the temple courts had been made "a den of robbers."[74] His shame at the irreverent lengths to which the commercialism of the temple precincts had gone is evident too, so that "he would not allow any one to carry anything through the temple."[75]

As for the act itself, by which Jesus singlehanded stopped the traffic, the bias of interpreters has commonly made of it whatever prejudice desired, from aggressive violence comparable with war to an exhibition of spiritual power that made physical force needless. The facts, however, do not seem difficult to come at. The "whip of cords," of which so much is frequently made, is unknown to Mark, Matthew and Luke, appearing only in John's Gospel, and there so spoken of that its use in driving out "the sheep and oxen" is a natural interpretation.[76] That Jesus used force, however, is evident in all the Gospels. "He overturned the tables of the money-changers and the seats of those who sold pigeons," say Mark and Matthew; and Luke says that "he began to drive out those who sold."[77] The decisive factor, however, surely lay in Jesus' popular support. The crowd was with him. They too resented the graft of which they were the victims, so that when the chief priests and the scribes, hearing of Jesus' act, "sought a way to destroy him; . . . they feared him, because all the multitude was astonished at his teaching," or as Luke puts it, "all the people hung upon his words."[78] Without this popular backing what Jesus did, overturning the tables and driving out the hucksters and the beasts, would have proved a futile gesture, immediately and forcefully suppressed.

The cleansing of the temple gave "the chief priests and the scribes and the elders" the chance for which they had waited. Here was an overt act of insubordination. Now the charge against Jesus could be shifted from religious heresy to political subversion. He was stirring up the people.[79] He was a peril to public order, regarded by others and, it might be, regarding himself as the Messiah. If he went unstopped, he would set himself up as "king of the Jews." At first the conspirators against him intended to postpone the final stroke until after Passover. "And the chief priests and the scribes were seeking how to arrest him by stealth, and kill him; for they said, 'Not during the feast, lest there be a tumult of the people.'"[80] As their plans gathered momentum, however, they changed their minds, and events moved swiftly—the bribery of Judas, the secret arrest of Jesus in the garden, when the crowd was absent, the extralegal informal hearing in the high priest's house where Jesus acknowledged his messiahship, and then the trial before the Roman Procurator, with concocted accusations hurled at him—"We found this man perverting our nation, and forbidding us to give tribute to Caesar, and saying that he himself is Christ a king"[81]—while the hirelings and hangers-on, whom the priests had gathered, cried, as they had been told to cry, "Crucify him!" and, if John's Gospel be correct, even shouted, "We have no king but Caesar."[82]

That Jesus was executed as a political offender is certain. The Gospels so record the matter although the Christian churches, when the Gospels were written, would naturally have wished to suppress the fact. Few things were more practically important to the churches of the Empire during the latter half of the first century than to make clear to the authorities the political harmlessness of Christianity. The influence of this motive is obvious in the New Testament.[83] Luke, for example, as any reader of the Book of Acts can see, is strongly moved by it, even to the point of omitting all mention of Paul's execution at Rome. As for Jesus' trial before the Roman Procurator, Mark's picture of Pilate's desire to release him—"Why, what evil has he done?"[84]—is expanded by Luke, as thrice the Procurator, appealing against Jesus' accusers, seeks his liberation, and in an effort to escape responsibility even sends him to Herod. Matthew even records that Pilate took water and washed his hands before the crowd, saying, "I am innocent of this man's blood; see to it yourselves."[85]

This picture of Pilate, devoted to justice, conscientiously sensitive, and reluctant to order an execution is so widely at variance from all the evidence we have about his character[86] that scholars naturally question it. How, for example, could Mark have so intimately known Pilate's mind, that he could say, "He perceived that it was out of envy that the chief priests had delivered him up"?[87] And did Luke have firsthand witnesses to substantiate the story, which he alone relates, of Herod's exoneration of Jesus, and of Pilate's words: "You brought me this man as one who was perverting the people;

and after examining him before you, behold, I did not find this man guilty of any of your charges against him; neither did Herod, for he sent him back to us. Behold, nothing deserving death has been done by him; I will therefore chastize him and release him"?[88]

Whatever Pilate's attitude may have been, the urgent desire of the Gospel writers to represent him as finding no evil in Jesus and as desiring to release him as harmless to the state, is obvious. All the more the fact stands clearly out that, wishing as they did to make the charge of sedition seem false even in the Procurator's eyes, the Gospel writers could not and did not obscure the central fact: Jesus finally was executed by the Romans as a political criminal, with the offensive charge nailed to his very cross, "The King of the Jews."

So the great pacifist was crucified as a criminal insurrectionist. Some who passed by, while he was on the cross, "derided him, wagging their heads," we read, and "so also the chief priests mocked him."[89] One wonders if any "daggermen" were also there, and if they felt the irony of crucifying as a dangerous revolutionist one who so stoutly had withstood the war they wanted, and had so disappointed their hopes of his militant leadership. Were they there, they too must have "derided him, wagging their heads."

## CHAPTER IX

# As Jews With a World-wide Outlook Saw Him

A COMMON supposition is that Jesus' personal ministry was carried on within an exclusively Palestinian Jewish setting, and that only after the crucifixion did his movement come into contact with the larger currents of the world's thought and life.

Palestine itself, however, was far from being an isolated Jewish province. From the days of the Syrian Greeks in the third century B.C., the Hellenistic world had both surrounded and penetrated Palestine—so much so that the Maccabean revolt in particular and the Pharisaic party in general are to be explained as measures of resistance against the Hellenization of the Jewish people. In Jesus' day Palestine was set in a matrix of Graeco-Roman cities. Syria to the north; the coast cities along the Mediterranean such as Joppa, Caesarea, Tyre and Sidon; Transjordania, as the ruins of temples and theatres in such towns as Jerash and Amman still show, were all predominantly influenced by Hellenistic culture.

Moreover, within Palestine itself some areas apparently were so Gentile in population as to be out-of-bounds for stricter Jews. When Jesus, sending his disciples on their first mission, said, "Go nowhere among the Gentiles, and enter no town of the Samaritans,"[1] the implication seems plain that there were recognized Gentile districts in Palestine—Tiberias and Taricheae, for example, cities on the Sea of Galilee, Scythopolis south of the Sea, and Sepphoris just north of Nazareth.

Galilee, thus surrounded by and infiltrated with Hellenistic influence, was certainly in some degree bilingual. Business could hardly have been carried on around the Sea of Galilee without the use of Greek. Some fifty years ago, in his *Historical Geography of the Holy Land*, George Adam Smith, perceiving that "Galilee was on the road to everywhere," confronted facts which since have been expanded, confirmed and emphasized: "The many roads which crossed Galilee from the Decapolis to the coast, the many inscriptions upon them, the constant trade between the fishermen and the Greek exporters of their fish, the very coins—everywhere thrust Greek upon the Jews of Galilee. The Aramaic dialect began now to be full of Greek words. It is impossible to believe that our Lord and His disciples did not know Greek."[2] Indeed, two of the disciples, Philip and Andrew, had Greek names; and to suppose that Matthew could have been a tax collector on the Sea of Galilee without understanding Greek seems incredible.

Moveover, Jerusalem too must have been bilingual. The most thorough study yet made of the use of Greek in ancient Palestine concludes: "The degree of a person's Hellenistic culture depended on his social standing. Probably the upper class knew Greek literature, the middle class was less conversant with it, while the knowledge of the lower class was limited to the vernacular only."[3] This seems to be confirmed by the fact that when Paul, under arrest in Jerusalem, addressed the crowd in front of the Roman barracks, they, thinking he might be an Egyptian, expected him to speak in Greek, and "when they heard that he addressed them in the Hebrew language, they were the more quiet."[4] Certainly the ruling elders in

[ 215 ]

Jerusalem needed Greek in dealing with Roman authorities. Of Rabban Gamaliel it was said, "Permission was given to the house of Rabban Gamaliel to teach their children Greek, owing to their relation with the [Roman] government." Rabbi Simeon, Gamaliel's son, even wrote, "There were a thousand pupils in my father's house; five hundred studied Torah and five hundred studied Greek Wisdom." And Simeon's son, Rabbi Juda Hanassi went further, saying, "Why speak Syriac in Palestine? Talk either Hebrew or Greek."[5]

This infiltration of Hellenistic influence into Palestinian Jewry was powerfully accentuated by the Jews of the dispersion. From Babylonia to Rome and beyond, Jews, either as forcibly displaced persons or as voluntary emigrants, had established themselves, especially in the great cities. In the time of Philo, Jesus' contemporary, Jews in Egypt were said to number a million, and Alexandria was so important a center of Jewish learning and influence that one Palestinian rabbi called it a "sister" of Jerusalem.[6] Doubtless many of these dispersed Jews fell away and were assimilated, but the tenacity with which the overwhelming number of them held to their faith and remained a distinct people is the real marvel. Nevertheless, they necessarily accommodated themselves to the Graeco-Roman world. In Egypt they so largely lost knowledge of Hebrew that the Scriptures were translated into Greek for use in the synagogues. Philo's words give a contemporary picture of the situation in Jesus' day: "No one country can contain the whole Jewish nation, by reason of its populousness; on which account they frequent all the most prosperous and fertile countries of Europe and Asia, whether islands or continents, looking indeed upon the holy city as their *metropolis* in which is erected the sacred temple of the Most High God, but accounting those regions which have been occupied by their fathers and grandfathers and great-grandfathers and still more remote ancestors, in which they have been born and brought up, as their country."[7]

That these Jews of the diaspora, though living as they often did in segregated communities, were profoundly affected by Graeco-Roman culture was inevitable. Not only in such matters as language, fashions and customs, recreations, tastes in literature and the drama, and methods in education, but in basic philosophical religious ideas, Hellenism invaded Judaism. Philo remained a loyal Jew, but the major presuppositions of his philosophy must be explained in the light of Greek thought. Though the statement is too condensed to be adequate, the fact is that Philo commonly thought as a Hellenistic philosopher and then deduced his Greek ideas by allegory from the Hebrew Scriptures.

These Hellenistic Jews of the diaspora have generally been set in sharp contrast with the strict, old-fashioned Jews of Palestine, but this distinction, while justified, can easily be exaggerated. From all over the Roman world multitudes of Jews came on pilgrimage to their holy city. Alike for financial reasons, since these pilgrims were one of the main supports of the city and the temple, and for religious motives—the maintenance of loyal faith and practice among the dispersed Jews—this and every other means of close relationship between Palestinian Jewry and the diaspora were cultivated. Hellenistic Judaism was no stranger in Palestine; Jesus must have encountered it. Early in the history of the first church in Jerusalem, "The Hellenists murmured against the Hebrews because their widows were neglected in the daily distribution."[8] These Hellenists were Jews from the Gentile world, or possibly Jewish proselytes, now Christianized, who were at home in Jerusalem, and who certainly had not all come there in the few months since Jesus died. There was, indeed, at least one Greek-speaking synagogue in the holy city—"The synagogue of the Freedman (as it was called), and of the Cyrenians, and of the Alexandrians, and of those from Cilicia and Asia."[9] The milieu in which Jesus worked was far more cosmopolitan than has generally been supposed.

Even in its central citadel Judaism had never been impervious to foreign influence. The orthodox Jewish angelology and demonology of Jesus' time had come mainly from Persia, and, as for the Essenes, "Pythagorism, Orphism, Chaldean astral religion, Parsiism and, apparently, even Buddhism all contributed ingredients much transformed on their way to the Jordan Valley."[10] The idea of a capsuled Palestinian Judaism unaffected by the world's life and thought is a myth. Some of the most important and most popular Jewish writings in the first century were from the diaspora and were deeply impregnated with Greek thought. As for Jesus himself, Dr. Klausner concludes that the reason why he "tended to set aside the ceremonial laws," was "because he had become influenced by Hellenistic Judaism through the medium of the Palestinian apocalypses."[11]

The passage in John's Gospel where "some Greeks," pilgrims at the temple festival, come to Philip, saying, "Sir, we wish to see Jesus,"[12] has been usually interpreted as representing a later situation—the Gentile world becoming the object of Christianity's mission—read back into the days of Jesus. Such may well have been the motive of this passage in John's Gospel, but in the story itself there is nothing inconsistent with the known situation in Palestine.

Jesus, while facing the narrower type of traditional Palestinian Judaism, faced, as well, the wider outlook of Hellenistic Judaism, and to suppose, as some critics hold, that words such as, "The field is the world," could not have been his, seems unwarranted. Putting ourselves into the place of these Jews at home in the wider world outside Palestine, we may well ask what they saw in him.

Jesus' views, in some important regards, were close of kin with the more liberal outlooks of Hellenistic Judaism. The attitude of the dispersed Jews toward the Gentile world had not been merely enmity, accommodation or self-defense. Active proselytism had become a major concern of faithful Jews. The ethical monotheism of the synagogue attracted many thoughtful Gentile minds, and the evidence makes clear the eagerness with which the Judaism of the diaspora sought converts and the success with which they were won.

This endeavor to present Judaism persuasively to Gentiles in the Graeco-Roman world led necessarily to a rethinking of Jewish requirements. What was essential Judaism? Were ethical monotheism and the moral law enough? How far were the ceremonial demands of the old tradition, such as circumcision and the observance of Kosher rules, necessary? The answers to such questions were not unanimous. To some Jews Gentiles were enemies of God and of his people, doomed to extermination in this world and without hope in the next; to others they were children of the one universal God, and to teach them the true religion and win them to its acceptance was Israel's duty and glory. In this second group, with its evangelistic zeal, there was a natural tendency to stress the major rather than the minor differences between Judaism and paganism, emphasizing Jewish monotheism and its moral law, and wherever possible simplifying its ritualistic and legalistic demands. This tendency can be exaggerated. Philo makes it clear, for example, that by "proselyte," he means one who has made a clean break with all non-Jewish religious affiliations, has accepted fully the Jewish people as his own, and is prepared to respect its customs and to observe its basic laws. Nevertheless proselytism naturally stressed the weightier as over against the lesser matters of the law.

When Paul, after spirited debate with the stricter sort, won from the first church in Jerusalem the reduction of ceremonial requirements to abstention "from what has been sacrificed to idols and from blood and from what is strangled and from unchastity,"[13] and when as a Christian evangelist he went on his mission requiring "no greater burden than these necessary things," it has been commonly supposed that this sort of compromise was new in Judaism. Such accommodation, however, was not unfamiliar to liberal Hellenized Jews. How far such liberalism went among Jewish propagandists, facing the crucial issue of monotheism against polytheism, is evidenced even in Palestinian rabbis, saying that to reject idolatry is to acknowledge the whole Jewish law.[14]

Such liberality explains the wide divergence of opinion among Palestinian Pharisees with regard to the growing number of Gentile proselytes and near-proselytes of many sorts. In Jesus' time Rabbi Shammai's school would have no commerce with any so-called convert who was not prepared to acknowledge and obey the whole traditional law of Israel. Rabbi Hillel's school, however, was more tolerant, following their master's motto: "Be one of the disciples of Aaron, a lover of peace, following after peace, loving all mankind, and drawing them to the law."[15] This difference of attitude runs on into the Talmudic period. There, on one side, was pride in the success of Jewish propaganda among the Gentiles and in great figures such as Rabbi Akiba and Rabbi Meir, who were said to be of proselyte ancestry, and on the other side such bitter sayings as that of Rabbi Helbo that proselytes—presumably those won by liberal policies—were as troublesome to Israel as a poisonous eruption is to the body.[16]

Was it not this latter attitude which the Gospel writer had in mind when he represented Jesus as saying "Woe to you, scribes and Pharisees, hypocrites! for you traverse sea and land to make a single proselyte, and when he becomes a proselyte, you make him twice as much a child of hell as yourselves"?[17] This harsh accusation was relevant to those who, like the rabbis of Shammai's school, made acceptance of all the legalistic minutiae which Jesus discarded a *sine qua non* of any Gentile's conversion. Such Pharisees, as Jesus said, "shut the kingdom of heaven against men."

There was another kind of Pharisee, however, whose main concern was for the far-flung body of the Jewish people across the empire, and for the Gentiles who were being drawn into their fellowship. At no point is the distinction between Sadducees and Pharisees more clear than in this regard. The Sadducees were tied to the Jewish state and temple; if collaboration with Rome would help sustain even the semi-independence of the state, they were collaborationists; when war at last broke out and the state was threatened with destruction, they fought with the Zealots to preserve it; and when at last the state and temple fell, the Sadducees were finished and passed out of history. The concern of the Pharisees, however, was centered in the law, and wherever in the whole world the law was honored and obeyed they saw the hope of Israel. When, therefore, the state and temple fell, the Pharisees, far from being finished, began their greatest era of influence. In this regard, as in others, Jesus was on the Pharisee's side, his religion resting not upon transient Jewish nationalism and temple sacrifice, but upon the deep bases of ethical monotheism and the law. "The liberal party, which was strong among the Hellenistic Jews, and had influential support even in Palestine," writes G. H. Box, "was willing to divest Judaism of its accidental elements and to insist upon essentials—the profession of faith in one God, the observance of the Sabbath-rest, and the abjuration of idolatry in all its forms as well as its immoral accompaniments. In a word, all that it insisted upon was ethical monotheism."[18]

The possible relationship of Jesus with such Jews, whose attitude was so akin to his, is naturally suggested. At Pentecost, almost immediately after Jesus had gone, the audience which was reported to have heard the disciples preach in Jerusalem contained "Parthians and Medes and Elamites and residents of Mesopotamia, Judea and Cappadocia, Pontus and Asia, Phrygia and Pamphylia, Egypt and the parts of Libya belonging to Cyrene, and visitors from Rome, both Jews and proselytes, Cretans and Arabians."[19] Can it be that Jesus never met such varied folk from the ends of the known world who flocked to Jerusalem for the festivals, or that his thought never reached out to face their problems? The sharp break commonly posited between the exclusively Palestinian ministry of Jesus and the almost immediate Hellenization of the Christian movement after he had gone is difficult to imagine. Jesus could not have been so isolated from the major currents in his people's life and thought. The problem of Judaism's universality and of the terms on which it could be realized was one of the most urgent religious questions discussed in Palestine, and liberal Hellenistic Jews, hearing Jesus, must have recognized in his teaching an endeavor to state the core of their religion in universal terms.

Nevertheless, this point of view faces difficulties and Matthew, most Jewish of the Gospels, presents them in full force.

As the record stands, we confront an apparent contradiction: Jesus limited his mission to Jews only, and yet Jesus had a world vision, his aim to "make disciples of all nations,"[20] and in him Isaiah's prophecy was fulfilled, "in his name will the Gentiles hope."[21] Matthew alone quotes Jesus as saying to the twelve, "Go nowhere among the Gentiles, and enter no town of the Samaritans, but go rather to the lost sheep of the house of Israel."[22] Matthew alone records the saying, "I was sent only to the lost sheep of the house of Israel."[23] In Matthew only does Jesus say that "not an iota, not a dot, will pass from the law until all is accomplished."[24] Matthew's insistence on Jesus' Jewishness is unmistakable, but apparently with no sense of inconsistency Matthew also stresses his universalism.

Praising a Roman centurion, Jesus says, according to Matthew, "I tell you, many will come from east and west and sit at table with Abraham, Isaac, and Jacob in the kingdom of heaven."[25] Condemning the Jews as faithless tenants of God's vineyard, Jesus represents God as saying to them, "I tell you, the kingdom of God will be taken away from you and given to a nation producing the fruits of it."[26] Matthew quotes Jesus as saying to his disciples: "You are the light of the world";[27] "The field is the world"; [28] "This gospel of the kingdom will be preached throughout the whole world, as a testimony to all nations."[29]

That this conflict in Matthew's Gospel between the restricted Jewishness of Jesus and his universalism reflects the later conflict in the church between the Jewish legalists and men like Paul seems certain. That Matthew's record represents the historic fact in one regard—that Jesus first offered his gospel to the Jews, that he thought of his mission as the preparation of his own people for the world-wide kingdom's coming, and that only after their rejection of him did his movement

[ 223 ]

turn to the Gentiles—seems likewise certain. Behind these explanations, however, does not the record reflect a real conflict in the mind of Jesus himself? Grant him the most universal outlook conceivable, he still had to begin with the Jews. There only could he find rootage for his message. Moreover, he was himself deeply, sincerely, loyally a Jew, and through Judaism only did he see hope of God's grace coming to the world. He may well have said everything he is quoted as saying to his disciples concerning the limitation of their first preaching missions.

Nevertheless, to stress his early concentration on gaining a foothold among his immediate fellow countrymen in such a manner as to obscure his world-wide outlook is to lose the large perspective of his mission. To be sure, he conceived himself as sent to "the lost sheep of the house of Israel," but those "lost sheep" for the most part did not live in Palestine. They were scattered over the whole known world, speaking Greek, reading their Scriptures in Greek, in cities like Alexandria conducting their synagogue services in Greek, and by hundreds of thousands, as pilgrims to the holy festivals, they thronged through Palestine, had at least one synagogue of their own in Jerusalem itself, and through their writings profoundly influenced the thought of Israel. To suppose that Jesus did not have them in mind seems incredible.

Universalism was in the great tradition of the Jewish people. In books like Ruth and Jonah, in prophets from Amos saying, "Are ye not as the children of the Ethiopians unto me, O children of Israel? Have not I brought up Israel out of the land of Egypt, and the Philistines from Caphtor, and the Syrians from Kir?"[30] to the Isaiah of the Exile saying, "I will also give thee for a light to the Gentiles, that thou mayest be my salvation

[ 224 ]

unto the end of the earth,"[31] Hebrew thought at its noblest had long been world-wide in its outlook. To picture Jesus as unacquainted with this or as rejecting it is unwarranted. That the later church, when the Gospels were written, when Christians were increasingly Gentile by birth and nurture, may have played up Jesus' universalism, adding new expressions to it, such as the postresurrection commission with its trinitarian formula, only with difficulty imaginable on Jesus' lips,[32] may be taken for granted. That he himself had the world in his mind, however, and that liberal Jews with a world-wide outlook found in him a kindred spirit and even during his personal ministry were attracted to his movement is the most natural explanation of the facts. The rise of Christianity from the very beginning must be explained not by reactionary Jews who rejected Jesus but by the more liberal Jews who accepted him.

This need not and should not be interpreted to mean that Jesus foresaw and commanded the early church's world-wide mission to the Gentiles. To ascribe the postresurrection words of Christ, "Go therefore and make disciples of all nations," to the historic Jesus runs counter to the attitude of Jesus himself as plainly set forth in the Gospels. To his disciples, starting on a preaching mission to their fellow countrymen, Jesus said: "You will not have gone through all the towns of Israel, before the Son of man comes."[33] Some think that this truly represents Jesus' very foreshortened view of the future at the beginning, and that he gradually changed his mind, saying later, "There are some standing here who will not taste death before they see the Son of man coming in his kingdom,"[34] and later still, "But of that day and hour no one knows, not even the angels of heaven, nor the Son, but the Father only."[35] In any case, not

[ 225 ]

the long-drawn-out missionary campaign of the churches to all nations but the swift coming of the kingdom was in Jesus' mind.

It is an anachronism, therefore, to make the words "universalism" and "particularism" mean in Jesus' time what they mean to moderns now. He was both a "particularist" and a "universalist"—a loyal Jew who could even picture his twelve disciples, in the day of his coming glory, sitting "on twelve thrones, judging the twelve tribes of Israel,"[36] and at the same time an interpreter of Judaism in terms so basically human and inclusive that they were universally applicable to all mankind. The early churches were not essentially mistaken in claiming the authority of Jesus for their international, interracial mission. He almost certainly did not foresee that outcome, but he prepared the way for it. In a profound sense he universalized Judaism.

The weightiest evidence for Jesus' world-wide outlook is to be found in the essential nature of his teaching, but the incidental evidence also is so plentiful that to eliminate it would tear the gospel record to shreds. The Samaritans were special objects of disdain among stricter Jews, so that John's picture of the Pharisees, denouncing Jesus as insultingly as possible, and saying,"You are a Samaritan and have a demon,"[37] may be taken as typical. One sacred book of Jesus' time called the Samaritans, "the foolish people that live in Shechem."[38] Jesus, however, made a good Samaritan his hero, in contrast with a priest and a Levite.[39] Not postponed to the Pauline churches but in Jesus himself began the liberal outlook which Paul expressed—"When Gentiles who have not the law do by nature what the law requires, they are a law to themselves, even though they do not have the law. They show that what the law requires is written on their hearts."[40]

In his references to the scriptures Jesus' interest in Gentiles is notable. He had pondered on Jonah's preaching to the Ninevites, on Solomon's influence on the Queen of Sheba,[41] on Elijah's service to the widow of Zarephath, on Elisha's healing of Naaman the Syrian,[42] and on Tyre, Sidon and even Sodom as having more chance in the day of judgment than Bethsaida and Capernaum.[43] That Jesus should have found in a Roman centurion more faith than he had found in Israel[44] is a single incident but it is revealing—no racial or national lines confined his appreciation and care. If John the Baptist could cry, "Do not presume to say to yourselves, 'We have Abraham as our father'; for I tell you, God is able from these stones to raise up children to Abraham,"[45] why should it be doubted that Jesus said, "I tell you, many will come from east and west and sit at table with Abraham, Isaac, and Jacob in the kingdom of heaven"?[46] If Isaiah represented God as saying, "My house shall be called a house of prayer for all peoples,"[47] why should it be doubted that Jesus quoted and enforced it?[48]

To be sure, Jesus was critical of Gentiles and their way of life: "In praying do not heap up empty phrases as the Gentiles do";[49] "And if you salute only your brethren, what more are you doing than others? Do not even the Gentiles do the same?"[50] "You know that those who are supposed to rule over the Gentiles lord it over them. . . . But it shall not be so among you."[51] Taken in conjunction with all the other evidence, however, such passages reveal in Jesus' thought not so much prejudice against Gentiles as awareness of them, interest in them, concern about them. Not Jews only but Gentiles were in the center of his attention.

[ 227 ]

Indeed, while he may have told his disciples on their first preaching mission not to approach Gentiles, he himself continually did approach them and was approached by them. If any area within Jesus' reach was thoroughly Gentile it was the Decapolis—ten Greek cities southeast of the Sea of Galilee— but Matthew tells us that "great crowds followed him from Galilee and the Decapolis,"[52] and Luke adds from "the seacoast of Tyre and Sidon."[53] Mark even describes a journey Jesus himself took into the Decapolis and his healing there.[54] The more the evidence is canvassed, the more clearly impossible it becomes to doubt Jesus' acquaintance with all sorts and conditions of people, Jews and Gentiles, and with the problems which they faced, especially the problem of universalism as against the narrower type of Judaism.

That he himself was troubled by the conflict between universalism and the endeavor to initiate his movement within Judaism, is evidenced in one of the most puzzling narratives in the Gospels:

And from there he arose and went away to the region of Tyre and Sidon. And he entered a house, and would not have any one know it; yet he could not be hid. But immediately a woman, whose little daughter was possessed by an unclean spirit, heard of him, and came and fell down at his feet. Now the woman was a Greek, a Syrophoenician by race. And she begged him to cast the demon out of her daughter. And he said to her, "Let the children first be fed, for it is not right to take the children's bread and throw it to the dogs." But she answered him, "Yes, Lord; yet even the dogs under the table eat the children's crumbs." And he said to her, "For this saying you may go your way; the demon has left your daughter." And she went home, and found the child lying in bed, and the demon gone.[55]

That Jesus thus called Jews children and non-Jews dogs—even though the word used means pet dogs—is so shocking and so inconsistent with the portrait of him in the Gospels that scholars have been tempted to suppose that Jesus has been misquoted. Some think that one of the disciples used the harsh comparison in the same spirit in which they tried to keep those who brought children to Jesus from bothering him—and that the words were mistakenly attributed to Jesus. Others think that the Syrophoenician woman herself, playfully urging her appeal, first claimed the right of the family's dogs to the children's crumbs, and that Jesus took up her words and made use of them, while all the time intending to help her. Others suppose that Jesus used the words, as he is quoted, not as an expression of his own opinion, but as a caricature of the orthodox Jewish attitude, which he discarded in helpfulness and friendliness to the woman.[56] These are only guesses whose chief value is to indicate that, if we had the whole conversation instead of the condensed narrative in the Gospels, its meaning might be clarified.

The historic setting of the narrative is of utmost importance in its interpretation. Jesus had so aroused the hostility of Herod that, facing the probability of John the Baptist's fate, he had fled from Galilee to the coasts of Tyre and Sidon. His public ministry was confronting failure; he himself in danger of death was turning to his one hope—the training of his disciples. He fled from Galilee to Phoenicia to escape publicity, and there "He entered a house, and would not have anyone know it." Even in that pagan land, however, he "could not be hid." This beseeching woman wanted him to begin there the same process that had brought the crowds swarming around him in Galilee. If he could not go on with that kind of ministry among his own people, how could he do it for the Phoenicians? He may well have been distraught, and out of his inner struggle may have come the comparison set in the picturesque speech always characteristic of him, which, put bluntly in our abbreviated record, sounds so unlike him. At any rate, whatever he said to the woman, she did not feel as badly about it as we do. Far from feeling insulted, she made a humorous answer, that brought the help she sought. Moreover, Mark and Matthew in preserving the story must have thought of it as an argument not against but in favor of the Gentile mission, for Jesus did heal the woman's daughter.

To set Jesus' universalism over against his Judaism betrays misunderstanding of what the world of Jesus' day was like and of what liberal Judaism was thinking. The Roman Empire had achieved among the nations such a degree of unity that the Stoics said, "The world is one city." To his own kind of world view Jesus came, not despite the kind of world he lived in, but as a sharer in it and in the best thinking of his people who were scattered all over it. He never doubted the primacy of Judaism in God's revelation of himself and in God's purpose for the world. No more did the New Testament churches doubt it, and whether in Pauline or Johannine thought, it still was true that "salvation is from the Jews."[57] Nevertheless, this salvation was for the whole of mankind. It was *through* Judaism that Jesus reached his conviction that "the field is the world."

His Jewish monotheism involved it. From the eighth century prophets on, the greatest of the Hebrew seers, believing in one God, had conceived of one world with all nations under the divine sovereignty and subject to the divine law. Monotheism among the Jews was not primarily speculative; it never dealt, as in modern times, with materialistic atheism as an alternative, but with polytheism; and as polytheism meant many peoples with many gods, so monotheism meant one world under one God. Let hatred and prejudice do their worst, and resentment against tyranny issue in bitter desire that the Gentiles should all perish, yet there were always those who could not escape the logic of monotheism. Among the books that almost certainly influenced Jesus was the *Testament of the Twelve Patriarchs,* in which the implications of faith in Israel's God were accepted and acclaimed: "He shall save Israel and all the Gentiles";[58] "The Lord shall reveal his salvation to all Gentiles";[59] "The Lord shall visit all Gentiles in his tender mercies forever";[60] The Gentiles shall be "multiplied in knowledge upon the earth and enlightened through the grace of the Lord."[61] Jews with such an outlook regarded the dispersion of their people across the world as providential, and heard God saying, "I will scatter this people among the Gentiles that they may do good to the Gentiles."[62]

That Jesus' God, therefore, was "Lord of heaven and earth,"[63] whose will was to be done "on earth as it is in heaven," and that his followers were to be the "salt of the earth" and the "light of the world," sprang directly from his Jewish heritage. Paul's logic was not a new discovery, revealed to him for the first time when he became a Christian, but was rooted in his spiritual tradition: "Is God the God of Jews only? Is he not the God of Gentiles also? Yes, of Gentiles also, since God is one."[64] To suppose that Paul saw this and that Jesus did not see it is incredible. Jesus was a universalist not despite his Judaism but because of it.

When Jesus, with this theological approach to his world view, dealt with God's ethical requirements, his universalism became even more evident. To the question, what does the "Lord of heaven and earth" require of men, Jesus gave an answer which only the more radical liberals, even among Hellenistic Jews, could have accepted. He described God's ethical demands in terms of righteousness so basic—sincerity, humility, self-sacrifice, inner rightness of spirit, and outward humaneness, all motivated by undiscourageable goodwill—that no racial or national lines had any relevance.

At the last judgment, said Jesus, one issue will decide the fate of men—have they fed the hungry, given drink to the thirsty, welcomed the stranger, clothed the naked, visited the sick and the inprisoned?[65] To meet this kind of requirement—to be a good Samaritan—involved nothing distinctively Jewish. A Gentile, redeemed to a right spirit, could aspire to this ideal and measure himself by this standard.

At this point also Jesus stood in the great tradition of the prophets. Had not Isaiah put ethical righteousness above all ceremonial, and had not Micah said: "What doth the Lord require of thee, but to do justly, and to love mercy, and to walk humbly with thy God?"[66] Priestly tradition and Pharisaic legalism, however, had supplemented these ethical demands of prophetic Judaism with a mass of requirements whose observance did make a Jew stand out as a Jew, distinct and unassimilable. Jesus himself conformed to many of these customary practices of his people. He was so fundamentally Jewish that Wellhausen could say, "Jesus was not a Christian; he was a Jew. He did not preach a new faith, but taught men to do the will of God; and, in his opinion, as also in that of the Jews, the will of God was to be found in the Law of Moses and in the other books of Scripture."[67] That Jesus tried his best to state his position thus in terms of the law's fulfillment instead of its abolition, and that he sought to work out his mission within the traditional culture of his people, seems clear. Was it not because of this that, after he had gone, two points of view clashed in the earliest church—one stressing Jesus' Jewishness and insisting that all Christians must be circumcised and obey all the law, and the other stressing Jesus' antilegalistic universalism? Both factors were in Jesus, their conflict necessarily unresolved while he was launching his movement in Palestine. When, however, Jesus stated the ethical requirements of God, as he saw them, he so dropped the legalistic and priestly specialties of Judaism, and so emphasized a kind of goodness to which racial and national distinctions were irrelevant that the stricter Pharisees could not miss seeing the peril with which he threatened them. He was universalizing ethics.

Men were to be humble and merciful, pure in heart and peacemakers, forgiving enemies and loving them, simple and sincere in speech and unostentatious in piety, generous without show, free from servitude to Mammon, finding life by sacrificially losing it, and so completely devoted to God's will that, having done their utmost, they still regarded themselves as "unworthy servants." Whatever one may think of such an ethic's practicability, it is certain that nothing exclusively Jewish characterizes it. Here, indeed, from the standpoint of the stricter Pharisees was the crux of Jesus' offending—he was opening the doors to the whole world on the basis of ethical monotheism and the moral law. Thus a modern Jewish scholar argues that the Jews could not have done otherwise than reject him: "A religion which possesses only a certain conception of God and a morality acceptable to *all* mankind, does not belong to any special nation, and, consciously or unconsciously, breaks down the barriers of nationality. This inevitably brought it to pass that his people, Israel, rejected him."[68]

Along with his monotheistic and ethical approach to universalism went Jesus' individualism. He cared for persons one by one, and his concern about them and desire to help them were stopped by no economic, national or racial lines. As in the case of the Roman centurion, or of the Samaritan leper, who alone

[ 233 ]

of ten cured returned to thank him,[69] his ministry of healing knew no boundaries of race or nation. When little children came to him, is it conceivable that Jewish babes alone were welcomed and all others rejected?

Two major approaches to a cosmopolitan world view were in evidence in Jesus' day, as in our own: one, moving by way of overall, outward facts of political and economic interdependence to see the world as one, and the other so valuing persons, as persons, regardless of color, race or nationality that all personalities, wherever found, are equally regarded as worth living and dying for. How far the outward approach may have influenced Jesus none can tell, but that the inward approach, by way of care for individuals, led him to a universal outlook seems plain. Jesus' thought of every soul as infinitely precious in the sight of God was one of his incontestable characteristics. Adolf Harnack even said: "Jesus Christ was the first to bring the value of every human soul to light."[70]

Jesus made every profound matter which he touched intimately personal—companionship with God inward and secret, goodness a quality of the heart, moral decision an act of will from deep within the individual. As for right relationships between persons the family was Jesus' norm—God our Father, we his children, and therefore "all brethren"[71]—and a good family is the one social group we know where, no matter how many children there are, each has standing in his own right, each is loved for his own sake, each possesses distinct, inalienable worth and meaning. Jesus carried this care for individuals to a point where customary morality was shocked and ordinary commonsense rebelled. He saw value and possibility in most unlikely persons—a prodigal, an adulteress, a thieving tax collector, a beggar whose sores the dogs licked. There is joy in

[ 234 ]

the presence of God, he said, over one such individual redeemed.

Such individualism is bound to have more than an individual consequence. If personality is in itself so valuable, racial
and national lines must be overpassed in dealing with it. Souls,
as such, are not Jewish, Gentile or Samaritan. The external approach to universalism lacks intensiveness; under its spell one
cares for man but not for men. Mankind may thus be regarded
as though it were one sea, the sea abiding, the waves transient.
Such a world view has extension of outlook without intensity
of meaning. To achieve a vital universalism involves beginning
with the individual. If each person is a child of God, infinitely
valuable, then all men everywhere must be that. If, however,
the individual is nothing, E. F. Scott's dictum is inescapable,
"Nothing may be multiplied by a hundred million, but it is still
nothing."[72]

Jesus' universalism traveled the inward road. He cared for
and helped persons regardless of racial, religious, economic or
national lines. "Whoever" was one of his favorite words—
thirty-six times in Matthew's Gospel it, or its equivalent, is reported in his sayings. "Every one then who hears these words
of mine and does them will be like a wise man";[73] "Every one
who acknowledges me before men, I also will acknowledge";[74]
"Whoever gives to one of these little ones even a cup of cold
water";[75] "Whoever does the will of my Father in heaven is my
brother, and sister, and mother";[76] "Whoever would save his
life will lose it, and whoever loses his life for my sake will find
it";[77] "Whoever humbles himself like this child, he is the greatest in the kingdom of heaven";[78] "Whoever would be great
among you must be your servant."[79] That means anybody.
Color, caste, race, nation make no difference. It is human

persons he is thinking of, individual souls anywhere and at any time.

Springing from his monotheism, from his idea of God's ethical demands, and from his care for individuals, Jesus' universalism was expressed in his conception of the kingdom. For a long generation now the phrase "kingdom of God"—or its equivalent, in accordance with Jewish usage, "kingdom of heaven"—has been given in modern thought a significance primarily sociological. It has been taken to mean a world-wide society, sometime in the future to arrive, utopian in its righteousness, brotherhood and peace. Present-day scholarship, however, has made clear this idea's inadequacy.

God's kingdom in the Gospels means primarily his sovereignty, and that is an eternal fact. He *is* sovereign now and forever. In its *initial* meaning the kingdom is not a new social order yet to come, not a redeemed political regime displacing the world's present empires, but an everlasting fact: "The Lord shall reign for ever and ever."[80] Acknowledged or unacknowledged, accepted by man or neglected and denied, this lordship of God is a fact.

The acceptance of the kingdom, therefore, is first of all personal. When, at his ministry's beginning Jesus faced the conflict in the world between God and Satan and, renouncing Satan, quoted Deuteronomy, "You shall worship the Lord your God, and him only shall you serve,"[81] he was acknowledging God's sovereignty, and as an ancient Jewish phrase put it, taking on himself the kingdom. When, at his ministry's end, he cried, "Not what I will, but what thou wilt,"[82] he was confirming with his willingness to die his acceptance of God as rightful sovereign.

While God's sovereignty, however, was thus an eternal fact,

its final fulfillment was yet to come. Someday this profound and in the end invincible truth of God's rightful kingship would be so asserted from on high and, whether voluntarily or forcibly, would be so accepted in the whole world, that God's will would be "done on earth as it is in heaven." From a messianic war to a superhuman Son of Man the imagination of the Jewish people canvassed the possibilities as to how God's victorious dominion would be finally achieved. Jesus surely did not think of the divine kingship as established by war, and how fully he shared any other picture of the kingdom's coming, current among his people, is now endlessly debated. Certainly he thought—at least in the early stages of his ministry—that it was coming soon.

Meanwhile—and, as his ministry continued, this apparently became more and more his emphasis—men and women could enter the kingdom now. The meaning of God's lordship, being an eternal fact, was not exhausted in its future consummation. Here and now it was operative in the world, and men and women, acknowledging it and loyal to it, could become "sons of the kingdom,"[83] and could be like leaven in the meal.[84] Though as inconspicuous as a grain of mustard seed,[85] the recognized sovereignty of God was nonetheless at work now. Wherever a victory over sin and evil was won the kingdom's presence was made evident: "If it is by the Spirit of God that I cast out demons, then the kingdom of God has come upon you."[86] However much this saying may have to be balanced by others, it certainly represents a major emphasis in Jesus' teaching. On the parchment discovered at Oxyrhynchus in Egypt Jesus is quoted as saying: "The kingdom of God is within you, and whoever knows himself will find it."[87] That this view of the present nature of God's sovereignty is not inconsistent with the apocalyptic view of its ultimate consummation is evident in

[ 237 ]

Paul who, thoroughly believing in apocalypticism, could also say: "The kingdom of God does not mean food and drink but righteousness and peace and joy in the Holy Spirit."[88]

Who, then, were qualified to enter the kingdom? Jesus' answers to that question reveal once more the universality of his idea of the divine requirements. Little children, with their trustfulness and humility—"to such belongs the kingdom of God."[89] Those who see that to love God and to love one's neighbor as one's self are "much more than all whole burnt offerings and sacrifices"—they are "not far from the kingdom of God."[90] "The poor in spirit"—"theirs is the kingdom of heaven."[91] He who "does the will" of God, instead of making pious professions only, "shall enter the kingdom of heaven."[92] Such souls are "sons of the kingdom" now, sown like seed in the world.[93] But those who serve Mammon and trust in riches, a camel can pass through a needle's eye more easily than they can "enter the kingdom of God."[94] As for those who, having put their hand to the plough, turn back when confronted with sacrifice, they are not "fit for the kingdom of God."[95]

Nothing whatever involving the legalism of the Pharisaic code or the ceremonialism of the temple is suggested as a requirement for entering the kingdom. The doors are open on terms that apply to all men and women everywhere who fulfill the conditions of ethical life and spiritual quality which Jesus lays down. Not from the later church's thinking, then, but from the essential nature of his own thinking came his admonition to all "workers of iniquity," that they would be cast out while "men will come from east and west, and from north and south, and sit at table in the kingdom of God."[96]

Had there been no receptive audience for such teaching, no good soil along with all the hard-packed, thorny, unresponsive ground for such seed to fall on, how can the consequence be explained? The earliest church we know had liberal elements in it, ready to reduce the law's requirements to the simplest terms and to proclaim a universal God and a universal ethic. Jesus' message took hold because some, at least, were prepared to understand it.

Stephen, the first Christian martyr,[97] is the kind of man whose opinion of Jesus we are trying to represent. He was almost certainly a Hellenistic Jew, well-known in the Greek-speaking synagogue in Jerusalem. He may well have seen, heard and even followed Jesus. According to an old tradition, noted by Epiphanius[98] in the fourth century, Stephen was one of the seventy disciples whom Jesus commissioned to preach,[99] and while this tradition deserves no credence, it may be true that Stephen had been won to Jesus' discipleship before the crucifixion. Certainly he dissociated himself from those who consented to the crucifixion as a "stiff-necked people, uncircumcised in heart and ears," who had "betrayed and murdered" the Christ.[100] Moreover, he understood Jesus very well and faced the enmity of the orthodox for the same reasons his Lord had faced it, accused of desire to "change the customs which Moses delivered to us," and of speaking "blasphemous words against Moses and God." Outspoken in his defense of the broader, deeper convictions of Jesus regarding the meaning of Judaism, he roused the enmity even of the Hellenistic synagogue and of Saul of Tarsus, still trying to be "a Pharisee of the Pharisees," and so died for his faith, praying as his Master had prayed, "Lord, do not hold this sin against them." Surely Stephen does not stand alone. Others, too, like him in breadth of outlook, must have recognized in Jesus their leader and their Lord.

[ 239 ]

That the stricter Pharisees had to reject him, or else surrender their whole system of thought and life, is obvious. That
there were Jews, however, often deeply influenced by Hellenistic thought, to whom his gospel brought personal liberation
and hope for the whole world seems obvious too.

# Epilogue

W E HAVE not adequately described Jesus' contemporaries by classifying them, as we have done, and by noting each group's distinctive response to him. This approach, while clarifying the immediate circumstances which our Lord confronted, and throwing light upon the meaning of many of his words and deeds, may also obscure an important matter. These contemporaries were not simply members of special social and religious classes; they were first of all individual personalities with timeless spiritual needs. Analyzing the response of these contemporary groups to Jesus emphasizes the fact that he was a man of his own time, speaking to his own generation, but he has proved to be a man of all times, speaking to all generations. The reason for that goes back to depths in him and to timeless elements in his message, which these same contemporaries began discovering.

The ancient situation in Palestine, in whose matrix Jesus' ministry was set and whose traditions and ways of thinking conditioned the phrasing of his gospel, has long since been outgrown, but not Jesus himself. In one realm after another, such as war, racial relationships, economic justice, the best conscience of the world is haunted by the fact that he is ahead of us, an unattained goal. The relevance to modern need of what he believed and stood for becomes ever more apparent as powerful competing ideologies oppose it and, as for personal life, our timeless needs still find in him their abiding supply. This eternal factor in Christ and his gospel was present from the start. He appealed to profundities in human nature, which passing centuries and changing cultures do not affect. He did deal with the problems presented by current Phariseeism, legalism, nationalism, and even with special problems such as the Jewish system of divorce, but his solutions had the dimension of depth, so that they have carried over, their truth applicable to situations utterly different from first-century culture.

This timeless profundity in Jesus was felt by his first followers before it was defined. They were impressed by his "authority"; they exclaimed, "What is this? A new teaching!" They were sure he was a "prophet," speaking for God, and at last they used the most superlative patterns of thought in their possession to explain him. Putting ourselves in their places, we may surmise that this powerful impression of permanent greatness in Jesus dawned on them as they confronted the manner of his teaching, and then the substance of his teaching, and then the stature of the personality through whom the teaching came.

Jesus had a way of putting things that time does not wear out. He might have discussed neighborliness in the abstract, like a lawyer analyzing its obligations in terms of current practice. Had he done so, we probably should never have heard of it. Instead, he personified neighborliness in the good Samaritan, making him stand out in vivid contrast with the unneighborly priest and Levite, so that not only did his contemporaries grasp his meaning, but we do also. Personal incarnations have a perennial continuance in the understanding of the race. Abstract condemnations of economic greed have been both frequent and transient, but the rich man who "feasted sumptuously every day," while "a poor man named Lazarus, full of sores," begged at his gate has not been transient;[1] nor that other rich man who said to his soul, "Soul, you have ample goods laid up for many years; take your ease, eat, drink, be merry."[2] Such incarnations walk the streets of New York and London as plainly as they walked the streets of Jerusalem.

Two qualities in Jesus' manner of teaching are outstanding: the poignancy of its immediate appeal and its continuing pertinence to all men, always and everywhere. Arguments aplenty can be conjured up to excuse an unforgiving spirit when one has been wronged. The merciless steward, however, who, having been pardoned a vast debt, seized "one of his fellow servants . . . by the throat," crying, "Pay what you owe," and then, refusing his plea for patience, cast him into prison, is not easily escapable.[3] Jesus' first hearers felt that. His attack on their unwillingness to forgive was not argumentative, theoretical, abstract, but came at them in incarnate form, so forcefully personified that willy-nilly they had to make up their minds whether to be that merciless steward or not. This quality in Jesus' manner of teaching, moreover, has made all men everywhere his contemporaries. Still that merciless steward and many another character in Jesus' parables challenge our consciences.

Behind the manner of Jesus' teaching was its substance. Grant the transient, contemporary elements that necessarily entered into the Master's message, from small details reflecting current customs to prevalent ideas of Gehenna and expectations of the speedy coming of the messianic age, still the profound residue remains—truth applicable always and everywhere to man's deepest moral and spiritual needs.

The sovereignty of God with whom "all things are possible";[4] the sternness of God before whom no unrighteousness can stand; the fatherhood of God—"Your Father is merciful";[5] the availability of God's help—"If you then, who are evil, know how to give good gifts to your children, how much more will your Father who is in heaven give good things to those who ask him?"[6] the forgiveness of God—"There is joy before the angels of God over one sinner who repents":[7] with such basic ideas Jesus' teaching started. One wonders at first that his contemporaries, accustomed from youth to similar doctrines, should have found such teaching "new." But new it was. Jesus was so convinced of its truth, felt it so deeply, lived it so consistently, brought to it such fresh developments of meaning, that, when he spoke, the message became incarnate in him, novel, challenging, convincing. He did not argue about God; he revealed him. God walks through his teaching, whether as king, or as judge, or as a householder entrusting talents to his servants, or as a "Father who sees in secret,"[8] no abstraction, no hypothesis at the end of an argument, but a real Being from whose presence none can escape, in whose plenty all wants can be supplied, and to do whose will is man's glory. "His aim is not to make God an article of faith, but the object of faith," writes Dr. Manson. "We are often concerned to make God probable to men; he set out to make God real to them."[9]

Along with this basic substance of Jesus' teaching about God went his insight into eternal truths about human life. "A man's life does not consist in the abundance of his possessions";[10] "No one can serve two masters. . . . You cannot serve God and mammon";[11] "Which of you by being anxious can add one cubit to his span of life?"[12] "Whoever seeks to gain his life will lose it, but whoever loses his life will preserve it";[13] "Whoever humbles himself like this child, he is the greatest in the kingdom of heaven"[14]—such insights are timeless. As for his distinctively ethical teaching, what we have said about its relevance to all races applies to its relevance to all generations. The framework of the Last Judgment, as Jesus pictured it—the Son of Man sitting on his "glorious throne" and, like a shepherd, parting sheep from goats—is local and contemporary, but its ethical gist is permanent: mercy to the needy as God's central requirement and love as the fulfilling of the law.[15]

Because this ethic was rooted in Jesus' faith in God, it was proclaimed in terms not alone of obligation but of hope. One of Jesus' most familiar phrases was "the will" of God. God was not primarily an object of speculation, nor even of belief, but was active purpose, the eternal Doer, immediately to be recognized in experience and wholeheartedly served. Here and now God was presently at work, revealed in nature, caring for even a sparrow's fall, the planner and achiever of all good deeds, the guarantor of a coming time when his will would be done on earth as in heaven. "My Father is working still, and I am working"[16] is John's statement of Jesus' undergirding faith. To his immediate listeners, therefore, he brought a demand for action in the name of the supreme Actor: "Go and do likewise";[17] "Which of the two did the will of his father?"[18] "Not every one who says to me, 'Lord, Lord,' shall enter the kingdom of heaven, but he who does the will of my Father who is in heaven."[19] And because divine purpose, issuing in divine action, was thus the central fact in the universe, as Jesus saw it, victory lay ahead—God's kingdom surely coming, involving the triumph of the righteous and their eternal life. His confidence was unshakable: "Every plant which my heavenly Father has not planted will be rooted up."[20]

The deep needs of human nature to which such faith is pertinent are as real today as ever. While, therefore, the forgiven sinners in the Gospels, the mended lives, the ordinary folk made extraordinary because they were carried out of themselves by a cause greater than themselves to which they gave themselves, wore first-century clothes and thought in first-century terms, they are nonetheless our contemporaries. They were subdued and mastered and enlisted by a truth that does not wear out.

It was the personality, however, through whom the teaching came, who supremely impressed the first disciples, and who still fascinates our imagination and challenges our conscience. Three names by which Jesus is called are familiarly remembered: a "physician" who cares for the sick; a "bridegroom" rejoicing with his bridal party; an incendiary, who has come "to cast fire upon the earth," to consume evil things whose doom God has decreed. But Jesus and his truth are thought of in a fourth way also, as a stone: "Every one who falls on that stone will be broken to pieces; but when it falls on any one it will crush him."[21] So those first disciples began to see him—impregnable, permanent, the decisive arbiter of what will last and what will pass away. Despised and rejected, crucified and hated, all the evil in men and nations arrayed against him and his gospel, he still maintains that position in the faith of his followers—a rock on which evil falling will yet be broken.

That he taught humility and impressed those who knew him best with his humble spirit is evident in the Gospels. As Ruskin said of the supreme artists, they could not be proud because "the greatness is not *in* them, but *through* them."[22] As Jesus saw the matter, it was not himself but God who was good, and who was using him in every good work he did. So John interpreted his self-consciousness: "The Father who dwells in me does his works."[23] But while thus humble about himself, he was uncompromising in affirming and defending the truth he stood for and in asserting his supreme authority as its representative:

[ 246 ]

"He who receives you receives me, and he who receives me receives him who sent me";[24] "So every one who acknowledges me before men, I also will acknowledge before my Father who is in heaven."[25] The earliest Christianity of the first disciples was thus devotion to a person—"Follow me," he said. It was not a formal creed nor an ethical code but a Man they believed in. He was to them that most powerful force in human experience, an incarnation, embodying and revealing in his own person the truths he represented. When they thought of God, it was more and more in terms of Jesus; when they thought of goodness, it meant likeness to him. So he became to them not only Teacher, but Lord and Savior, revealer of the divine, ideal of the human, who having died for their sakes still lived, and to whom, in God's good time, the future belonged.

This, too, has stood the test of passing centuries and, amid the many conflicts which divide his followers today, one constant element alone binds them together—loyalty to a Personality.

Jesus, as his contemporaries saw him, cannot be thought of, therefore, in his stark historicity as an uninterpreted person. His very first disciples began interpreting him and, so far as the four Gospels are concerned, this theological rendering of Jesus, which came to its climax in John, began in Mark. By various paths those first followers came to him, wanting renewed faith, forgiveness of sin, healing of body and spirit, a leader to follow, a cause to serve, a hope to give them courage; and, finding these timeless needs supplied by Jesus, they began asking, Who is he? and answering in terms of the mental categories they had inherited. This, too, is a perennial process and still goes on. For the deep and abiding needs of man, in the twentieth century as in the first, call for a living, personal revelation and symbol of God, for pardon, power, faith in divine

[ 247 ]

purpose and courage in serving it, for inward peace, a cause worth ultimate self-sacrifice, and for hope here and hereafter. The process which started in the experience of the first disciples has proved to be endless: man's profoundest spiritual wants finding their satisfaction in this Eternal Contemporary, with the question rising, Who is he?

> Yea, in the night, my Soul, my daughter
> Cry,—clinging Heaven by the hems;
> And lo, Christ walking on the water
> Not of Gennesareth, but Thames![26]

# REFERENCES

## CHAPTER I

### A REAL MAN, NOT A MYTH

1. Acts 5:33–39.    2. Sanhedrin, 43a.
3. The soldier's name, according to this tale, was *Pantheras;* the word for virgin is *Parthenos.* Jewish scholars like Klausner and Christian scholars like Goguel agree that this Jewish canard was at first a wordplay on "Son of the Virgin." See *Jesus of Nazareth,* by Joseph Klausner, p. 23 f.; *The Life of Jesus,* by Maurice Goguel, p. 73 f.
4. See *Christianity in Talmud and Midrash,* by Robert Travers Herford.
5. See e.g., Klausner, *op. cit.,* p. 56 ff.    6. *Annals* XV. 44.
7. *Life of Claudius,* 25.
8. *The Search for the Real Jesus,* by Chester Charlton McCown, p. 69.
9. *Encyclopaedia Britannica,* article on Buddha.
10. The First Epistle of Clement, chaps. 5 and 47: *The Ante-Nicene Fathers,* ed. by Roberts and Donaldson, I, 5; cf. I Corinthians 11, 17 ff.
11. II Corinthians 5:16 (A.R.V.).    12. Galatians 1:18–19.
13. Acts 12:12.    14. Acts 12:12.    15. Galatians 4:4.
16. I Corinthians 11:23 f.    17. Galatians 2:20.
18. Cf. the "we" sections of Acts, chaps. 16:10–17; 20:5–15; 21:1–18; 27:1–28.
19. Philemon 24.    20. Colossians 4:14.    21. II Timothy 4:11.
22. II Corinthians 10:1.    23. Romans 15:1–3.
24. II Corinthians 3:18 (Henry Drummond).    25. Luke 14:11.
26. Romans 12:16.    27. Matthew 25:40.    28. II Corinthians 11:29.
29. Matthew 5:10.    30. II Corinthians 12:10.    31. Matthew 6:25.
32. Philippians 4:6.    33. Mark 7:15.    34. Romans 14:14.
35. Matthew 7:1.    36. Romans 14:13.    37. Mark 11:23.
38. I Corinthians 13:2.    39. Matthew 5:44.    40. Romans 12:14, 17.
41. Mark 12:28 f.    42. Romans 13:10.    43. I Corinthians 11:1.
44. Ephesians 4:21 M.    45. Galatians 4:19.    46. Philippians 2:3–5.
47. Matthew 5:3.    48. Luke 6:20, 21, 24.
49. Roberts and Donaldson, eds., *op. cit.,* I, pp. 154–5.    50. Mark 10:18.
51. Matthew 19:17.    52. Mark 11:12–14, 20–21; Matthew 21:18–19.
53. Mark 5:1–20; Matthew 8:28–34.
54. Mark 10:46–52; Matthew 20:29–34.
55. Mark 14:47; Luke 22:51.    56. John 2:1–11; 9:1–7; 11:1–44.

REFERENCES

57. Mark 13:30 f; 9:1.    58. Roberts and Donaldson, eds., *op. cit.*, I, 153.
59. Mark 2:27.    60. Matthew 19:14.    61. Mark 2:17.
62. Luke 6:32 f.    Cf. *The Poetry of Our Lord*, by Charles Fox Burney.
63. Luke 1:1–4.    64. Roberts and Donaldson, eds., *op. cit.*, I, 155.
65. Luke 1:1–4.    66. Mark 6:1–6; Luke 4:16 f.
67. Matthew 21:12–13; Mark 11:15–17; Luke 19:45; John 2:13–17.
68. Matthew 6:9 f; Luke 11:2–4.    69. Matthew 7:12; Luke 6:31.
70. Matthew 27:51–53.    71. Church History, Eusebius, 6, 14, 6.
72. E.g., Mark 5:41; 7:11, 34; 14:36; 15:34.    73. Mark 12:42.
74. Mark 11:13.    75. Mark 7:3.    76. Mark 10:11 f.; cf. Matthew 5:31 f.
77. See *The Gospel of Luke*, by William Manson, p. xi.
78. *Ibid.*, p. xxvii f.    79. Acts, chap. 21 ff.    80. Acts 21:17–18.
81. Acts 21:8–9.    82. Colossians 4:10, 14; Philemon 24.
83. Church History, Eusebius 6, 14, 7.    84. Matthew 15:24.
85. Cf. *The Gospel before the Gospels*, by Burton Scott Easton, chap. iv.


CHAPTER II

AS THE CROWDS SAW HIM

1. John 6:2.    2. John 6:15.    3. John 1:11.
4. John 7:1; cf. 7:11, 30; 8:48–59.    5. Mark 1:28.    6. Mark 2:2.
7. Mark 3:9.    8. Mark 3:31, 32.    9. Mark 3:20.    10. Mark 1:33.
11. Mark 5:31.    12. Mark 3:7–8.
13. Josephus, *History of the Jewish War*, 3:2; *Life*, 45.
14. *Itinerarium Antonini Placentini: Corpus Scriptorum Ecclesiasticorum Latinorum*, Vol. 39, p. 162.    15. Strabo 16:2, 34.    16. Mark 6:14–16.
17. Luke 13:31.    18. Luke 13:32.    19. Luke 13:33.    20. Mark 7:24.
21. Matthew 21:9.    22. John 12:19.    23. Mark 12:37 M.
24. Luke 22:2.    25. Luke 23:27.    26. Luke 23:48.
27. H.D.A. Major, in *The Mission and Message of Jesus*, p. xxx.
28. *The Jewish Encyclopedia*, V, 522.    29. Mark 6:56 M.    30. Luke 4:16.
31. Acts 23:8.    32. Matthew 11:19.    33. M. Sota 3, 4.
34. Sota 22b.    35. Deuteronomy, Rabba 2, 24.    36. Mark 4:10–13.
37. Mark 1:27 M.    38. *Antiquities* 17:2, 4.    39. Matthew 23:24.
40. Matthew 7:3–5.    41. Matthew 7:6.    42. Matthew 5:29–30.
43. Matthew 18:6.    44. Matthew 18:23 f.    45. Mark 11:23.
46. Luke 17:6.    47. Matthew 10:16.    48. Matthew 19:24.
49. Matthew 8:22.    50. Mark 10:21.    51. Matthew 8:10.
52. Matthew 7:16.    53. Matthew 10:30.    54. Matthew 7:9, 10.
55. Berachoth 55b; Baba Mezia 38b.    56. Matthew 7:28.
57. Romans 11:24.    58. δύναμεις, δύνατα ἔργα, τέρατα, σημεῖα.
59. Luke 11:15.    60. Mark 13:22.    61. Luke 11:19.
62. See Joseph Klausner, *Jesus of Nazareth*, p. 266.    63. Acts 13:6 f.

64. Klausner, *op. cit.*, p. 266.     65. Mark 1:44; 3:12; 5:43; 7:36.
66. Matthew 12:28.     67. Matthew 11:4–6; Luke 7:20–22.
68. Luke 5:26.     69. Mark 2:12.     70. Mark 5:1–20.
71. Luke 6:6–11.     72. Matthew 9:34.     73. Matthew 11:20–24.
74. Mark 5:43.     75. Luke 11:29 M.     76. Luke 11:29–32.
77. Mark 8:11, 12.     78. Mark 5:22–24; 35–43.     79. Matthew 12:39 f.
80. *The Apocryphal New Testament*, by M. R. James; especially *The Gospel of Thomas* and *The Gospel of Pseudo-Matthew*.     81. Matthew 21:18–21.
82. Mark 16:18.     83. Major, Manson and Wright, *op. cit.*, p. 107.
84. Luke 16:31.     85. Luke 10:17–20.     86. Mark 8:27–28.
87. Acts 15:5.     88. Epistle of Ignatius to the Magnesians, X.
89. *Jesus the Nazarene, Myth or History?* by Maurice Goguel, p. 38.
90. E.g., John 8:37–59.     91. Mark 14:61.     92. Matthew 11:20–24.
93. Matthew 23:37.
94. See *The Historic Mission of Jesus*, by C. J. Cadoux, p. 183 f.

CHAPTER III

AS THE SCRIBES AND PHARISEES SAW HIM

1. *Antiquities* 13:10, 6; 18:1, 4.     2. *Antiquities* 13:10, 6.     3. Mark 7:8.
4. Mark 12:18–23.     5. Matthew 2:4; 16:21; Luke 19:47; 23:10.
6. Mark 11:18; cf. 11:27; 14:1.     7. Mark 2:16.
8. Matthew 12:34; 23:33; cf. Matthew 3:7.     9. Acts 15:5.
10. Acts 23:6.     11. Mark 12:28–34.     12. John 3:1 f.
13. Galatians 2:12 f.     14. Acts 21:18–26.     15. *Antiquities* 20:9, 1.
16. Matthew 13:52.     17. Matthew 8:19.     18. Matthew 5:17, 18.
19. Matthew 23:2, 3.     20. II Enoch 42:13.
21. *Testament of the Twelve Patriarchs*, Benjamin 5:4.     22. *Ibid.*, Joseph 18:2.
23. *Ibid.*, Issachar 7:2.     24. *Ibid.*, Benjamin 8:2.
25. Judith 16:16.     26. Mark 2:18–20.     27. Luke 6:1–5.
28. Mark 7:1–5.     29. Luke 15:1, 2.     30. Mark 7:14–19.
31. Galatians 5:6.     32. *Jesus of Nazareth*, by Joseph Klausner, p. 376.
33. *Saints and Strangers*, by George F. Willison, p. 47.
34. *The Churchman*, January 15, 1944, letter in protest against *Churchman's* liberality.     35. Matthew 23:23.     36. Matthew 23:24.
37. Mark 7:1–5.     38. Mark 7:6–8 M.     39. Sota, 4b.
40. Numbers 30:2.     41. Matthew 5:34, 37.     42. Matthew 23:16–22 M.
43. Mark 7:9–13 M.     44. Shabbath 22, 6.
45. See *The Pharisees and Jesus*, by A. T. Robertson, p. 45 f; *The Jewish World in the Time of Jesus*, by C. A. H. Guignebert, p. 796; *The Jewish People in the Time of Jesus Christ*, by Schuerer, Div. II, Vol. II, pp. 96–105.
46. Magnalia, Bk. III, p. 178 (London, 1702).
47. *The Puritan Oligarchy*, by Thomas Jefferson Wertenbaker, p. 170.

# REFERENCES

48. *The Memorial History of Boston*, by Justin Winsor, II, 470 n.
49. Shabbath 31a.     50. *Judaism*, by George Foote Moore, I 80 f.; see *The Jewish Encyclopedia*, III, 115 f.
51. *The Mission and Message of Jesus*, by Major, Manson and Wright, p. 99.
52. M. Hagigah 1, 8.     53. M. Sota 3, 4.     54. Moore, *op. cit.*, II, 194, n. 2.
55. Mark 2:27.     56. See Klausner, *op. cit.*, p. 278.
57. *History of the Jewish War*, 1:5, 2.     58. Yoma 85 f.     59. Mark 2:23 f.
60. Mark 3:1–6.     61. Matthew 12:12 M.     62. Luke 13:14 M.
63. Yoma 85 f.     64. Luke 13:10–17 M.     65. Matthew 12:1–4 M.
66. Mark 10:2–9 M.     67. Matthew 9:10–13.
68. Matthew 12:1–8; Hosea 6:6.     69. *Abot de Rabbi Nathan*, IV, 5.
70. Luke 4:25–27.     71. Exodus 3:6.     72. Mark 12:18–27.
73. Matthew 5:21–22.     74. Mark 2:22.     75. Luke 15:1–32.
76. Mark 9:33–37.     77. Luke 10:25–37.     78. Luke 7:36–50.
79. Luke 11:2.     80. Matthew 7:6.
81. *The Complete Works of James Whitcomb Riley*, V, 124, ed. by Edmund Henry Eitel.     82. Matthew 23:4.     83. Jer. Sota, 19a.     84. Luke 18:11.
85. Berakoth 28b.     86. Leviticus, Rabba 1, 5.     87. Matthew 7:18 M.
88. Matthew 23:26.     89. Luke 11:39 G.
90. *The Teaching of Jesus*, by T. W. Manson, p. 300.     91. Baba Kamma 83b.
92. Acts 26:5.

## CHAPTER IV

### AS THE SELF-COMPLACENT SAW HIM

1. Philippians 3:6.     2. Luke 15:29.     3. Mark 10:17–22.
4. Luke 19:1–10.     5. Luke 10:38–42.     6. Mark 5:18–19.
7. Luke 18:12 f.     8. Luke 7:36–50.     9. Matthew 5:21, 22.
10. Luke 11:42.     11. Luke 5:14.     12. Psalm 51:10.
13. Jeremiah 31:33.     14. Revelation 1:10.
15. Song of Songs, Rabba 1, 2.
16. *Studies in Pharisaism and the Gospels*, by Israel Abrahams, second series, p. 12.
17. Hebrews 4:15.     18. Mark 10:18.     19. Mark 10:21.
20. Luke 10:30–37.     21. Matthew 25:42, 43.
22. Matthew 21:28–31.     23. Matthew 12:43–45.     24. Matthew 23:15.
25. Josephus, *History of the Jewish War*, 2:10, 4.     26. Luke 18:11.
27. Abodah Zarah 20b.     28. Matthew 23:5–7.     29. Luke 15:7.
30. Sota 5a.     31. Luke 18:9.     32. Matthew 21:31.
33. Matthew 5:38–48 M.     34. Proverbs 25:21.     35. Job 31:29–30.
36. Discourses of Epictetus, IV, 1.     37. Plato's *Georgias*, 468 f.
38. Samyutta Nikaya 7.1.2; 11.1.4.     39. Dhammapada 197.
40. Kakacupama Suta: Majjhima Nikaya 1.129.     41. Matthew 5:20.
42. Romans 12:21.

# REFERENCES

43. *Rabbinic Literature and Gospel Teachings*, pp. 103 f.
44. Luke 19:41 f.    45. Matthew 23:37.
46. *The Life of Jesus*, by Ernest Renan, chap. 5.    47. Matthew 5:39.
48. Matthew 6:34.    49. John 12:27.    50. Matthew 5:48.
51. Luke 6:36.
52. *The Four Gospels*, a New Translation, by Charles Cutler Torrey.
53. Hebrews 5:14.    54. Ephesians 4:13.    55. I Corinthians 14:20.
56. E.g., Matthew 18:23–35.    57. E.g., Luke 7:36–50.
58. Matthew 6:29.    59. Mark 10:13–16.    60. Matthew 9:14, 15.
61. Matthew 6:16.    62. Matthew 22:2.    63. Luke 15:7, 10.
64. Matthew 6:1.    65. Matthew 5:14–16.    66. Matthew 11:28–30.
67. Matthew 16:24.    68. Matthew 6:34.    69. Matthew 25:1–13.
70. Luke 6:35.    71. Matthew 5:9.    72. Luke 12:51.
73. Matthew 5:45.    74. Luke 12:5.    75. Matthew 5:17.
76. Matthew 5:21, 22.
77. *Akiba, Scholar, Saint and Martyr*, by Louis Finkelstein, p. 103.
78. *Ibid.*, pp. 138–139.    79. pp. 15–16.    80. Luke 17:7–10.
81. *Othello*, Act II, scene 3.    82. Luke 6:22–23.    83. Yoma, 86b.
84. Matthew 18:21–22.    85. Aboth 11, 9.    86. Matthew 7:1.
87. Matthew 26:63.    88. Matthew 7:24 M.

## Chapter V

### As Religious and Moral Outcasts Saw Him

1. Sota 22a.
2. *The Beginnings of Christianity*, by Jackson and Lake, Pt. I, Vol. I, Appendix E, p. 439 f.    3. Pesachim 49a.    4. Kethuboth IIIb.
5. Pesachim 49b.    6. Aboth 11, 6.    7. Pesachim 49b.
8. Jackson and Lake, *op. cit.*, Pt. I, Vol. I, p. 444.    9. Mark 2:15.
10. Baba Bathra, chap. I, 8a.    11. John 7:48, 49.    12. Matthew 7:28.
13. Mechilta 57b.    14. Matthew 9:33.    15. John 7:15.
16. Cf. *The Teaching of Jesus*, by T. W. Manson, p. 47 f.
17. Mark 12:14, 32.    18. *Against Apion* 1, 12; 2, 18.
19. *Life In Palestine When Jesus Lived*, by J. Estlin Carpenter, p. 53 f.; *Rabbinic Literature and Gospel Teachings*, by C. G. Montefiore, p. 6.
20. Matthew 9:36.    21. Luke 7:34.    22. Cf. Carpenter, *op. cit.*, p. 83.
23. Luke 3:12, 13.    24. Luke 19:8.    25. Luke 18:9.
26. Matthew 5:46.    27. Carpenter, *op. cit.*, p. 83.    28. Luke 19:9.
29. Matthew 9:9.    30. Matthew 23:23 M.    31. Matthew 11:25 M.
32. *The Jewish Encyclopedia*, I, p. 484.    33. Luke 7:34.
34. John 7:53–8:11.    35. *Church History*, Eusebius, 3, 39.
36. de conjug. adult. 2, 7. Cf. *The Mission and Message of Jesus*, by Major, Manson and Wright, pp. 793–796.    37. Luke 5:30–32.    38. John 12:47.

# REFERENCES

39. Exodus, Rabba 31.      40. Midrash on Psalm 120.      41. Matthew 25:41.
42. Matthew 18:6.
43. Tos. Sanhedrin 13³; cf. *Judaism*, by George Foote Moore, II, 387.
44. Luke 19:10.      45. Montefiore, *op. cit.*, p. 222.      46. Matthew 16:13, 14.
47. Luke 15:1–10.      48. Luke 15:10.      49. Luke 15:20.
50. Matthew 18:27.      51. Matthew 18:12–14 M.      52. Aboth 3, 14.
53. M. Sanhedrin IV, 5.      54. Matthew 7:13, 14.
55. Mark 10:23–27.      56. Luke 15:1, 2.

## Chapter VI

### As Women and Children Saw Him

1. Matthew 13:55, 56; Mark 6:3.      2. Matthew 7:9, 10.
3. Matthew 11:16, 17.      4. Luke 11:7.      5. Matthew 18:1–4.
6. Matthew 18:5, 6.      7. Matthew 21:15, 16.
8. Matthew 19:13–15; Mark 10:13–16; Luke 18:15–17.      9. John 16:32.
10. Cf. *The Mission and Message of Jesus*, by Major, Manson and Wright, p. 460.
11. Matthew 25:40.      12. Mark 3:31–35.
13. *Rabbinic Literature and Gospel Teachings*, p. 47.      14. Luke 7:11–17.
15. Luke 7:36–50.      16. Luke 10:38–42.      17. Luke 13:10–17.
18. Luke 23:27, 28.      19. Luke 8:1–3.      20. Mark 15:40–41.
21. *Op. cit.*, p. 217.      22. Luke 17:35.      23. Luke 11:25.
24. Luke 15:8–10.      25. Matthew 6:30.      26. Matthew 13:33.
27. Matthew 6:19–21.      28. Mark 2:21, 22.      29. Luke 12:6.
30. Galatians 3:28; cf. I Corinthians 11:2–15; I Timothy 2:11–15.
31. Luke 18:1–8 M.      32. Luke 21:1–4.      33. Luke 4:25, 26.
34. Mark 12:40.      35. Leviticus, Rabba III, 5.
36. Cf. *The Jewish Encyclopedia*, XII, 514.      37. Luke 20:47 M.
38. Exodus, Rabba, XXX.      39. Proverbs 31:10–31.
40. The Wisdom of Ben Sira (Sirach) 26:21–24.      41. *Ibid,.* 42:9, 11–14.
42. Matthew 5:28.      43. Luke 10:38–42.
44. Major, Manson and Wright, *op. cit.*, p. 748.
45. Mark 14:3–9; Matthew 26:6–13; John 12:1–8.      46. Mark 14:4–7 M.
47. John 7:53–8:11 (cf. chap. IV).      48. Luke 7:36–50.
49. John 4:5–30.
50. On the possibility that the five husbands may be allegorically interpreted, see Major, Manson and Wright, *op. cit.*, p. 746 f.      51. Deuteronomy 24:1.
52. *Studies in Pharisaism and the Gospels*, by Israel Abrahams, first series, p. 72.
53. *The Synoptic Gospels*, by C. G. Montefiore, Vol. 1, p. 235.
54. Mark 10:2–9.      55. I Corinthians 7:10–11.      56. Matthew 19:9.
57. Matthew 19:10–12.      58. Mark 10:11.
59. Abrahams, *op. cit.*, first series, p. 76.      60. Malachi 2:15–16.
61. Luke 14:26.      62. Genesis 29:30–31.      63. Matthew 10:37.

# REFERENCES

64. Mark 3:21.     65. Mark 3:31–35.     66. John 7:5.     67. Mark 10:29.
68. Luke 12:51–53.     69. Matthew 10:36 (Micah 7:6).
70. John 19:25–27.     71. Mark 15:40; Matthew 27:55, 56.
72. Luke 3:23.     73. Isaiah 7:14.     74. *First Apology*, 21.
75. Acts 1:13–14.     76. Galatians 1:18–19.     77. Mark 5:25–34.
78. Matthew 15:21–28.     79. Luke 8:1–3.     80. Mark 10:15–16.
81. Luke 11:27–28.     82. *Unpopular Opinions*, p. 148.


CHAPTER VII

As His First Disciples Saw Him

1. Matthew 9:9; 10:3; Mark 2:14; 3:18.     2. Luke 6:16; Acts 1:13.
3. Revelation 21:14.     4. Luke 9:51–56.     5. Matthew 15:16.
6. Mark 10:35–41.     7. Mark 9:33–37.     8. Luke 22:24.
9. Matthew 16:23.     10. John 15:15.     11. Mark 1:16–17.
12. Mark 2:14.     13. John 1:40–42.     14. Mark 1:16–38.
15. *The Life and Teaching of Jesus The Christ*, by Arthur C. Headlam, p. 11.
16. Matthew 13:10.     17. Matthew 15:12.     18. Matthew 15:15 M.
19. Mark 8:32.     20. Mark 3:14.     21. Mark 6:31.     22. Luke 22:32.
23. Matthew 26:50.     24. Mark 5:18–19.     25. Luke 9:57–58.
26. Luke 9:61–62.     27. Luke 6:12–13.     28. II Timothy 1:12.
29. Matthew 13:3 f.; Mark 4:1 f.; Luke 8:4 f.     30. Mark 4:34.
31. Matthew 5:13–14.     32. Mark 10:42–44.     33. Matthew 23:8.
34. Mark 10:29 f.     35. Luke 10:18.     36. Luke 12:32.
37. Mark 4:31 f.     38. Matthew 13:33.     39. Luke 22:15.
40. Luke 22:28.     41. John 17:6–11.     42. Matthew 10:23.
43. Matthew 24:36–44.     44. Mark 13:9–13.     45. Matthew 24:36.
46. Luke 14:27.     47. Luke 14:26.     48. Matthew 5:11.
49. Luke 17:3.     50. Matthew 18:15–17.     51. Mark 10:39.
52. Luke 14:25–33.     53. Matthew 10:17–18.     54. Mark 1:35–36.
55. Matthew 6:7.     56. Luke 9:29.     57. Luke 11:1.
58. Luke 11:5–8.     59. Luke 18:1–8.     60. Luke 11:9–13.
61. Luke 12:6–7.     62. *Timaeus:*VIII.     63. Luke 9:18.
64. Matthew 6:6.     65. Mark 1:7.     66. Mark 1:11.     67. Mark 1:24.
68. Mark 3:11.     69. Mark 8:29.     70. Mark 9:7.     71. Mark 1:25.
72. Mark 3:12.     73. Mark 8:30.     74. Luke 9:21.     75. Matthew 16:20.
76. Mark 14:61–62.     77. Luke 7:16.     78. Mark 6:15.
79. Mark 8:27–28.     80. Matthew 21:11.     81. Matthew 21:46.
82. Mark 6:4.     83. Luke 13:33.
84. E.g., Matthew 7:21; 15:13; 16:17; 18:19; 18:35, etc.
85. Luke 10:22; Matthew 11:27.     86. John 3:35; 10:15; 13:3; 17:25.
87. Matthew 5:9.     88. Matthew 5:45.     89. Testament of Judah, 24:1.
90. Testament of Naphtali 4:5.     91. Sibylline Oracles 3:655, 656.

REFERENCES

92. Testament of Simeon 7:2; Testament of Issachar 5:7; The Book of Jubilees 31:18 f.    93. Testament of Reuben 6:7 f.; Testament of Levi 8:14.
94. Testament of Dan 5:10.    95. Sibylline Oracles 3:653.
96. Testament of Levi 18:4.    97. Assumption of Moses 1:14.
98. Daniel 7:13–14; I Enoch 48:2–6; 49:2.    99. Zechariah 9:9.
100. Daniel 7:13.    101. Sanhedrin 98a.
102. Isaiah 42:1–4; 49:1–6; 50:4–9; 53: 1–12.
103. See *Judaism*, by George Foote Moore, I, 551.
104. See *Jesus the Messiah*, by William Manson, Appendix B, the Targum on Isaiah 53.    105. IV Maccabees 6:27–29.    106. Acts 8:27–39.
107. I Peter 2:22–25.    108. Hebrews 9:29.    109. Luke 4:16 f.
110. Matthew 11:2 f.; cf. Isaiah 35:5.    111. Luke 22:37.
112. Isaiah 53:11–12.    113. Mark 10:45.    111. Mark 9:12.
115. Mark 14:21.    116. Mark 14:24.    117. Mark 9:31–32.
118. On the difficulties involved in interpreting the phrase "Son of man," as used in the Gospels, see *Jesus the Messiah*, by William Manson, p. 158 f.; *The Historic Mission of Jesus*, by C. J. Cadoux, p. 90 f. On problems associated with Jesus' resurrection see *The Mission and Message of Jesus*. by Major, Manson and Wright, p. 211 f.; also. the author's book, *A Guide to Understanding the Bible*, chap. vi.    119. Zechariah 11:12–13.
120. Mark 14:10–11; Matthew 26:14–16; Luke 22:3–6.
121. Matthew 27:3–10.    122. Acts 1:16–19.    123. Luke 24:21.

CHAPTER VIII

AS MILITANT NATIONALISTS SAW HIM

1. Psalm 137:5–6.    2. *Antiquities* 18:1, 6.    3. *History of the Jewish War*, 3:3, 2.
4. *Antiquities* 14:15, 5.    5. *Antiquities* 17:10, 9.
6. *The Provinces of the Roman Empire*, II, 203.    7. Acts 5:36–37.
8. *Akiba, Scholar, Saint and Martyr*, by Louis Finkelstein, p. 269.
9. John 6:15.    10. Matthew 4:8–9.    11. Luke 19:11.    12. Luke 6:15.
13. Matthew 10:4.    14. Cf. Acts 21:20; Galatians 1:14.    15. Mark 3:17.
16. Luke 9:54.    17. Mark 10:35 f.
18. Mark 8:33 (cf. "Begone, Satan!" Matthew 4:10).
19. Luke 22:35–38.    20. Mark 14:47.    21. Luke 12:49.
22. Windisch, Der Mess. Krieg, p. 95.    23. Mark 11:17.    24. Mark 15:7.
25. Luke 19:41–44.    26. Mark 13:2.
27. Matthew 23:37–38; cf. Luke 13:34–35.
28. Mark 13:1–37; Matthew 24:1–44; Luke 21:5–36.    29. Vs. 14.
30. Mark 13:14–19.    31. Luke 21:20.    32. Luke 21:24.
33. Luke 13:1–5.    34. Luke 12:54–56.

35. Mark 12:1–11; Matthew 21:33–46; Luke 20:9–19.
36. Matthew 23:34–36.    37. Luke 23:28–31.    38. Matthew 24:6.
39. Matthew 26:52.    40. Mark 12:13–17.    41. Mark 14:56–59.
42. Matthew 11:12.    43. Luke 16:16.    44. Chaps. III and IV.
45. Matthew 5:41.    46. Matthew 5:9.    47. Luke 19:42.
48. Finkelstein, *op. cit.*, p. 60.    49. Yoma, 39b.    50. Baba Bathra 10b.
51. Isaiah 49:6.    52. Micah 4:3.    53. II Enoch 50:3 f.
54. The Assumption of Moses 10:7–10.    55. II Esdras 6:55–59.
56. Matthew 10:34–37.    57. Luke 12:51.    58. Luke 22:35–38.
59. Luke 22:50–51.    60. Matthew 26:51–52.    61. John 18:36.
62. Luke 19:27.    63. Matthew 22:7.    64. Luke 14:31–32.
65. Mark 3:27.    66. Luke 16:1–9.    67. Luke 17:7–10.
68. Matthew 25:14–30.    69. Matthew 8:5–9.    70. Mark 3:22.
71. Cf. *The Gospel of Mark*, by B. Harvie Branscomb, pp. 271–277.
72. *Studies in Pharisaism and the Gospels*, by Israel Abrahams, first series, chap-XI.    73. Kerithoth 1:7.
74. Mark 11:17; Matthew 21:13; Luke 19:46.    75. Mark 11:16.
76. John 2:13–15.    77. Mark 11:15, Matthew 21:12; Luke 19:45.
78. Mark 11:18; Luke 19:48.    79. Luke 23:5.
80. Mark 14:1–2; cf. Matthew 26:4–5.    81. Luke 23:2.
82. John 19:15.    83. Eg., Romans 13:1–7; Titus 3:1–2; I Peter 2:13–14.
84. Mark 15:14.    85. Matthew 27:24.
86. E.g., Philo. Leg. ad. Caium, 38.    87. Mark 15:10.
88. Luke 23:14–16.    89. Mark 15:29–31.

## Chapter IX

### As Jews with a World-wide Outlook Saw Him

1. Matthew 10:5.
2. Eighth ed., chap. 28.
3. *Greek in Jewish Palestine*, by Saul Lieberman, p. 21.    4. Acts 22:2.
5. T. B. Sota 49b.
6. *A Social and Religious History of the Jews*, by Salo Wittmayer Baron, I, 156.
7. *Against Flaccus*, 7, 46.    8. Acts 6:1.    9. Acts 6:9.
10. Baron, *op. cit.*, I, 222.    11. *Jesus of Nazareth*, by Joseph Klausner, p. 117.
12. John 12:20 f.    13. Acts 15:22–29.
14. Sifre (Midrash) Numbers, Sec. 111; Deuteronomy, Sec. 54. cf. *Judaism*, by George Foote Moore, I, 325.    15. Aboth 1, 2.    16. Yebamot 47b.
17. Matthew 23:13–15.
18. *The Journal of Theological Studies*, XIII, 324.    19. Acts 2:9–11.
20. Matthew 28:19.    21. Matthew 12:18–21.    22. Matthew 10:5–6.
23. Matthew 15:24.    24. Matthew 5:18.    25. Matthew 8:11.

# REFERENCES

26. Matthew 21:43.    27. Matthew 5:14.    28. Matthew 13:38.
29. Matthew 24:14.    30. Amos 9:7.    31. Isaiah 49:6.
32. Matthew 28:19.    33. Matthew 10:23.    34. Matthew 16:28.
35. Matthew 24:36.    36. Matthew 19:28.    37. John 8:48.
38. The Wisdom of Ben-Sira (Sirach) 50:25; 26.    39. Luke 10:30 f.
40. Romans 2:14–15.    41. Luke 11:30–32.    42. Luke 4:25–27.
43. Matthew 11:20–24.    44. Matthew 8:5 f.    45. Matthew 3:9.
46. Matthew 8:11.    47. Isaiah 56:7.    48. Mark 11:17.
49. Matthew 6:7.    50. Matthew 5:47.    51. Mark 10:42.
52. Matthew 4:25.    53. Luke 6:17.    54. Mark 7:31 f.
55. Mark 7:24–30.
56. Cf. *The Gospel of Mark*, by B. Harvie Branscomb, p. 132.    57. John 4:22.
58. Testament of Asher VII, 3.    59. Testament of Benjamin X, 5.
60. Testament of Levi, IV, 4.    61. Testament of Levi, XVIII, 9.
62. Baruch, 1.1.4.    63. Matthew 11:25.    64. Romans 3:30.
65. Matthew 25:31–46.    66. Micah 6:8.
67. *Einleitung in die drei ersten Evangelien*, p. 113. Berlin, 1905.
68. Klausner, *op. cit.*, p. 390.    69. Luke 17:11 f.
70. *What is Christianity?* tr. by Thomas Bailey Saunders, 1912, p. 73.
71. Matthew 23:8.    72. *The Ethical Teaching of Jesus*, by Ernest Findlay Scott, p. 13.
73. Matthew 7:24.    74. Matthew 10:32.    75. Matthew 10:42.
76. Matthew 12:50.    77. Matthew 16:25.    78. Matthew 18:4.
79. Matthew 20:26.    80. Exodus 15:18.    81. Matthew 4:10.
82. Mark 14:36.    83. Matthew 13:38.    84. Matthew 13:33.
85. Mark 4:30 f.    86. Luke 11:20–21.
87. *The Sayings of Jesus from Oxyrhynchus*, by H. G. E. White.
88. Romans 14:17.    89. Mark 10:14, 15.    90. Mark 12:32–34.
91. Matthew 5:3.    92. Matthew 7:21.    93. Matthew 13:37 f.
94. Mark 10:23 f.    95. Luke 9:62.    96. Luke 13:27–29.
97. Acts 6:8–8:3.    98. Haer. XX.4.    99. Luke 10:1.
100. Acts 7:51–53.

## Epilogue

1. Luke 16:19–31.    2. Luke 12:13–21.    3. Matthew 18:23–35.
4. Matthew 19:26; Mark 10:27.    5. Luke 6:36.    6. Matthew 7:11.
7. Luke 15:10.    8. Matthew 6:4.
9. *The Teaching of Jesus*, by T. W. Manson, p. 72.    10. Luke 12:15.
11. Matthew 6:24.    12. Matthew 6:27.    13. Luke 17:33.
14. Matthew 18:4.    15. Matthew 25:31–46.    16. John 5:17.
17. Luke 10:37.    18. Matthew 21:28–31.    19. Matthew 7:21.
20. Matthew 15:13.    21. Luke 20:17–18.

## REFERENCES

22. *Modern Painters*, chapter on "Of Modern Landscape."     23. John 14:11.
24. Matthew 10:40.     25. Matthew 10:32.
26. "In No Strange Land" in *The Collected Poetry of Francis Thompson*, *p*. 412. Reprinted by permission of Sir Francis Meynell and the publishers, Messrs. Burns, Oates & Washbourne, Ltd.

# Selected Bibliography

MATHEWS, SHAILER. *New Testament Times in Palestine*, 175 B.C.–135 A.D. Macmillan, 1934.

CHARLES, R. H. *Religious Development between the Old and New Testaments*. Thornton and Butterworth, 1934.

MOORE, GEORGE FOOTE. *Judaism in the First Centuries of the Christian Era*. Harvard University Press, 1927–30.

BARON, SALO WITTMAYER. *A Social and Religious History of the Jews*. Columbia University Press, 1937.

GUIGNEBERT, CH. *The Jewish World in the Time of Jesus*. Kegan Paul, Trench, Trubner & Co., 1939.

GRANT, FREDERICK. *The Economic Background of the Gospels*. Oxford University Press, 1926.

HERFORD, ROBERT TRAVERS. *Christianity in Talmud and Midrash*. Williams and Norgate, 1903.

WALKER, THOMAS. *The Teaching of Jesus and the Jewish Teaching of His Age*. George Allen and Unwin, 1923.

MONTEFIORE, C. G. *Rabbinic Literature and Gospel Teachings*. Macmillan, 1930.

CHARLES, R. H. *Apocrypha and Pseudipigrapha of the Old Testament*. Clarendon Press, 1913.

JAMES, M. R. *The Apocryphal New Testament*. Clarendon Press, 1926.

BRANSCOMB, B. HARVIE. *Jesus and the Law of Moses*. R. R. Smith, 1930.

McCOWN, CHESTER CHARLTON. *The Search for the Real Jesus*. Charles Scribner's Sons, 1940.

# SELECTED BIBLIOGRAPHY

SCHWEITZER, ALBERT. *The Quest of the Historical Jesus.* A. & C. Black, 1910.

CASE, SHIRLEY JACKSON. *The Historicity of Jesus.* University of Chicago Press, 1912.

SCOTT, ERNEST FINDLAY. *The Validity of the Gospel Record.* Charles Scribner's Sons, 1938.

LIGHTFOOT, R. H. *History and Interpretation in the Gospels.* Harper & Brothers, 1935.

EASTON, B. S. *The Gospel before the Gospels.* Charles Scribner's Sons, 1928.

TAYLOR, VINCENT. *The Formulation of the Gospel Tradition.* Macmillan, 1935.

GRANT, FREDERICK. *Form Criticism: A New Method of New Testament Research.* Willett, Clark & Co., 1934.

GOGUEL, MAURICE. *The Life of Jesus.* Macmillan, 1944.

KLAUSNER, JOSEPH. *Jesus of Nazareth.* Macmillan, 1925.

MACKINNON, JAMES. *The Historic Jesus.* Longmans, Green & Co., 1931.

STRACHAN, R. H. *The Historic Jesus in the New Testament.* Student Christian Movement Press, 1931.

MAJOR, MANSON AND WRIGHT. *The Mission and Message of Jesus.* E. P. Dutton & Co., 1946.

CASE, S. J. *Jesus: A New Biography.* University of Chicago Press, 1927.

CADOUX, C. J. *The Historic Mission of Jesus.* Harper & Brothers, 1943.

KNOX, JOHN. *The Man Christ Jesus.* Harper & Brothers, 1942.

MANSON, T. W. *The Teaching of Jesus.* Cambridge University Press, 1943.

BRANSCOMB, B. HARVIE. *The Teachings of Jesus.* Abingdon-Cokesbury Press, 1931.

LINDSAY, A. D. *The Moral Teaching of Jesus.* Harper & Brothers, 1937.

SCOTT, ERNEST FINDLAY. *The Ethical Teaching of Jesus.* Macmillan, 1936.

MANSON, WILLIAM. *Jesus, the Messiah.* The Westminster Press, 1946.

CADBURY, HENRY J. *Jesus, What Manner of Man.* Macmillan, 1947.

COLWELL, ERNEST CADMAN. *An Approach to the Teaching of Jesus.* Abingdon-Cokesbury Press, 1946.

WILDER, AMOS NIVEN. *Eschatology and Ethics in the Teaching of Jesus.* Harper & Brothers, 1939.

SIMKHOVITCH, V. G. *Toward the Understanding of Jesus.* Macmillan, 1921.

CADBURY, H. J. *The Peril of Modernizing Jesus.* Macmillan, 1937.

SMITH, B. T. D. *The Parables of the Synoptic Gospels.* Cambridge University Press, 1937.

DODD, C. H. *The Parables of the Kingdom.* Charles Scribner's Sons, 1936.

ABRAHAMS, ISRAEL. *Studies in Pharisaism and the Gospels.* Macmillan, first series, 1917; second series, 1924.

HERFORD, ROBERT TRAVIS. *Pharisaism: Its Aim and Its Method.* G. P. Putnam's Sons, 1912.

MONTEFIORE, C. G. *Some Elements of the Religious Teaching of Jesus.* Macmillan, 1910.

OTTO, R. *The Kingdom of God and the Son of Man.* Zonderman Publishing House, 1938–39.

SHARMAN, H. B. *Son of Man and Kingdom of God.* Harper & Brothers, 1943.

McNEILE, ALAN HUGH. *The Gospel According to St. Matthew.* Macmillan, 1915.

SMITH, B. T. D. *The Gospel According to Matthew.* Cambridge University Press, 1927.

RAWLINSON, A. E. J. *St. Mark.* Methuen & Co., 1931.

BRANSCOMB, B. HARVIE. *The Gospel of Mark.* Harper & Brothers, 1937.

CREED, J. M. *The Gospel According to St. Luke.* Macmillan, 1930.

EASTON, BURTON SCOTT. *The Gospel According to St. Luke.* Charles Scribner's Sons, 1926.

LUCE, H. K. *The Gospel According to St. Luke.* Cambridge University Press, 1933.

MONTEFIORIE, C. G. *The Synoptic Gospels.* Macmillan, 1909.

STREETER, B. H. *The Four Gospels.* Macmillan, 1930.

SCOTT, ERNEST FINDLAY. *The Fourth Gospel, Its Purpose and Theology.* T. & T. Clark, 1908.

COLWELL, ERNEST CADMAN. *John Defends the Gospel.* Willett, Clark & Co., 1936.

SMART, W. A. *The Spiritual Gospel.* Abingdon-Cokesbury Press, 1945.

[ 263 ]

MacGregor, G. H. C. *John*, in *The Moffatt New Testament Commentary*, Harper & Brothers, 1928.

Strachan, R. H. *The Fourth Gospel: Its Significance and Environment.* Student Christian Movement Press, 1941.

INDEXES

# INDEX I

# INDEX II

## Passages from the Old Testament

# INDEX III

[ 274 ]

# INDEX IV

## PASSAGES FROM THE APOCRYPHA AND PSEUDEPIGRAPHA

[ 282 ]

Gearhartville St Severin's
at 11 $\frac{oo}{am}$

Hawk Run — Good Shepherd
at 9 $\frac{oo}{am}$